National Minimum Wage

Low Pay Commission Report 2008

Presented to Parliament by the Secretary of State
for Business, Enterprise & Regulatory Reform
by Command of Her Majesty
March 2008

Cm 7333   £30.00

Contents

Chairman's Foreword

One of the notable achievements of the National Minimum Wage has been that, for the best part of the last decade, it has ensured, probably for the first time, that the wages of the lowest paid in the UK have shown a modest but meaningful uplift when compared to increases in the average wage and with no consequent loss of jobs. This has helped to improve the pay of a number of groups of workers and to narrow the pay gap between men and women but has made no impression on the gap between the highest and lowest wage earners. The achievements of the minimum wage are often most clearly illustrated in graphic form. For example, Figure 2.6 on page 24 shows starkly the effect on the pay of the lowest paid by contrasting the situation before and after the introduction of the National Minimum Wage; and Figure 3.2 on page 72 graphically illustrates the effect on the gender pay gap.

This year, when we met in January 2008 to review the available evidence as a prelude to agreeing our recommendations, we were faced with a situation more complex than usual. Looking back over the year gone by, most of the evidence generated supported a positive and optimistic view of the labour market. However, looking forward to 2008–09, the prospects looked much less positive as a result of the uncertainty brought about by the crisis in global financial markets. In the circumstances and after much discussion and debate, we took the view that a degree of caution was advisable and this is reflected in a recommendation that is lower than the predicted increase in average earnings. We are conscious, above all, of the need to protect jobs.

Ten years ago, as the minimum wage was about to be introduced, it was just this fear of job losses that dominated discussion. Indeed in June 1997, the Economist magazine printed an article on Britain's forthcoming National Minimum Wage entitled 'Devilish Details'. The article concluded with the following observation, "Coming up with a minimum wage that will not seriously harm the economy and destroy jobs will require the wisdom of Solomon – or extraordinary luck." At that time the Economist was not alone in being sceptical about the likely impact of a National Minimum Wage on the UK labour market. In fact, since the introduction of the National Minimum Wage in April 1999, the number of jobs in the whole economy has increased by over two million and there are well over half a million more jobs in the sectors most likely to be affected. So far, therefore, the evidence suggests that either we have been very lucky, or the Low Pay Commission is packed with men and women blessed with an unusual degree of wisdom, or the author of the Economist article got it wrong. Of course it could be all three.

In fact, since the introduction of the National Minimum Wage, the Low Pay Commission has been at the forefront of the search for evidence of any damage caused by the minimum wage to the economy or to jobs. So far we have not found any significant negative effects, either in the work we have done ourselves or in the work we have commissioned from others. And we have looked long and hard in all the places that are most likely to reveal such an effect. This is not to say that the minimum wage is incapable of negative impact; merely that, so far, the UK minimum wage has successfully avoided the dangers.

Indeed, this year we have commissioned a further series of studies (details can be found in Appendix 2 to this report) to inform our recommendations for next year. These projects will look in particular at the effect of the larger than average earnings increases of 2003 onwards across a wide range of variables including staff turnover and retention, employment and hours, competitiveness, vulnerable sectors and regional impact. I expect that the findings of these projects will be a significant factor affecting our views as we ponder the recommendations we will make to Government about the minimum wage this time next year.

Next year we are also likely to be taking a closer look at the impact of the minimum wage on young workers. In particular, at the prompting of the Prime Minister, we will be asked to examine the position of apprentices, many of whom are currently not covered by the legislation.

This year's report is deliberately shorter and more concise than most previous Low Pay Commission reports. We hope that this will make our work a little more accessible to the non-academic reader, but I am conscious that reading our report from cover to cover is likely to remain a minority activity, whatever changes we make. If you have views on the streamlined format of this report, or suggestions as to how we might improve future reports, we would be delighted to hear from you.

With the retirement last year of six long-serving Commissioners, the make up of the Low Pay Commission has changed markedly since this time last year. The six new Commissioners have proved to be worthy successors to their eminent predecessors and just as committed to an evidence-based approach. It has been a pleasure to work with such colleagues, as it has been to work with the members of our Secretariat, who have served us well.

Paul Myners
February 2008

The Commissioners

Paul Myners (Chairman)
Chairman of Land Securities Group PLC
and Chair of the Trustees of Tate

Susan Anderson
Director,
Human Resources Policy, CBI

Professor Bob Elliott
Professor of Economics and Director of
the Health Economics Research Unit,
University of Aberdeen

Neil Goulden
Chief Executive,
The Gala Coral Group

John Hannett
General Secretary,
Usdaw

Ian Hay OBE
Chairman,
Food Trade Association Management

Professor Stephen Machin
Professor of Economics at University
College London and Research Director,
Centre for Economic Performance,
London School of Economics

Frances O'Grady
Deputy General Secretary,
TUC

Heather Wakefield
National Secretary for UNISON's Local
Government Service Group

The Secretariat
Chris Dee, OBE, Secretary
Jay Arjan
Tim Butcher
Hazel Hector
Heather Holt
Mouna Kehil
Tony Studd
Sonia Wilson

Executive Summary

Chapter 1: Introduction

In our terms of reference we were asked to monitor, evaluate and review the impact of the minimum wage and to consider its effect on business, especially on small firms and firms in low-paying sectors. We were also asked to consider the impact on different groups of workers. To help meet our remit we commissioned two research reports and carried out three in-house research projects. We also visited a number of organisations throughout the UK to listen to local people affected by the minimum wage. In addition, we received over sixty written submissions from a variety of organisations and individuals and we heard oral evidence over a two day period.

Chapter 2: The Impact of the National Minimum Wage

Since the introduction of the National Minimum Wage we have carefully monitored its impact on the economy in general and the labour market in particular. We have done so again this year and focused on those sectors most likely to be affected by the minimum wage. We looked particularly at the impact of the minimum wage on earnings and for any sign that it had affected employment. In addition, we looked for an impact on other economic variables such as profits, prices, productivity, investment and business creation.

We estimate that the rise of the minimum wage to £5.35 in October 2006 covered around 5.0 per cent of jobs held by adults (up to 1.2 million jobs). It led to an increase in the proportion of jobs paid at the minimum wage, and the rise was most evident in the low-paying sectors. As a result, there was an increase in the 'bite' of the minimum wage – defined as its relative level when expressed as a proportion of the average hourly wage. The 'bite' of the minimum wage rose to 51.1 per cent of medium hourly earnings in April 2007.

We also found some evidence that the uprating of the minimum wage in October 2006 may have squeezed differentials.

The subsequent 3.2 per cent increase in the minimum wage to £5.52 on 1 October 2007 was, as anticipated, in line with pay settlements and below average earnings growth but, contrary to expectations, it was also below the increase in the Retail Price Index. We estimate that the 2007 uplift covered about 4 per cent of jobs held by adults (about a million jobs). It is, however, too early to assess properly the impact of the October 2007 upratings.

The UK economy performed better during 2007 than had been anticipated at the time of our last report, with generally positive developments on employment and hours. Employment in the UK reached record levels in 2007, and unemployment fell. Jobs in the low-paying sectors increased slightly faster than jobs in the economy overall. The number of hours worked increased, as did vacancies, although there was also a small rise in redundancies. Our commissioned research found few effects from the minimum wage on employment or hours.

Other business variables – such as profits, productivity, investment and the net number of businesses created – performed positively during 2007 and we could find little evidence of negative impact that might be ascribed to the minimum wage. There was some research evidence that firms may have passed part of the higher costs of the minimum wage onto customers.

Employers and trade unions provided differing perspectives on the impact of the minimum wage. Employers tended to stress that the minimum wage was affecting more sectors, employers and workers than before. The impact on small businesses was of particular concern for some, as were the costs associated with the Government's enhancement of holiday entitlement for others. Affordability and the erosion of pay differentials were some of the other issues which some employers believed stemmed from minimum wage increases, affecting their ability to reward staff and maintain staff incentives. It was argued that these developments had a negative effect on jobs, hours worked, and future business decisions, such as whether to invest or recruit more staff. Some also maintained that the erosion of differentials was having a negative impact on staff's willingness to undergo training.

On the other hand, unions argued that, to date, employers had been able to manage increases in the minimum wage with little difficulty and pointed to the continued increase in jobs in affected sectors. They maintained that businesses should be able to fund a further increase in the minimum wage given the generally robust levels of profitability. Unions also pointed out that the rate of business start-ups was greater in the low-paying sectors than in the economy as a whole. Moreover, they argued that the forthcoming increase in annual leave would impact on only half of the year in which the present recommendations would have effect and they contended that paying low wages raised business costs by increasing staff turnover and the need to retrain.

The quality of the official data which is available to us is crucial to our decision-making process. We were concerned that changes made by the Office for National Statistics to some of their surveys affected the quality of the data we use, particularly on earnings at detailed industry level. Changes to the availability of data on employee jobs also restricted our analyses of employment in the low-paying sectors. We have therefore recommended that the Government take steps to address this erosion of the quality of the key national data.

Chapter 3: Groups of Workers

We were asked in our terms of reference to consider the impact of the minimum wage on different groups of workers, including different age groups, people with disabilities, workers from ethnic minority groups, women and migrant workers. Paying particular attention to these groups of workers is important as they are disproportionately represented in the low-paying sectors and occupations and therefore more likely to be affected by the minimum wage.

Women, ethnic minority groups and people with work-limiting disabilities have become more involved in the labour market over the last ten years and there is no evidence of an adverse impact on their employment due to the minimum wage. The closing of the gender pay gap has been particularly pronounced at the very bottom of the distribution since 1999, which suggests that the minimum wage has had a positive impact on women's pay.

By definition, people with work-limiting disabilities are less likely to participate in the labour market, but their employment rate has slowly increased over the last ten years and, since 2004, it has increased slightly more rapidly than for other groups.

The impact of the minimum wage on people from ethnic minority groups has varied markedly between the different ethnic groups. In recent years the employment rate of ethnic minority groups as a whole has increased more than the employment rate of white workers. However, recently they have also experienced a small increase in unemployment. Evidence suggests that the minimum wage has improved the earnings of ethnic minority workers at the lower end of the distribution.

Since its introduction, we have carefully considered the impact of the minimum wage on young people to ensure that there is no detrimental impact on their participation in education or on their labour market prospects. This year the long-term increase in inactivity and unemployment rates of 16–17 year olds not in full-time education showed signs of reversing. However, the employment rate of the 18 to 20 year old age group has been in continuous decline since 2000, accompanied by a steady increase in inactivity and, since 2004, a sharp rise in unemployment. It is the labour market position of 18 year olds, and to a lesser extent that of 19 year olds, that has deteriorated the most. It is difficult to explain why young people have not fared better in the workplace, but it may in part be due to the arrival of large numbers of predominantly young migrant workers and the increase in the number of people of pension age becoming or remaining economically active.

The Government has consistently rejected our previous recommendations that 21 year olds should be entitled to the adult rate of the National Minimum Wage. We have again weighed the evidence and concluded unanimously that lowering the entitlement to the adult rate to the age of 21 would not have a detrimental impact on their employment prospects. Most employers already pay 21 year olds at least the adult rate. We therefore again recommend that 21 year olds should be entitled to the adult rate of the National Minimum Wage. Should the Government maintain its opposition to this proposal, we are asking for an explanation of the nature of their disagreement and for a description of the changes that would be required for the Government to agree to our proposal.

We welcome the Prime Minister's announcement that we will be asked to undertake a review of apprenticeships and we look forward to carrying this out in the coming year.

In recent years there has been a substantial increase in the number of migrant workers in the UK and we have monitored the impact of this influx on unemployment and wage inflation at the lower end of the labour market. On the evidence available, it appears that migrant workers are contributing to the success of the UK economy by filling gaps in the labour market and that, in general, they have not displaced UK nationals in the workplace. The effect of migrant workers on wage inflation is less clear, but most indications are that any impact has been minimal.

For this report, we again received some evidence of non-compliance with the minimum wage in respect of work experience placements. We believe that more effective guidance and enforcement is the answer. Similarly, we consider that the confusion which has arisen about the application of the minimum wage when a worker is required to sleep at their place of work (known as 'sleepovers') should be addressed by a review of the existing guidance. We recommend that the Government should review the official guidance on both these issues.

We also received evidence that many homeworkers and those paid through fair piece rates continue to face difficulties in enforcing their right to be paid at least the minimum wage. Although the fair piece rates system has been in place for around three years, evidence about how it works in practice remains scarce. The information we have received suggests that awareness and proper use of the new arrangements may be low. We therefore recommend that the Government takes stock and evaluates whether the current fair piece rates arrangement is meeting its objectives.

Chapter 4: Compliance and Enforcement

The evidence we have received over a number of years leads us to believe that the vast majority of employers support and comply with minimum wage legislation. It is difficult to determine the extent of non-compliance but we do know that there are still workers being underpaid, and there is anecdotal evidence that the level of non-compliance might be rising, in particular as a result of the arrival of significant numbers of migrant workers, many of whom are unfamiliar with the English language and British institutions.

We appreciate that in many cases where underpayment arises it is through genuine error and, when brought to an employer's attention, it is put right. We believe that such problems could largely be resolved through greater awareness of the minimum wage rates, as well as the availability of clear, practical and up-to-date guidance on those operational aspects of the minimum wage that are known to cause confusion. However, swift and firm action needs to be taken against those employers who intentionally flout their minimum wage responsibilities.

We recognise and welcome the significant steps that the Government has taken, and the new measures that are in train, to strengthen the minimum wage enforcement regime. We are particularly pleased that additional resources have been allocated to enforcement. This should have a tangible impact. We will monitor developments with interest. We also welcome the Government's decision to act on our recommendations to introduce fair arrears and penalties for all non-compliant employers. These steps, taken together, should send a strong clear message to employers who might be tempted to underpay their workers.

This year we have decided not to make any recommendations on minimum wage enforcement. We believe that it is more appropriate to allow time for the initiatives already under way to be developed, and for those in the pipeline to be implemented. In our view, the coming year should be regarded as a period of consolidation in respect of enforcement, with an emphasis on raising awareness, co-ordination of the different strands of the work in progress and on ensuring that appropriate means to evaluate the outcomes are in place.

Chapter 5: Setting the Rates

We have examined the impact of the minimum wage, considered the position of those workers most affected and reviewed compliance and enforcement. We now turn to the macroeconomic picture and the prospects for the economy in 2008 before addressing the issue of the appropriate minimum wage rates for October 2008.

Although the world economy has grown strongly in recent years, it was clear, when we met in January 2008 to agree our recommendations, that the financial crisis and credit concerns in the US had led to severe problems in financial markets across the world and most forecasters were suggesting that global growth would slow in 2008. Moreover, it was also clear that, although UK output had grown at or above trend during 2006 and 2007, the UK would not be immune from the general economic upheaval. By the end of 2007 consumer spending showed signs of slowing, business investment had tailed off and growth in Government spending had weakened.

We also considered the implications of the Government's decision to increase the statutory entitlement to annual leave, the second phase of which will be introduced from April 2009. The majority of firms will be unaffected but, for those where all workers will be entitled to the full four day increase, we estimated that the direct cost was likely to be equivalent to about 1.6 per cent on the wage bill. However, we were conscious that our calculations were based on estimates derived from uncertain data.

Our formal consultation revealed views about the appropriate level of the minimum wage for 2008 that largely followed the pattern of previous years. The majority of unions supported a substantial increase, while most employers called for restraint. The CBI thought that the minimum wage had reached an appropriate level. It described the overall economic outlook for the UK as uncertain and warned against an above average increase in a slowing economy. The TUC, on the other hand, did not agree that the minimum wage had reached its highest sustainable level. It maintained that the fundamentals of the UK economy were sound and could support a minimum wage of more than £6 an hour (an increase of 8.7 per cent) by October 2008.

In last year's report we said that, subject to developments in the economy and in the labour market, the increase we were likely to recommend for 2008 would be around the predicted rise in average earnings. Independent forecasts predict that average earnings growth will be about 4 per cent in 2008. Retail price inflation is forecast to fall to 2.6 per cent. Employment is expected to continue to grow, albeit more slowly.

Against this background, we weighed the evidence and agreed that, on balance, the uncertain economic outlook made a degree of caution advisable despite the generally encouraging labour market data. We therefore recommend that the adult rate of the minimum wage should be increased from £5.52 to £5.73 an hour in October 2008. This is slightly below the predicted increase in average earnings. We see this recommendation as balancing the generally positive messages in the data with the need for caution implied by the uncertain economic outlook.

In reaching this decision we have, as our remit required, taken account of the forthcoming increase in annual leave entitlement. However, as the available evidence is imperfect and as it should be possible to get a clearer indication of the actual impact in the next few months, we intend to keep the matter under review during the coming year.

In line with our approach to the adult rate, we recommend that in October 2008 the Youth Development Rate should increase from £4.60 to £4.77 an hour and the 16–17 year old rate should increase from £3.40 to £3.53 an hour.

As the recommended minimum wage rates for October 2008 are slightly below the forecast increase in average earnings, we estimate that, if the Government accepts our recommendations, the new rates would achieve a level of coverage a little below that of the 2007 uprating. The direct impact of our recommendations on the average wage bill is likely to be modest. There will be little impact on the public sector wage bill, but the Exchequer is likely to benefit from reduced benefits and increased tax receipts as the minimum wage increases.

Our long-term aim is to create and maintain a minimum wage that helps as many low-paid workers as possible without significant adverse impact on employment or the economy. Looking forward, we expect the increases we recommend for October 2009 to be particularly influenced by three factors: the nature of the broad economic environment; the findings of the research programme we have instigated to assess the impact of the series of increases in the minimum wage implemented from 2003 onwards; and developments in the low-paying sectors. We expect that the rates we will recommend next year for October 2009 will be broadly around the predicted increase in average earnings, but our decision will ultimately depend on the evidence.

Recommendations

National Minimum Wage Rates

We recommend that the adult rate of the minimum wage should be increased from £5.52 to £5.73 an hour in October 2008. (Paragraph 5.41)

We recommend that the Youth Development Rate should increase from £4.60 to £4.77 an hour and the 16–17 rate should increase from £3.40 to £3.53 an hour in October 2008. (Paragraph 5.44)

21 Year Olds

We recommend again that 21 year olds should be entitled to the adult rate of the National Minimum Wage. Should the Government maintain its opposition to this proposal, we would welcome an indication of the exact nature of its opposition and a specification of what would need to change for the Government to adopt a positive approach to this recommendation. (Paragraph 3.36)

The Data

We recommend that the Government take steps to reverse the cuts to the sample of the Annual Survey of Hours and Earnings and prevent further erosion of the quality of the key data provided by the Office for National Statistics. (Paragraph 2.26)

Accommodation Offset

We recommend that the value of the accommodation offset should rise from £4.30 per day to £4.46 per day from October 2008. (Paragraph 5.50)

Guidance

We recommend that the Government reviews the existing official guidance on sleepovers as soon as practicable (Paragraph 3.74) and updates the material concerning work experience placements in the official guide to the minimum wage. (Paragraph 3.65)

Fair Piece Rates

We recommend that the Government takes stock and evaluates whether the fair piece rates arrangement is meeting its objectives. (Paragraph 3.69)

List of Figures

List of Tables

Chapter 1

Introduction

Terms of Reference

1.1 In this report, like its predecessors, we review the impact of the National Minimum Wage, consider the economic outlook for the UK and weigh the available body of evidence before making a number of recommendations to the Government for the future.

1.2 Our terms of reference asked us to:

- Monitor, evaluate and review the National Minimum Wage and its impact, with particular reference to the effect on pay, employment and competitiveness in the low-paying sectors and small firms; the effect on different groups of workers, including different age groups, ethnic minorities, women and people with disabilities and migrant workers; the effect on pay structures; and taking into account any forthcoming changes to the statutory annual leave entitlement;

- Review the levels of each of the different minimum wage rates and make recommendations for October 2008; and

- Contribute to Government consultations and reviews on major policy issues impacting the National Minimum Wage.

Responding to the recommendation in our 2007 Report that the Low Pay Commission be invited to review the apprentice exemptions, the Government told us that it thought it would be inappropriate for the Commission to review the apprentice and pre-apprentice exemptions as, at the time, it was consulting on plans to raise the participation age in education, which included plans to expand apprenticeships.

1.3　We were asked to report to the Prime Minister and the Secretary of State for Trade and Industry by the end of February 2008. In June 2007, as part of a series of changes to the machinery of Government, the newly created Department for Business, Enterprise and Regulatory Reform (BERR) assumed the responsibilities for the National Minimum Wage previously managed by the Department of Trade and Industry (DTI). Accordingly, we are now reporting to the Secretary of State for BERR.

Research

1.4　In order to inform our thinking for this report we commissioned two new research projects focusing on some of the key parts of our remit. One project investigated the impact of the October 2006 upratings, the other looked at the impact of the minimum wage on prices. In addition, we conducted two in-house projects. The first examined the changes in pay composition of the low paid since 1997; the second sought to understand some of the hidden complexities behind official data recording the number of workers paid below the adult rate of the minimum wage. Details of these research projects and a summary of the findings are set out in Appendix 2. We will shortly publish the research reports on our website (www.lowpay.gov.uk) and make them available in certain libraries.

1.5　We organised a research workshop in October 2007 which enabled the researchers working on these projects to share their emerging findings with each other and the Commission. Guest speakers were invited to give presentations and the Commission Secretariat presented some of its work on changes in pay composition.

Statistics

1.6　From the outset, our recommendations have been evidence-based. Accordingly, we place great store on our analyses of official data. It is with great regret, therefore, that we note that changes introduced during the course of the past year by the Office for National Statistics (ONS) have impaired our ability to conduct some of the analyses that we previously relied upon to monitor the impact of the minimum wage. We discuss these concerns in more detail in Chapter 2.

Visits

1.7   Meeting those directly affected by the minimum wage is a crucial part of the Commission's preparations for making recommendations to the Government. In 2007 our programme of visits focused on the low-paying sectors and we talked with representatives from organisations both large and small. We held meetings with some firms and a range of associations that represent firms in the sectors most affected by the minimum wage. We also met union officials and other individuals who represent those working in low-paying jobs. We travelled to a number of different urban and rural areas of England and to Belfast in Northern Ireland; Aviemore in Scotland; and Cardiff in Wales.

Consultation

1.8   In addition to our visits, we have consulted widely during the preparation of this report, especially throughout the low-paying sectors. We undertook a written consultation exercise between July and October. We used our extensive mailing list and website to reach interested parties and encouraged individuals, firms and organisations to submit their evidence to us. We received over 60 written submissions from employer organisations, trade associations, unions, voluntary organisations, pressure groups, individuals, academics and the Government.

1.9   We also held two day-long sessions to gather oral evidence from key interested groups. This gave an opportunity for a number of important stakeholders to expand on points they had made in written evidence. At the oral evidence sessions we discussed the evidence presented by the CBI, the TUC, and delegations representing key low-paying sectors including hospitality, retail, social care, cleaning and support sectors as well as a group of young people.

1.10   Additionally, the Secretariat met with many other interested organisations throughout the year.

Timing

1.11   We met over two days in mid-January 2008 to review all of the relevant evidence and to agree the recommendations contained in this report.

Conclusion

1.12   In conclusion, we would like to record our gratitude to the wide range of organisations and individuals who made time to write or speak to us in order to pass on their views, comments and advice. Their efforts have made an important contribution to our work and have informed our recommendations. The evidence they have produced has helped to make this report better informed and more relevant. The lists of organisations we visited and of those that provided written submissions and gave oral evidence are set out in Appendix 1.

The Impact of the National Minimum Wage

Introduction

2.1 Since its introduction in 1999, we have carefully monitored the impact of the National Minimum Wage to determine its effects on the economy in general and on the labour market in particular. A legally enforced minimum wage set at a reasonable level raises the wage costs faced by at least some employers and this is likely to have consequences across a range of economic variables. This chapter sets out to establish whether and to what extent the National Minimum Wage has had an impact on wages and, having done so, considers how it has affected other economic outcomes.

2.2 Two things are clear from economic theory. The first is that, in the presence of a wage effect from a minimum wage, employers will need to adjust on some margin. Something has to give. Raising the wages of low-paid workers can affect a number of economic variables, principal among which are: employment, prices, productivity and profits. The second implication is that the level at which the minimum wage is set is crucial to the magnitude of those economic effects and to the scale of any negative impact.

2.3 When setting the National Minimum Wage in the UK we have sought to set it at a level that minimises any harmful outcome. Our focus has been firmly on ensuring limited adverse effects on employment and the evidence to date suggests that the strategy has been successful.

2.4 This chapter also looks at the impact on those industries, firms and workers which are more likely to be affected by the minimum wage. We start by giving a brief overview of those sectors and workers.

Who is Affected Most by the National Minimum Wage?

2.5   It is well established that different industries and occupations have different wage distributions with some paying more than others. In our 2007 Report, we described in detail how we define the low-paying sectors[1], but it is basically those industries or occupations that employ a high number of minimum wage workers or those in which a high proportion of jobs are paid at the minimum wage. Figure 2.1 gives a breakdown of the number of jobs in each of our industry-defined low-paying sectors and the proportion of those that are paid at or below the minimum wage[2]. It is important to note that while we may classify a sector as low-paying, it clearly does not follow that all jobs in that sector will be low-paid. Many of the workers in these sectors will be earning well above the minimum wage, but each sector also has a substantial proportion of low-paid jobs. It is important to bear in mind as well that these low-paying sectors account for only 70 per cent of all employees paid at or below the minimum wage. Therefore, roughly 30 per cent of low-paid employees work in industries that we do not identify as low-paying sectors.

2.6   In terms of jobs, retail (including the motor trade) was the largest low-paying sector in September 2007 with 3.4 million jobs (40 per cent of all jobs in the low-paying sectors). However, in April 2007, only 7.5 per cent of these retail jobs were paid at or below the minimum wage[3]. Hospitality was the next largest sector with 1.8 million jobs (22 per cent of all jobs in the low-paying sectors). In this sector, 17.2 per cent of the workforce were paid at or below the minimum wage. The third largest low-paying sector, social care, had 1.2 million jobs (14 per cent of all jobs in the low-paying sectors), but only 5.1 per cent of these were paid at or below the minimum wage. Together the jobs in these three sectors accounted for three-quarters of all employee jobs in the low-paying sectors. They also accounted for over 50 per cent of all minimum wage employees. However, the two low-paying sectors with the largest proportion of employees paid at or below the minimum wage were hairdressing (22.2 per cent) and cleaning (19.3 per cent), although together these accounted for just 7 per cent of all minimum wage jobs.

---

[1]   See Appendix 5 of our 2007 Report.
[2]   Minimum wage jobs are defined throughout this section as those paid below the downrated value of the forthcoming minimum wage (£5.52 in October 2007). That is, adult jobs paying below £5.40, jobs for 18–21 year olds paying less than £4.50 and jobs for 16–17 year olds paying less than £3.32.
[3]   The latest data at industry level are September 2007 for jobs and April 2007 for earnings.

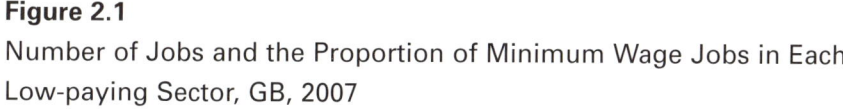

Figure 2.1

Number of Jobs and the Proportion of Minimum Wage Jobs in Each Low-paying Sector, GB, 2007

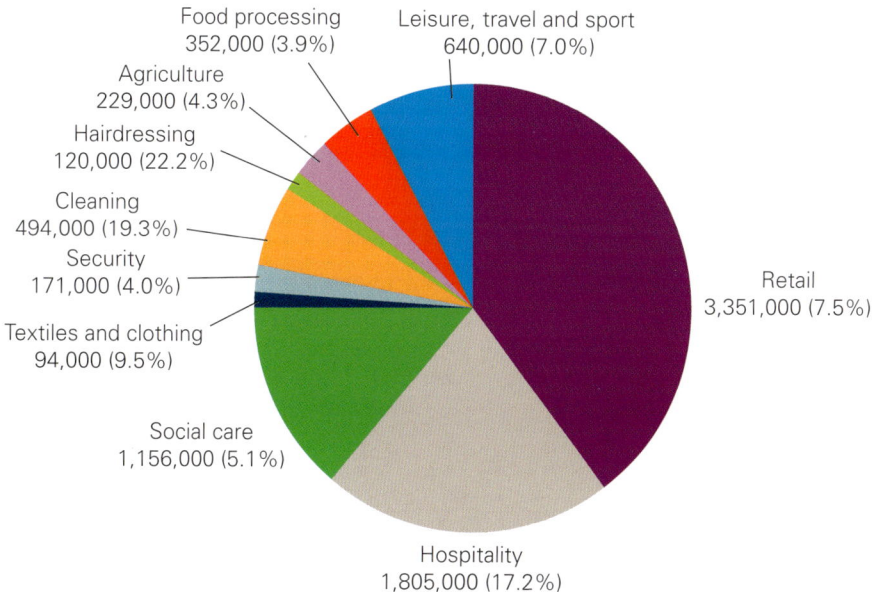

Food processing
352,000 (3.9%)

Leisure, travel and sport
640,000 (7.0%)

Agriculture
229,000 (4.3%)

Hairdressing
120,000 (22.2%)

Cleaning
494,000 (19.3%)

Security
171,000 (4.0%)

Textiles and clothing
94,000 (9.5%)

Social care
1,156,000 (5.1%)

Hospitality
1,805,000 (17.2%)

Retail
3,351,000 (7.5%)

Source: ONS employee jobs series, not seasonally adjusted, GB, September 2007 and ONS Annual Survey of Hours and Earnings (ASHE) 2007 methodology, low-pay weights, UK, April 2007.
Note: Figures in parentheses are the proportion of jobs in April 2007 that paid below the downrated value of the forthcoming minimum wage (£5.52 in October 2007). That is, adult jobs paying below £5.40, jobs for 18–21 year olds paying less than £4.50 and jobs for 16–17 year olds paying less than £3.32.

2.7   In our review of the low-paying sectors, we also looked at low-paying occupations because some areas of low-paid employment (such as childcare and office work) could not be identified using industry classifications. We have therefore used occupational definitions to investigate the impact on jobs and earnings in these occupations. Over the year to September 2007[4], there were on average around 355,000 jobs in low-paying childcare occupations and 308,000 jobs in low-paying office work occupations. About 8 per cent of jobs in childcare and 4 per cent of jobs in office work were paid at or below the minimum wage in April 2007.

2.8   Evidence from our consultation exercises and from official data suggests that smaller firms are more likely to be affected by the minimum wage than larger ones. In April 2007, more than 10 per cent of jobs in micro firms (with 1 to 9 employees) and 7 per cent in other small firms (10 to 49 employees) were estimated to be paying at or

---

[4]   Average over the year (the fourth quarter 2006 through to the third quarter of 2007) calculated using Labour Force Survey microdata.

below the minimum wage. In contrast, only 4 per cent of jobs in large firms (250 employees or more) were paid at or below the minimum wage. Minimum wage jobs are also more likely to be found in the private sector than in the non-profit sector. They are least likely to be found in the public sector although many public sector bodies now contract out services, such as cleaning and security, to private sector organisations.

2.9   In our 2007 Report, we reported that around two-thirds of minimum wage jobs were held by women and around 60 per cent of all minimum wage jobs were part-time. This remains the case. In April 2007, 64 per cent of minimum wage jobs were held by women and 61 per cent were part-time. Minimum wage jobs were also more likely to be temporary or casual than permanent. Some ethnic minority groups, such as Pakistanis and Bangladeshis, those with disabilities, those under 25 and those over 60 were also more likely to be employed in minimum wage jobs.

2.10   In this chapter we first consider recent developments in the broader UK economy and how they differ from those forecast at the time we made our recommendations in our 2007 Report.

Economic Outcome Compared with Expectations

2.11   In January 2007, when we discussed our recommendations for uprating the minimum wage in October 2007, we concluded that reasons for caution outweighed other considerations[5]. As a result, we recommended that the adult minimum wage should increase by 3.2 per cent. Similar percentage increases were also recommended for both youth rates (3.4 per cent for 18–21 year olds and 3.0 per cent for 16–17 year olds). These upratings were expected to be in line with median pay settlements, a little below average earnings growth and a little above retail price inflation.

---

[5]   See LPC 2007 Report, paragraphs 7.38–7.43.

Table 2.1

Actual Outturn Compared with Forecasts, UK, 2007[1]

	Latest Data (Whole year 2007 unless stated otherwise)	Forecasts Used in 2007 Report (February 2007)	
		2007	2008
GDP Growth[2]	3.1	2.5	2.5
Employment growth[3]	0.9	0.8	0.7
Claimant Unemployed (millions)[4]	0.81	1.00	1.01
Average earnings (AEI including bonuses, GB)[5]	4.0	4.3	4.3
Price Inflation Retail Price Index (RPI)[4]	4.2	2.9	2.6
Retail Price Index excluding mortgage interest payments (RPIX)[4]	3.1	2.5	2.5
Consumer Price Index (CPI)[4]	2.1	2.0	2.0

Source: Latest data from ONS (January 2008) and Forecasts from HM Treasury (February 2007). GDP growth (ABMI); Total employment as measured by Workforce Jobs (DYDC); Claimant unemployed (BCJD); Average Earnings Index including bonuses (LNNC), all seasonally adjusted, RPI (CZBH); RPIX (CDKQ); CPI (D7G7), not seasonally adjusted, UK (GB for AEI), 2006–2007.

Notes:

1. Figures for actual data are consistent with the forecasts unless stated otherwise.
2. Data and forecasts are for whole year growth.
3. Latest data are for Quarter 3 2007. Forecasts refer to annual growth.
4. Data and forecasts are for Quarter 4 2007.
5. Latest data are for the three months to November 2007. Forecasts refer to whole year growth.

2.12   Table 2.1 reveals how the forecasts compare with the outturn. It shows that in 2007 the economy performed better than had been expected. Throughout 2007, the UK's macroeconomic performance was strong and stable with GDP growth at 3.1 per cent. Consumer spending held up more strongly than anticipated at the start of the year, as consumers used savings and increased borrowing to offset reductions in their real disposable income. Government expenditure growth slowed in 2007 but business investment was strong over the year (although it weakened towards the end of 2007). The year concluded with continued uncertainty as the impact of the US financial difficulties led to disruptions in international and domestic financial markets. There was some evidence that, as a result, credit conditions had tightened in both the corporate and household sectors and were expected to tighten further into 2008. In addition, retail sales growth appeared to have slowed sharply by the end of 2007, leading most commentators to revise their forecasts for UK GDP growth in 2008 downwards. We shall comment further on these forecasts in Chapter 5.

2.13   Amid this uncertainty, the UK labour market remained remarkably robust. Employment growth in 2007 was slightly stronger than had been forecast. After the sluggish growth observed in the first quarter of 2007, employment recovered strongly and reached record highs in the three months to November 2007[6], and much of that increase was in full-time and permanent employee jobs. The available data suggest that growth in the low-paying sectors was at least as strong as in the economy as a whole in the year to September 2007. Although the forecasts anticipated an increase in unemployment, both headline unemployment and claimant unemployment fell over the year. However, the labour market for low-skilled workers, especially young people, performed less well than the market as a whole.

2.14   The performance of the forecasts for price inflation in 2007 was mixed. Despite rising prices for energy, fuel and food, by the end of 2007 consumer price inflation, as measured by the Consumer Price Index (CPI), had fallen back close to the Bank of England target of 2 per cent. Business services prices also remained relatively muted to the end of the third quarter of 2007. In contrast, retail price inflation measures (RPI and RPIX) were higher than forecast. In addition, producer prices for both inputs and outputs rose sharply in the last quarter of 2007.

2.15   Recent ONS data (up to December 2007) suggest that the economy continued to grow above trend, that household spending was holding up, retail sales had been robust, productivity growth was strong and the labour market was buoyant with unemployment falling and employment at record levels. Further, RPI price inflation had not fallen as quickly as forecast and has been at 4 per cent or thereabouts throughout 2007. In such circumstances and with RPI widely referred to in wage negotiations, one might expect that wage pressures would be increasing. But there has been little evidence that these factors have led to higher wage pressures (whether measured by official average earnings data or using pay settlements data from independent private sector sources). Although pay settlements have increased, they have done so only moderately. Moreover, official data from ONS suggest that average wage growth (including and excluding bonuses) has been steady. Indeed, the growth in average earnings was also lower than RPI price inflation across manufacturing, private sector

---

[6]   The latest data at the time the recommendations were agreed.

services and the public sector. As a result, average wage growth has been lower than we had anticipated in January 2007.

2.16　Between 1999 and mid-2006, Figure 2.2 shows that growth in the Average Earnings Index (AEI) including bonuses was typically about one percentage point higher than the average of the median level of pay settlements[7], which have tended to be more or less in line with price inflation as measured by RPI. Over the last year, however, average earnings including bonuses have grown between 3.5 and 4.1 per cent, compared with around 3.5 per cent for pay settlements. RPI, on the other hand, has grown between 3.8 and 4.8 per cent. Only the ONS wage series, Average Weekly Earnings (AWE)[8], showed signs that wage inflation had increased. However, this is an experimental series and ONS regards the AEI as the best short-term measure of average wage growth.

2.17　Several explanations have been put forward to explain why average earnings are relatively subdued. Among the most plausible is the argument that the supply of labour has been greater than the growth in demand. There are three major factors contributing to the faster growth of supply: the large increase in the number of migrants entering the UK; the substantial rise in the number of workers of pensionable age looking for work, and the small but significant decrease in the numbers on disability and sickness benefits. Pressures on wages have probably reduced as a result.

---

[7]　The AEI captures the totality of changes in all elements of pay such as bonuses, pay progression, overtime, interim adjustments and pay restructuring outside the annual pay review, as well as changes in workforce composition. Pay settlements, on the other hand, only capture consolidated increases in basic pay and performance-related pay rises.

[8]　The AEI and AWE are both based on data from the Monthly Wages and Salary Survey (MWSS), but they differ in terms of weighting, estimation, imputation, the handling of outliers and the treatment of smaller firms. See Appendix 3 for further detail.

Figure 2.2

Comparison of Growth in Average Earnings (GB) with Median Pay Settlements and Price Inflation (UK), 2001–2007

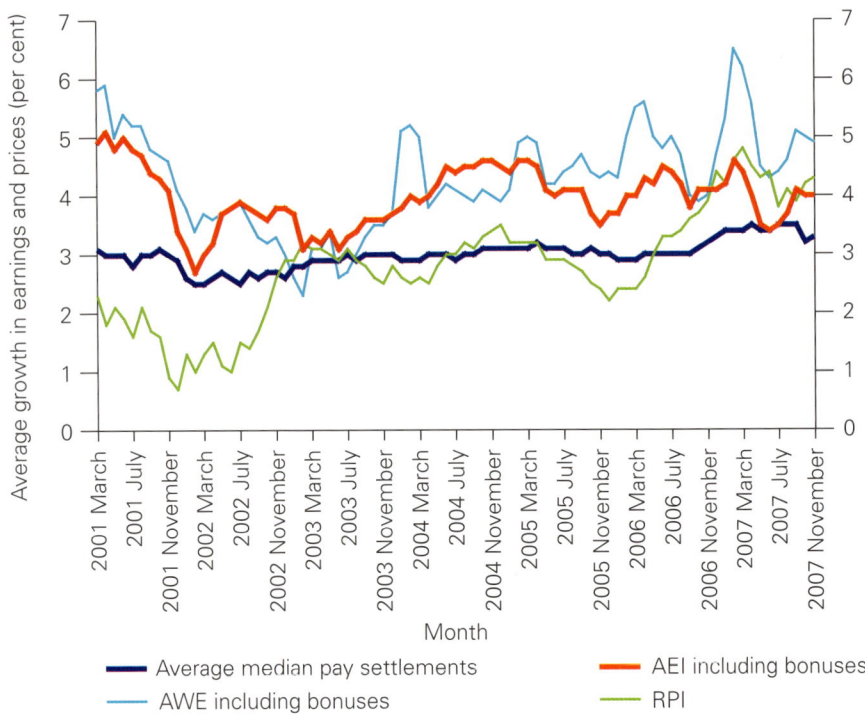

Source: ONS, AEI including bonuses (ONS code LNNC), Average Weekly Earnings (ONS website, 3 month average growth for whole economy), RPI (ONS code CZBH). LPC estimates of average median pay settlements from IRS, IDS, LRD and EEF pay databank records, monthly, seasonally adjusted, UK (GB for AEI), 2001–2007.

Notes:

1. The AEI growth rates shown are 3-month average percentage changes compared with the same period a year earlier.
2. The RPI growth rates are percentage changes over a year earlier. These figures are not seasonally adjusted.
3. Pay settlements are medians over 3 months. The IDS monthly series began in December 2002. The average of median pay settlements prior to that time uses IRS, LRD and EEF.

2.18   The increase in the National Minimum Wage in October 2007 of 3.2 per cent was, as expected, in line with pay settlements and below average earnings growth. However, the upratings were also below the increases in RPI. Our expectation that the recommended uprating would produce a small increase in wages above RPI for those at the bottom of the pay distribution was therefore not realised. The wage rises of the average employee were also below RPI.

The Quality of the Data

2.19   Before we proceed to look at the impact on earnings and employment, we must first register a concern about official data. From the outset, the Commission has relied heavily on data from the Office for National Statistics (ONS) to inform its analysis of earnings and other developments in the labour market. After problems in the early years with data that proved inadequate to assess the impact of the minimum wage, ONS worked hard to upgrade the quality of the material and succeeded in improving considerably the quality of official data on low pay. Throughout the years, we have worked closely with ONS to improve our understanding of the data and its limitations, benefiting from the expertise of its staff, and developing good working relations that have resulted in joint research and in our needs often being taken into account in ONS work plans.

2.20   It is therefore disturbing to report that this year we once more have concerns about the quality of official data. In March 2007, ONS announced major changes to several of its business surveys including reductions in the sample of the Annual Survey of Hours and Earnings (ASHE), a crucial data set on which we rely heavily. Along with other main users, we had been formally consulted about a proposed 10 per cent cut in the sample of ASHE. We objected, pointing out how vital this series was to our ability to monitor the impact of minimum wage upratings. Notwithstanding our protests, ONS implemented a cut at an even higher level of 20 per cent with no further consultation and in the face of strong opposition from the user community. Our further objections proved in vain.

2.21   Although we remain confident that the ASHE estimates are robust at the aggregate level, this significant reduction in the ASHE sample has reduced the reliability of estimates at detailed industry and occupation level and therefore impaired our ability to analyse what is happening in some individual low-paying sectors.

2.22   At the same time, ONS also introduced some methodological changes, which are designed to improve the quality of the data going forward. However, they cause a further break in this earnings series, coming on top of the discontinuity introduced in 2004 as a result of the ONS earnings review. Consistent earnings data are only available within each of the periods 1997–2004, 2004–2006 and 2006–2007[9]. This means that we are unable to compare the latest data for 2007, on a consistent basis, with 2005, let alone with the period before the introduction of the minimum wage.

2.23   In a further change, the annual re-benchmarking of the employee jobs series has caused a break in that series, with the result that measures of annual changes in employment between March 2006 and June 2007 are no longer reliable. The employee jobs series is our main source for monitoring changes in employment by industry and so this further impedes our analyses of the low-paying sectors. We were not informed of this discontinuity until we received the revised data. ONS have also cut the sample of two constituent surveys by 12–15 per cent; however, better targeting has limited the adverse impact.

2.24   Over time, the results obtained from our disaggregated analyses of the LFS microdata (based on population estimates for Spring 2003) become more divergent from those results published on the ONS website at the aggregate level (based on the latest population estimates). The latest population estimates, which allow for the recent large increases in migration, are much higher than those in 2003. Further, as noted in our 2007 Report, the move in the reporting period for the LFS from seasonal to calendar quarters has caused a break in the microdata series. While we recognise the reasons for these changes, they have severely limited our ability to carry out analyses that compare the present with the period prior to the introduction of the minimum wage. The problem could be resolved by the production of a revised historical series and in January 2006, at the time this change was introduced, ONS indicated that they intended to produce a back series as soon as possible. To date, however, only a very limited back series has been made available but we welcome the assurances given to us by ONS that it

---

[9]   Further details of the sample cuts and methodological changes are given in Appendix 3.

will shortly provide a full back series with current population weights. It is important that we have this data for use in our next report.

2.25 Because of these changes (and others in recent years), many of which we acknowledge are designed to lead to longer term improvements in data quality, we no longer have consistent time series data on either earnings or employment at a disaggregated level that cover the relatively short period from 1999 to present. That is, the data currently available prevent us from being able to assess, on a consistent basis, the impact on earnings and employment of the minimum wage from its introduction to the present day.

2.26 The recommendations we make to Government are based on careful analysis of the best available data. When the quality of the data declines, no amount of excellent analysis can make good the deficit. **We recommend that the Government take steps to reverse the cuts to the sample of the Annual Survey of Hours and Earnings (ASHE) and prevent further erosion of the quality of the key data provided by the Office for National Statistics.**

Impact of the 2006 and 2007 National Minimum Wage Upratings on Earnings

Background

2.27 We start our analysis of the impact on earnings by setting out a table showing how the rates of the National Minimum Wage have increased since its introduction in 1999. Table 2.2 reveals that increases in the minimum wage were largest in October 2001 but were also relatively large in October 2003, October 2004 and October 2006. As noted above, the increase in the minimum wage in October 2007 was more modest at 3.2 per cent for adult workers.

Table 2.2
National Minimum Wage Hourly Rates, UK, 1999–2008

	16–17 Rate		Youth Development Rate (Age 18–21)		Adult Rate (Age 22 and over)	
	NMW	Change (%)	NMW	Change (%)	NMW	Change (%)
April 1999–May 2000	–	–	£3.00	–	£3.60	–
June 2000–September 2000	–	–	£3.20	6.7	£3.60	0.0
October 2000–September 2001	–	–	£3.20	0.0	£3.70	2.8
October 2001–September 2002	–	–	£3.50	9.4	£4.10	10.8
October 2002–September 2003	–	–	£3.60	2.9	£4.20	2.4
October 2003–September 2004	–	–	£3.80	5.6	£4.50	7.1
October 2004–September 2005	£3.00		£4.10	7.9	£4.85	7.8
October 2005–September 2006	£3.00	0.0	£4.25	3.7	£5.05	4.1
October 2006–September 2007	£3.30	10.0	£4.45	4.7	£5.35	5.9
October 2007–September 2008	**£3.40**	**3.0**	**£4.60**	**3.4**	**£5.52**	**3.2**

Coverage of the 2007 Minimum Wage Upratings

2.28   We now look at how many workers were covered by the latest uprating of the minimum wage (October 2007). We confine our analysis here to the adult rate as young workers are covered in Chapter 3. We define a worker as covered if their hourly rate increases as a direct result of the uprating of the minimum wage. We explained the methods that may be used to calculate coverage in some detail in the 2007 Report.

2.29   The latest ASHE earnings data which enable us to estimate coverage were collected in April 2007. Figure 2.3 shows that around 5.2 per cent of jobs (1.196 million) held by those aged 22 and over were paid below the forthcoming October 2007 minimum wage of £5.52. This total was made up of around one per cent of jobs (231,000) which paid below £5.35, the minimum wage in April 2007. About 2.4 per cent of jobs held by adults (565,000) were paid at the minimum wage[10]. A further 400,000 jobs were paid above the £5.35 minimum wage but below the forthcoming rate (£5.52)[11].

---

[10]   Using a 5 pence pay band (those paid at least £5.35 an hour but less than £5.40 an hour).
[11]   Those paid at least £5.40 an hour but less than £5.52 an hour.

Figure 2.3

Hourly Earnings Distribution for Employees Aged 22 and Over, UK, 2007

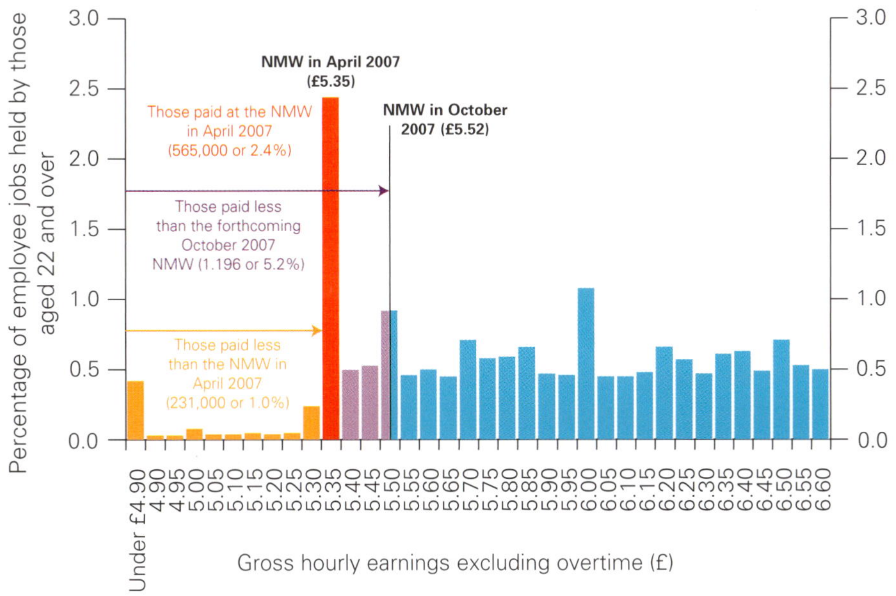

Source: LPC estimates based on ASHE 2007 methodology, low-pay weights, UK, April 2007.

2.30 Not all those paid below £5.52 will have directly benefited from the minimum wage uprating. As explained in our previous report, we would expect some to have received pay rises that would have taken their pay above £5.52 before October. This requires us to make assumptions about how wages would have been adjusted in the absence of a minimum wage. One assumption is that wages would have increased in line with average earnings. An alternative is that they would have increased in line with prices. Assuming the former, we estimate that about 3.4 per cent of jobs (0.8 million) held by adults were covered by the 2007 uprating. Assuming that the wages of the lowest paid would have risen in line with prices, we estimate coverage in the range of 0.87 million to 1.04 million (3.8 to 4.5 per cent), depending on the price index used. These estimates for the 2007 uprating can be compared with our final estimates that around 4.8 per cent of jobs held by adults (1.1 million jobs) were covered by the 2006 minimum wage uprating. Using the prices assumption, this rises to over 5 per cent, or approximately 1.2 million jobs.

Jobs Paid Below the National Minimum Wage

2.31   ONS data consistently record that some workers are paid below the minimum wage. Estimates for April 2007 from ASHE indicate that 292,000 jobs were held by people aged 16 or over with hourly pay below the appropriate National Minimum Wage rate. This represents 1.2 per cent of all UK jobs. The fourth column of Table 2.3 shows that the percentage of jobs held by adults aged 22 and over paid below the minimum wage in April each year has been stable at about 1 per cent since the October 2003 uprating.

2.32   These figures should not be interpreted as the number of workers being denied their legal right to the minimum wage. Some workers will be legitimately paid below the minimum wage. Inputting or counting errors will also result in an apparent underpayment. It seems unlikely that an employer in the formal sector would without a legitimate reason record an employee as being paid less than the National Minimum Wage in response to an official Government survey.

2.33   But these are not the only explanations and therefore this year, together with ONS, we decided to carry out some research, using both ASHE and the LFS, in order to get a better understanding of the reasons behind the recorded underpayment. The research (Holt, 2008a and Jenkins and Johnson, 2008) found that it was not possible to identify precisely how many of those recorded as earning below the minimum wage could be explained by legitimate exemptions or measurement errors. Their best estimate was that non-compliance could not be ruled out as an explanation for between a half and three-quarters of the number of jobs estimated to be paid below the minimum wage, though the limitations of the data made this a very tentative estimate.

Jobs Paid At the National Minimum Wage

2.34   The fifth and sixth columns in Table 2.3 show the number and percentage of jobs paid at or within ten pence of the minimum wage[12]. This has tended to fluctuate from 1.8 per cent of all jobs held by adults to 2.9 per cent (about 400,000 to 700,000 jobs), depending on the size

---

[12]   Jobs paid at the minimum wage are defined in this section as those paying within the same ten pence pay band as the National Minimum Wage (the National Minimum Wage being the lower bound). It differs from the five pence bands used elsewhere in this chapter.

of the minimum wage increase. In April 2007, after the large October 2006 uprating, it was at its highest at 2.9 per cent. The figure for the five pence band used elsewhere in this report is 2.4 per cent.

Table 2.3

Jobs Held By Adults (Aged 22 and Over) Paying Below the Existing National Minimum Wage and the Forthcoming National Minimum Wage, UK, 1999–2007

Data year (April)	Adult minimum wage rate (in April) (£)	Number of jobs held by adults paying less than the adult rate in April (000s)	Percentage of jobs held by adults paying less than the adult rate in April	Number of jobs held by adults in April paying the adult rate (ten pence band) in April (000s)	Percentage of jobs held by adults in April paying the adult rate (ten pence band) in April	Proposed October adult minimum wage rate (£)	Number of jobs held by adults in April paying less than the forthcoming October rate (000s)	Percentage of jobs held by adults in April paying less than the forthcoming October rate
1999	3.60	458	2.1	723	3.3	3.60	458	2.1
2000	3.60	195	0.9	551	2.5	3.70	746	3.3
2001	3.70	207	0.9	394	1.8	4.10	1,326	5.9
2002	4.10	290	1.3	630	2.8	4.20	920	4.1
2003	4.20	211	0.9	445	2.0	4.50	1,022	4.5
2004	4.50	232	1.0	558	2.5	4.85	1,399	6.2
2004	4.50	233	1.0	408	1.8	4.85	1,209	5.3
2005	4.85	233	1.0	484	2.1	5.05	1,147	5.0
2006	5.05	239	1.0	544	2.4	5.35	1,289	5.6
2006	5.05	238	1.0	544	2.4	5.35	1,289	5.6
2007	5.35	231	1.0	681	2.9	5.52	1,196	5.2

Source: ONS central estimates using ASHE without supplementary information and LFS for 1999–2004. LPC estimates using ASHE with supplementary information, low-pay weights, UK, 2004–2006 and ASHE 2007 methodology, low-pay weights, UK, April 2006–2007.
Note: Prior to 2004, all our analyses were conducted in ten pence pay bands using the ONS central estimate methodology. In contrast to elsewhere in this report, where five pence pay bands are used, we use ten pence pay bands in this table.

Jobs in April Paid Below the Forthcoming October Minimum Wage

2.35   The final two columns in Table 2.3 show that, on average in April each year, 5 to 6 per cent of the workforce (about 1.1 to 1.4 million) is paid below the hourly rate at which the minimum wage is due to be set in six months' time. As we would expect, the larger the planned increase, the higher the percentage affected.

The Bite of the National Minimum Wage

2.36   Since the introduction of the minimum wage, the adult rate has increased by 53.3 per cent from £3.60 in April 1999 to £5.52 in October 2007. Over the same period, average earnings have increased by around 41 per cent and prices have increased by between 14 per cent and 27 per cent, depending on the index used. As demonstrated in

Table 2.2, minimum wage increases have not been smooth. Figure 2.4 shows that, between its introduction in April 1999 and October 2004, the adult rate of the National Minimum Wage grew in line with average earnings but it then outpaced increases in average earnings in the period to October 2006. However the last uprating, in October 2007, was lower than the increase in average earnings.

Figure 2.4

Increases in the Adult National Minimum Wage Compared With Changes in Prices (UK) and Average Earnings (GB), 1999–2007

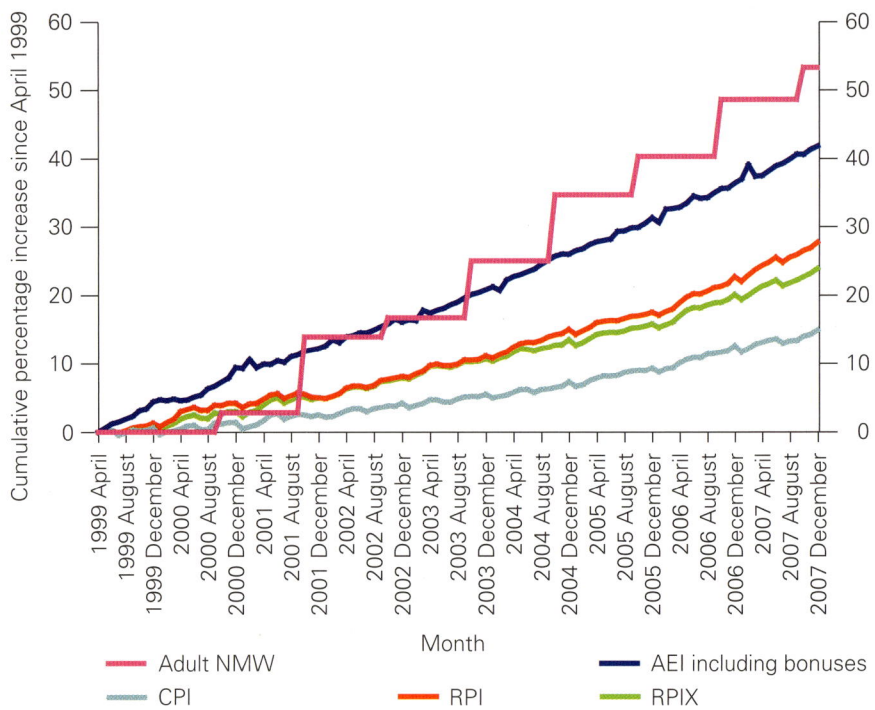

Source: LPC estimates based on ONS data, AEI including bonuses (ONS code LNMQ), RPIX (ONS code CHMK), RPI (ONS code CHAW) and CPI (ONS code D7BT), monthly, not seasonally adjusted (seasonally adjusted for AEI), UK (GB for AEI), 1999–2007.

2.37   The adult minimum wage was over half UK median hourly earnings for the first time in 2007 but was still below 40 per cent of the mean hourly wage[13]. Table 2.4 shows that the 'bite' of the minimum wage, measured against the mean or the median, has fluctuated, noticeably increasing after the large uprating in October 2001, but was not much higher in 2003 than it had been in 1999. Between 2001 and 2005, however, the 'bite' measured against the median increased by over five percentage points although it remained flat in 2006. The 'bite' on all these measures

---

[13] In contrast to previous reports, following advice from ONS, we use ASHE standard weights instead of the low-pay weights. This has the effect of reducing our estimates of the bite.

peaked in April 2007 after the October 2006 upratings. The minimum wage was over 51 per cent of median earnings and nearly 40 per cent of average earnings. It also approached 90 per cent of the lowest decile. Since then, we would expect the bite to have moderated in light of the more modest 3.2 per cent uprating in October 2007.

Table 2.4

The National Minimum Wage as a Percentage of Various Points on the Earnings Distribution, UK, 1999–2007

| | | Adult NMW (£) | Adult minimum wage as % of | | | | | |
			Lowest decile	Lowest quartile	Median	Mean	Upper quartile	Upper decile
ASHE without supplementary information	1999	3.60	83.9	65.1	45.7	36.6	30.4	21.1
	2000	3.60	81.2	64.2	45.4	35.7	29.8	20.6
	2001	3.70	80.3	63.0	44.2	34.7	29.0	19.9
	2002	4.10	85.2	67.5	47.2	36.5	30.8	21.0
	2003	4.20	82.4	65.8	46.5	35.9	30.5	20.8
	2004	4.50	84.9	67.6	47.5	37.2	31.3	21.4
ASHE with supplementary information	2004	4.50	85.6	68.3	48.1	37.7	31.6	21.7
	2005	4.85	88.0	69.9	49.4	38.5	32.3	22.1
	2006	5.05	87.5	69.9	49.4	38.4	32.3	22.1
ASHE 2007 methodology	2006	5.05	87.5	70.0	49.7	38.5	32.5	22.3
	2007	5.35	89.2	71.8	51.1	39.6	33.6	22.9

Source: LPC estimates based on ASHE without supplementary information, standard weights, UK, April 1999–2004, ASHE with supplementary information, standard weights, UK, April 2004–2006 and ASHE 2007 methodology, standard weights, UK, April 2006–2007.
Notes:
1. Direct comparisons before and after 2004 and those before and after 2006 should be made with care due to changes in the data series.
2. Those jobs where pay was affected by absence in the reference period were removed before the percentiles of gross hourly pay excluding overtime were calculated.

Impact on the Distribution of Earnings

2.38   As the 2007 National Minimum Wage upratings were introduced on 1 October 2007 – too recently for data to be available to allow us to assess its impact fully – we concentrate in this section on the National Minimum Wage upratings introduced in October 2006. The relative value of the minimum wage was at its highest in October 2006 and therefore we would expect that the impact of the minimum wage would be most apparent in the earnings data for April 2007. In October 2006, the minimum wage for adults increased by 5.9 per cent, which was substantially greater than average wage growth (around 4.1 per cent). Although young people are considered in more detail in Chapter 3, it should be noted that the minimum wage increased by 4.7 per cent for youths aged 18–21 and by 10 per cent for those aged 16–17. The latter age group had received no increase in October 2005.

2.39   One effect of the adult minimum wage on the hourly earnings distribution for adult workers can clearly be seen in Figure 2.5. There is a concentration of the adult workforce at the National Minimum Wage in both April 2006 and April 2007. Such pronounced spikes were not present in the wage data prior to the introduction of the minimum wage. As a result of the large minimum wage upratings in October 2006, the concentration is higher in 2007 when 2.4 per cent of jobs paid at £5.35 an hour. After the 4.1 per cent increase in October 2005, only 1.9 per cent of jobs were paid at the minimum wage (£5.05 an hour) in April 2006.

Figure 2.5

Hourly Earnings Distribution for Employees Aged 22 and Over, UK, 2006–2007

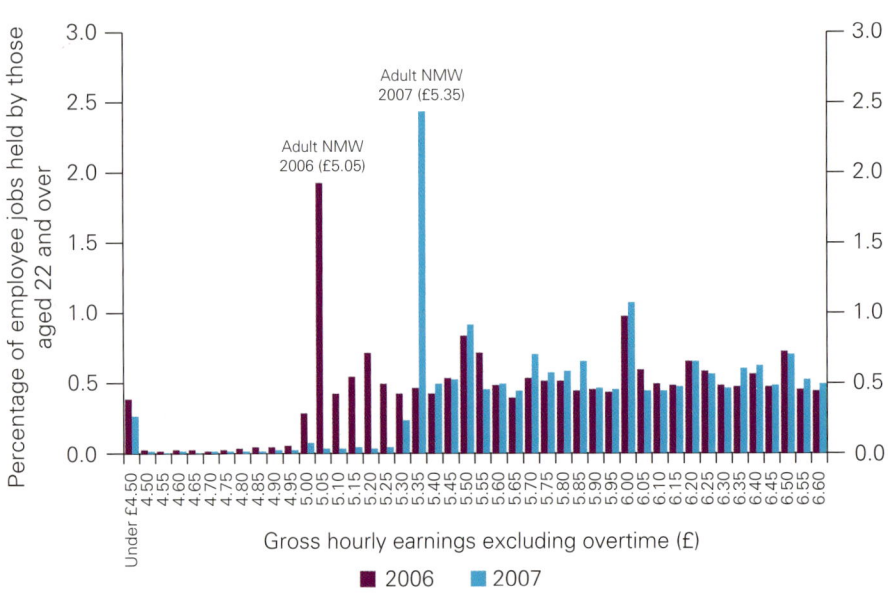

Source: LPC estimates based on ASHE 2007 methodology, low-pay weights, UK, April 2006–2007.
Note: NMW label shows the adult minimum wage rate in April of the given year.

Differentials

2.40   Our analysis above confirms that the October 2006 upratings increased the bite of the minimum wage and had a significant impact on the earnings distribution. We now focus on whether this impact extended to affecting wage differentials.

2.41   Dividing employees into 100 equally sized groups (percentiles) and ranking these groups by their hourly earnings from the lowest paid on the left to the highest paid on the right, Figure 2.6 shows how the earnings at each of these percentiles have changed on average each year compared with those at the median (earners in the middle of the distribution at the 50th percentile) for three periods: 1992–1997 (prior to the introduction of the minimum wage), 1998–2004 (covering the introduction of the minimum wage) and 2004–2007 (covering the more recent minimum wage upratings). For ease of comparison, the earnings at the median are normalised to zero. For example, over the period prior to the introduction of the minimum wage, 1992–1997 (depicted by the pink line), the lowest decile (those employees at the tenth percentile) had wage increases that were, on average, 0.6 per cent lower per annum than the wage increases for those at the median. However, in each of the other periods, 1998–2004 (depicted by the light blue line) and 2004–2007 (represented by the dark blue line), the earnings of the lowest decile increased, on average, by 0.7 per cent more each year than for those in the middle of the distribution.

2.42   Over the period prior to the introduction of the minimum wage, 1992–1997, the wages of the lowest paid increased by less than those at the median, whose wages in turn increased by less than the wages of those at the top of the earnings distribution. Following the introduction of the minimum wage, over the period 1998–2004 those at the bottom of the earnings distribution received higher pay rises than those in the middle of the distribution. Since 2004, the increases in the minimum wage appear to have had a slightly smaller effect than those from the earlier period (1998–2004). However, those at the bottom of the earnings distribution still received higher pay rises than those in the middle of the distribution. Moreover, the earlier minimum wage increases (1998–2004) appear to have had a knock-on effect up to around the 25th percentile, that is, those up to the 25th percentile received increases higher than those at the median. However, the impact declines between the 5th and 25th percentile and is smaller than the increase in the minimum wage. The more recent increases (2004–2007) appear to have had an impact, albeit small, further up the distribution. This provides some evidence of spill-over effects of the minimum wage on the earnings distribution. It also suggests that differentials just above the minimum wage may have been squeezed.

Figure 2.6

Annual Increase in Hourly Earnings minus the Increase in Median Earnings by Percentile for Employees Aged 22 and Over, UK, 1992–2007

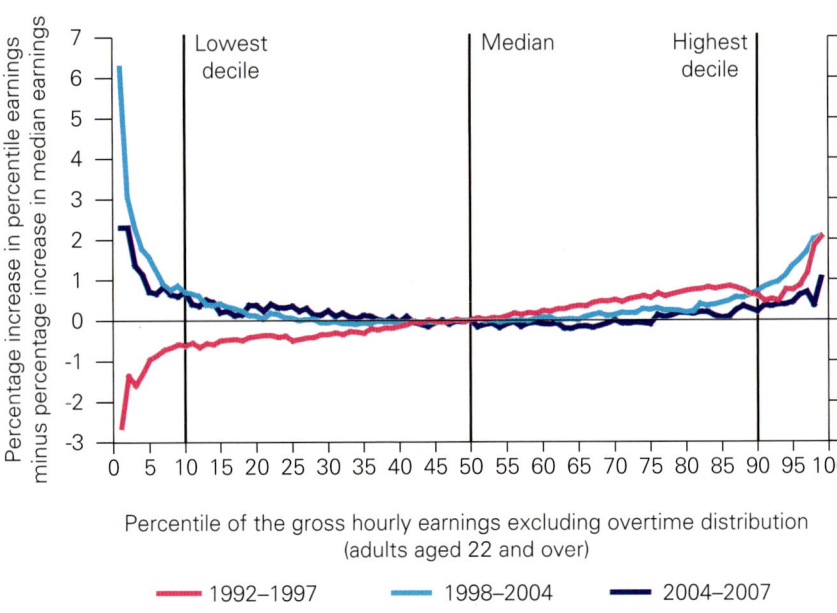

Percentile of the gross hourly earnings excluding overtime distribution (adults aged 22 and over)

1992–1997   1998–2004   2004–2007

Source: LPC estimates based on unweighted New Earnings Survey (NES), April 1992–1997, ASHE without supplementary information, standard weights, UK, April 1998–2004, ASHE with supplementary information, standard weights, UK, April 2004 and ASHE 2007 methodology, standard weights, UK, April 2007.

Notes:

1. Comparisons have been made here for illustrative purposes only as no consistent earnings time series data are available from 1992 to 2007. This analysis uses ASHE with supplementary information for 2004 and ASHE 2007 methodology for 2007. These two series are not strictly comparable although the data for 2006 are similar in both.

2. Those jobs where pay was affected by absence in the reference period were removed before the percentiles were calculated.

2.43   The highest earners have continued to experience large increases in their earnings relative to the average increase. Indeed, Brewer, Sibieta and Wren-Lewis (2008) recently found that the incomes of the top percentile grew at an average real rate of 3.1 per cent a year between 1997 and 2006 (a slowdown on the growth of about 3.8 per cent a year between 1979 and 1997). This compares with average real growth of about 2.3 per cent for the lowest decile between 1997 and 2006 (an improvement on the 0.8 per cent increase between 1979 and 1997). Further, the authors found that the incomes of the very rich (the top 0.1 per cent) grew even faster than the top percentile between 1997 and 2005.

2.44 In our analyses of the minimum wage we have usually focused on percentage changes. However, differentials are often considered by employees and employers in monetary pounds and pence terms. Table 2.5 compares the adult National Minimum Wage in April of each year with the wages at the lowest decile, quartile and median for those aged 22 and over.

2.45 In percentage terms, the upratings of the minimum wage since 2001 have generally been larger than the increase in the median wage. However, in cash terms, the rise in the minimum wage has nearly always produced smaller increases than the rise in median wages. Only the very large uprating in October 2001 led to a cash increase in the minimum wage (40 pence) that exceeded the cash increase in the median wage (32 pence).

2.46 More pertinently to our analyses of differentials, we can see from Table 2.5 that the cash increase in the minimum wage has generally been greater than the cash increase in the lowest decile and lowest quartile in those years of high minimum wage increases (October 2001, 2003, 2004 and 2006 – years 2002, 2004, 2005 and 2007 in the table). The exception was that the increase in the lowest quartile (37 pence) was slightly greater than that of the minimum wage (35 pence) following the October 2004 uprating observed in the 2005 data.

Table 2.5

Percentage and Cash Increases in the National Minimum Wage Compared with Selected Points on the Earnings Distribution, UK, 2000–2008

Age 22 and over	ASHE excluding supplementary information					ASHE including supplementary information			ASHE new methodology		
	2000	2001	2002	2003	2004	2004	2005	2006	2006	2007	2008
NMW (in April)	3.60	3.70	4.10	4.20	4.50	4.50	4.85	5.05	5.05	5.35	5.52
Cash increase (pence)	0	10	40	10	30	30	35	20	20	30	17
Percentage increase	0.0	2.8	10.8	2.4	7.1	7.1	7.8	4.1	4.1	5.9	3.2
Lowest decile	4.40	4.60	4.80	5.05	5.27	5.23	5.50	5.73	5.75	5.97	–
Cash increase (pence)	14	20	20	25	22	–	27	23	–	22	–
Percentage increase	3.3	4.5	4.4	5.1	4.4	–	5.1	4.2	–	3.8	–
Lowest quartile	5.54	5.79	6.00	6.30	6.59	6.51	6.88	7.17	7.16	7.40	–
Cash increase (pence)	8	25	21	30	29	–	37	29	–	24	–
Percentage increase	1.4	4.5	3.6	5.0	5.0	–	5.7	4.2	–	3.4	–
Median	7.85	8.24	8.56	8.90	9.34	9.22	9.69	10.11	10.06	10.37	–
Cash increase (Pence)	9	38	32	35	44	–	47	42	–	31	–
Percentage increase	1.2	4.9	3.9	4.0	4.9	–	5.1	4.3	–	3.1	–

Source: LPC and ONS Annual Survey of Hours and Earnings (ASHE) without supplementary information, 1998–2004, ASHE with supplementary information, 2004–2006 and ASHE 2007 methodology, 2006–2007.

Note: Data are not available for ASHE with supplementary information in 2003 or ASHE 2007 methodology in 2005, hence these increases on the previous year cannot be calculated. ASHE for 2008 is not yet available.

2.47   We have commissioned research to investigate further the impact of the minimum wage on wage differentials. It should report in time for its findings to be included in our next report.

Earnings in the Low-paying Sectors

2.48   Having looked at earnings in the economy as a whole, we now consider the impact of the minimum wage on earnings in the most affected sectors. Table 2.6 below shows the proportion of jobs held by those aged 18 and over[14] in each low-paying sector paid at or below the prevailing adult minimum wage in April 2006 and April 2007. It shows an overall rise, from 6.5 to over 8 per cent, in the proportion of jobs in the industrial low-paying sectors paid at the minimum wage in the year to April 2007. Most sectors experienced an increase. In retail the proportion rose from just over 4 to nearly 7 per cent. Textiles and clothing also experienced a rise, from 5.5 to 7.9 per cent. Conversely, falls in the proportion of jobs paid at the minimum wage occurred in security and childcare.

2.49   Overall, the proportion of jobs in the low-paying sectors that were paid below the minimum wage remained virtually unchanged at 5.5 per cent. The three sectors with the highest proportion of jobs paid below the adult rate in April 2007 were hospitality, hairdressing and childcare. Given the number of young people working in these sectors, this probably reflects the widespread use of the development rate and the apprentice exemptions.

---

[14]   For the low-paying sectors we look at ASHE data for jobs held by those aged 18 and over rather than for those aged 22 and over. A large proportion of the workforce in many low-paying sectors, particularly retail and hospitality, are aged between 18 and 21 years old.

Table 2.6

Percentage of Employee Jobs Held by those Aged 18 and Over Paid at the Adult Minimum Wage or Below by Low-paying Sector, UK, 2006–2007

Sector	April 2006		April 2007	
	% Paid at £5.05	% Paid below £5.05	% Paid at £5.35	% Paid below £5.35
Retail	4.2	5.0	6.9	4.5
Hospitality	15.2	13.5	16.3	13.5
Leisure, travel and sport	5.1	6.1	6.0	7.0
Cleaning	17.6	2.0	18.9	3.0
Security	4.4	0.3	3.4	1.1
Social care	3.6	2.3	4.2	2.2
Agriculture	2.7	3.1	2.8	3.3
Textiles and clothing	5.5	1.7	7.9	2.4
Hairdressing	8.7	16.7	8.8	17.6
Food processing	3.6	1.3	4.1	0.5
Office work[2]	2.3	3.0	3.3	2.8
Childcare[2]	4.3	7.2	3.8	7.3
All low-paying industrial sectors	**6.5**	**5.6**	**8.2**	**5.5**
Whole economy	**2.2**	**2.3**	**2.8**	**2.3**

Source: LPC estimates based on ASHE 2007 methodology, low-pay weights, UK, April 2006–2007.
Notes:
1. This table also includes those aged 18–21 paid at or below the adult rate in 2006 and 2007.
2. These sectors are defined using occupations. The other sectors are based on industry. The definitions are explained in detail in Appendix 5 of our 2007 Report.

2.50 Research we commissioned for this report by Incomes Data Services (IDS, 2007a) looked at the impact of the minimum wage across six low-paying industries (retail; hotels; fast food, pubs and restaurants; leisure; social care; and childcare). It found that the National Minimum Wage continues to have a substantial impact on the lowest rates of pay across all six industries. The minimum wage was the lowest rate of pay in one third of the social care organisations and in three quarters of the hotels surveyed. The research also found that in some sectors the minimum wage rate affected core staff (in particular in fast food establishments, pubs and restaurants and the leisure sector). In other sectors, such as social care, the impact of the minimum wage was felt mainly by support staff, such as cleaners and porters, who were below the main customer service grade. In the retail sector, trainee and starter rates were particularly affected.

2.51 We turn next to examine the impact of the National Minimum Wage on earnings in specific low-paying sectors. We focus on those industrial low-paying sectors which account for the largest numbers of minimum wage jobs (retail, hospitality, social care and cleaning), together with the childcare occupational sector.

Retail

2.52   Figure 2.7 (and Table 2.6) shows that there was a significant increase in the proportion of retail jobs paid at the National Minimum Wage between April 2006 and April 2007, up from just over 4 per cent to nearly 7 per cent. Although small retail firms continued to be most affected, the impact on large retail firms increased substantially between 2006 and 2007 and, for the first time since the introduction of the minimum wage, the highest peak in the earnings distribution for large firms was at the adult rate.

Figure 2.7

Hourly Earnings Distribution for Employees Aged 18 and Over in the Retail Sector, UK, 2006–2007

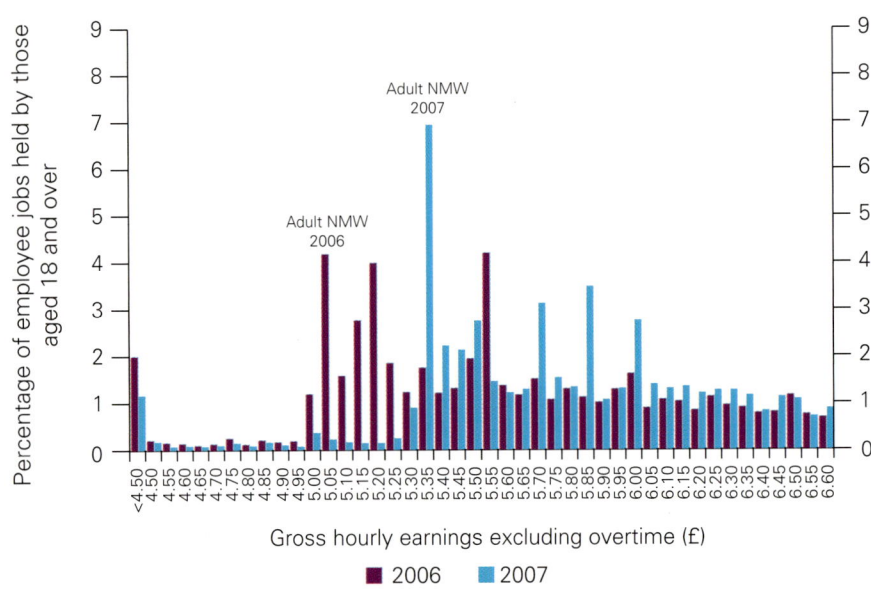

Source: LPC estimates based on ASHE 2007 methodology, low-pay weights, UK, April 2006–2007.
Note: NMW label shows the adult minimum wage rate in April of the given year.

2.53   There is some evidence that pay differentials in the sector have been squeezed, with a 13 per cent reduction in the gap between the minimum wage and the first quartile in the earnings distribution. IDS (2007a) found that the gap between the established rates of pay (normally payable after six to twelve months of starting) and the adult minimum wage had narrowed between 2003 and 2006. It noted that the largest gap between the National Minimum Wage and minimum starter rates had been maintained by relatively small retailers, although many large multiple retailers had also maintained a differential. IDS also found that many retailers had recently taken action to address the erosion of differentials between their sales assistants' rates and those of supervisors and managers.

Hospitality

2.54 Table 2.6 also shows that the proportion of jobs paid at the minimum wage in hospitality increased from 15.2 per cent to 16.3 per cent between April 2006 and April 2007. This is also illustrated in Figure 2.8. The increase in the minimum wage was felt across firms of all sizes but was most evident in small firms (those employing fewer than 50 employees), where over 18 per cent of jobs paid at the minimum wage in April 2007 (up from just under 16 per cent in April 2006).

2.55 The earnings data provide some evidence of a compression of differentials. Between April 2006 and April 2007 the differential between the adult minimum wage and the fourth decile reduced from 30 pence to 25 pence an hour. IDS (2007a) found that in fast food, pubs and restaurants a key impact of the October 2006 uprating was a narrowing of pay bands, squeezing pay differentials between team members and supervisors.

> At just over three-quarters of the hotels surveyed, the lowest rate of pay was £5.35 an hour. The most common jobs affected by the uplift in the National Minimum Wage were kitchen porters, luggage porters, and waiting staff.
>
> **IDS Research, 2007**

Figure 2.8

Hourly Earnings Distribution for Employees Aged 18 and Over in the Hospitality Sector, UK, 2006–2007

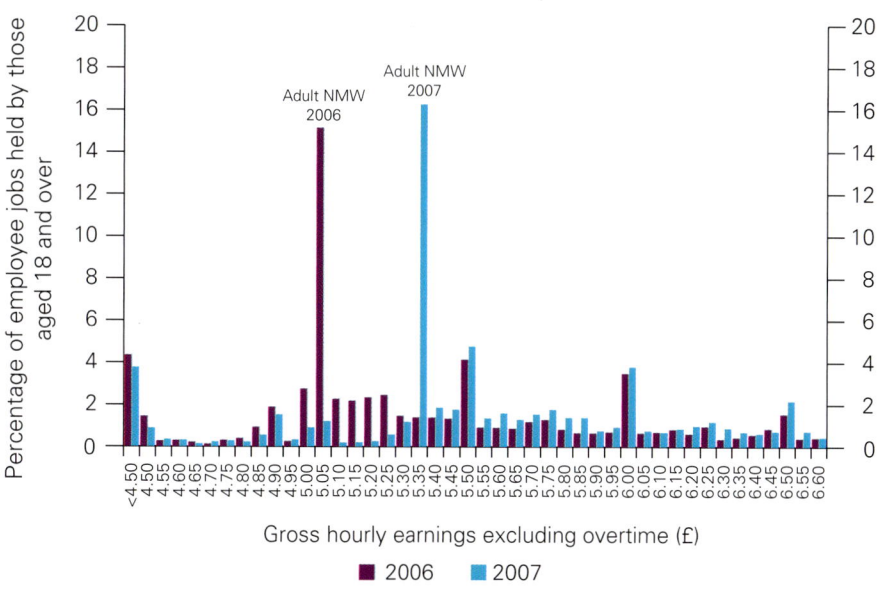

Source: LPC estimates based on ASHE 2007 methodology, low-pay weights, UK, April 2006–2007.
Note: NMW label shows the adult minimum wage rate in April of the given year.

Social Care

2.56   The social care sector, as a whole, is less affected by the minimum wage than either retail or hospitality but is the fourth largest affected sector in terms of the number of minimum wage jobs. Although minimum wage jobs account for a small proportion of all jobs in social care, Table 2.6 and Figure 2.9 show that there has been a slight increase in the proportion paid at the adult minimum wage between 2006 and 2007, from 3.6 to 4.2 per cent. The impact of the minimum wage in social care is far greater in the private sector, where in April 2007, 7 per cent of jobs were paid at this level, compared to 2 per cent of jobs in the voluntary sector, and fewer than 1 per cent in the public sector.

Figure 2.9

Hourly Earnings Distribution for Employees Aged 18 and Over in the Social Care Sector, UK, 2006–2007

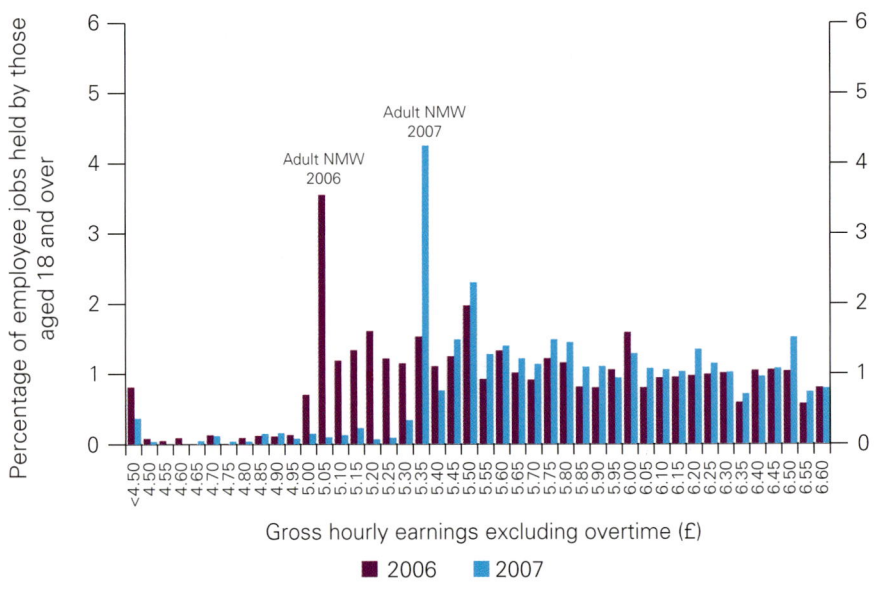

Source: LPC estimates based on ASHE 2007 methodology, low-pay weights, UK, April 2006–2007.
Note: NMW label shows the adult minimum wage rate in April of the given year.

2.57   There was some limited evidence of an erosion of differentials. The differential in the hourly rate between the fifth percentile (equating to the prevailing adult rate of the National Minimum Wage) and first quartile, reduced from 81 pence to 76 pence between April 2006 and April 2007. However, there was virtually no change in the differential between the minimum wage and median earnings. This suggests that employers in this sector may also have taken action to maintain pay differentials for more senior staff. IDS research indicated that one third of organisations in social care had to raise pay rates to comply with the October 2006 minimum wage upratings – the same proportion as last year – with a median increase of 25 pence per hour. However, the number of staff affected in any organisation was generally fewer than one in ten, although in some cases it was much higher.

2.58   IDS also found that the minimum wage was becoming the lowest pay rate in a growing number of social care organisations: one-third in 2007, compared to one-quarter in 2006. Nearly half of the social care organisations that took part in the survey said that they were experiencing recruitment problems, and a third reported difficulties with retention, particularly for non-supervisory level care staff. The reasons given for this included low pay and lack of sufficient skills.

Childcare

2.59   Earnings figures for childcare, in Table 2.6 and Figure 2.10, show a small fall between April 2006 and April 2007 in the proportion of jobs paid at the minimum wage, to just under 4 per cent. If we look specifically at nursery nurses we find that the proportion of jobs paid at the minimum wage fell from 4.8 per cent in April 2006 to 3.2 per cent in April 2007.

Figure 2.10

Hourly Earnings Distribution for Employees Aged 18 and Over in the Childcare Sector, UK, 2006–2007

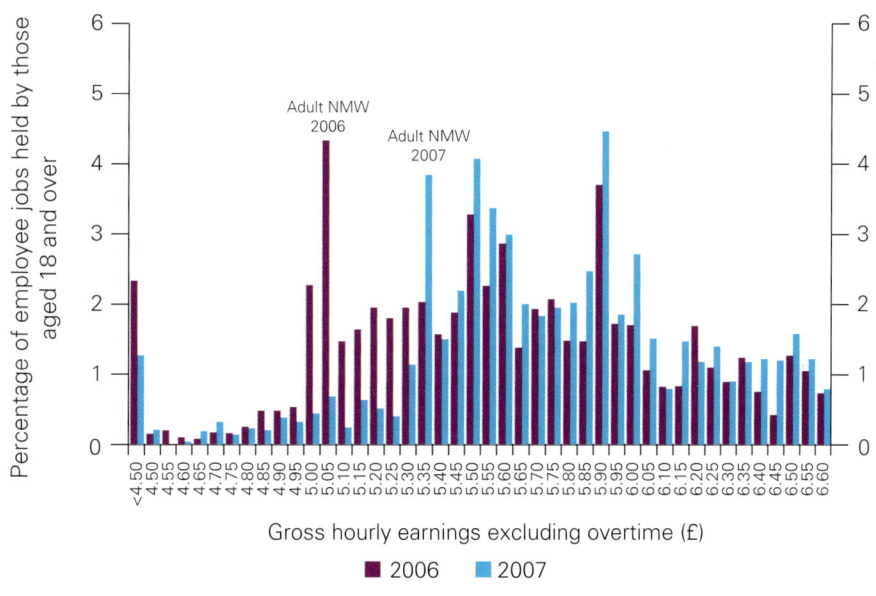

Source: LPC estimates based on ASHE 2007 methodology, low-pay weights, UK, April 2006–2007.
Note: NMW label shows the adult minimum wage rate in April of the given year.

2.60   As with social care, the minimum wage has greatest impact on childcare jobs in the independent sector. In April 2007, 7.6 per cent of childcare jobs in the voluntary sector paid at the minimum wage, as did 7.1 per cent of jobs in the private sector. While for public sector childcare organisations, only 1.7 per cent of jobs were paid at the minimum wage. This may be part of the explanation of the appearance of two spikes in the earnings data higher than the spike at the minimum wage, at £5.50 and £5.90. These spikes may also reflect pressures to increase pay for more experienced and qualified staff.

2.61   Evidence of the continued impact of the minimum wage on the independent sector (private and voluntary) comes from our commissioned research (IDS, 2007a) which found that just under two-thirds of respondents reported increasing pay rates in order to comply with the 2006 upratings, about the same as in its 2006 survey. IDS also found that slightly fewer respondents had recruitment and retention problems than in 2006. However, where problems arose, they tended to relate to experienced and qualified staff, sometimes leaving for higher pay in local authority funded nurseries (such as Sure Start Children's Centres).

The pay of more senior staff has had to be reviewed to keep differentials in place.

Staff were now not interested in training as the differences in pay did not justify the extra work.

Comments from nurseries, IDS Research, 2007

2.62   Just under two-thirds of the IDS survey respondents said that they had to raise the rates of higher paid staff to maintain differentials. The research cited evidence of a longer-term erosion of differentials, with the differential between the median starting rate for nursery nurses and the prevailing adult minimum wage having fallen from 8 per cent to 3 per cent between 2002 and 2007, while for senior nursery nurses it fell from 22 to 11 per cent over the same period. One effect reported to IDS was that a reduction in differentials had led to less interest in training.

2.63   Age-related pay is common in the childcare sector. ASHE data show that in private sector nurseries 19 per cent of nursery nurse jobs are paid below the adult rate of the National Minimum Wage, reflecting the number of employees under the age of 22.

Cleaning

2.64   With around 95,000 minimum wage jobs, the cleaning sector is one of the most affected industries. In April 2007, nearly 19 per cent of jobs in the cleaning sector were paid at the adult minimum wage. Figure 2.11 and Table 2.6 also show that it was 17.6 per cent in April 2006. The earnings data for the cleaning sector also suggest an impact on pay differentials, with the hourly pay differential between those on the minimum wage and those paid at the median falling by nearly 14 per cent between 2006 and 2007. However, the earnings distribution demonstrates that the differential between the second most common rate of pay and the minimum wage rose by over 40 per cent between April 2006 and April 2007 (from £5.50 to £6.00 an hour respectively).

Figure 2.11

Hourly Earnings Distribution for Employees Aged 18 and Over in the Cleaning Sector, UK, 2006–2007

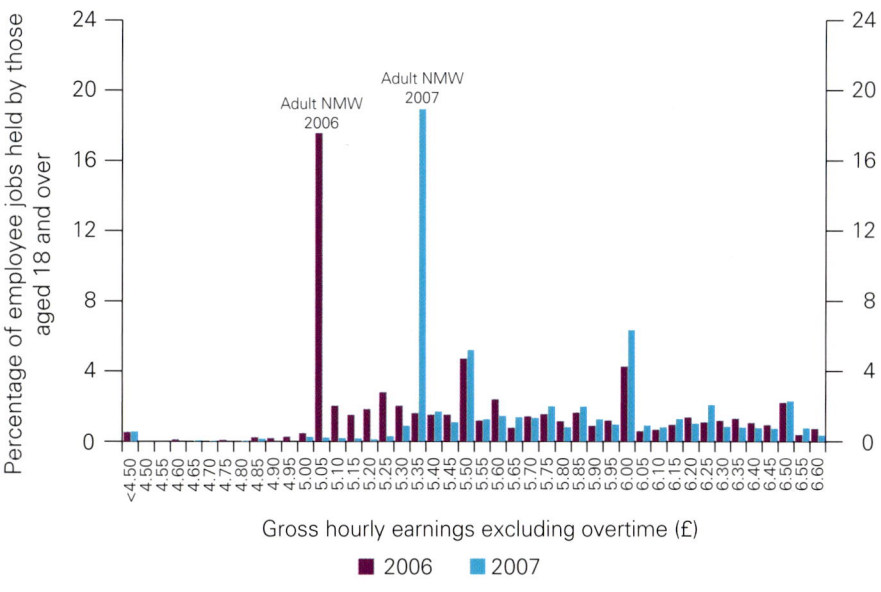

Source: LPC estimates based on ASHE 2007 methodology, low-pay weights, UK, April 2006–2007.
Note: NMW label shows the adult minimum wage rate in April of the given year.

2.65   Similar impacts of the minimum wage on earnings distributions are also observed for small firms and the groups of workers identified earlier in this chapter, with a discernable 'spike' at the level of the minimum wage. We next consider the views of those affected.

Stakeholders' Views and Evidence on the Impact of the National Minimum Wage on Earnings and Differentials

2.66   On our regional visits, in the responses to our written consultation and again during oral evidence sessions, the subject of the impact of minimum wage upratings on pay differentials was a recurring theme. The CBI reported their members' concerns that substantial increases in the minimum wage had eroded pay differentials and damaged firms' ability to reward and motivate their employees. In some instances, they said, pay rises at the lowest end had become decoupled from performance, and there was little incentive for the lower paid to take on more responsibility or undertake training.

2.67   The Cleaning and Support Services Association (CSSA) reported a contraction of pay differentials as a result of minimum wage increases, with its own survey showing a rise of 3 per cent to almost 44 per cent of cleaning staff paid at the National Minimum Wage. The British Shops and Stores Association (BSSA) reported that its 2007 wages survey had found that an inability to maintain differentials had often led to a loss of more experienced staff to higher paid sectors. Similarly, in oral evidence the British Hospitality Association (BHA), Business in Sport and Leisure (BISL) and the British Beer and Pub Association (BBPA), told us that the minimum wage had eroded pay differentials and reduced necessary incentives for supervisors, who were increasingly required to fulfil statutory responsibilities (for example, enforcing the ban on smoking).

2.68   Some respondents gave evidence that the minimum wage had caught up with agreed industry pay rates. For example, the British Furniture Manufacturers reported that increases in the minimum wage had outstripped the industry wage increases negotiated with the GMB, so that in recent years the minimum wage has overtaken two of the three rates in the industry agreement. The Food and Drink Federation reported that, while the minimum wage initially had a minor impact, it was now affecting pay levels and the structure of remuneration for its members. Members reported pressure to maintain differentials for basic pay rates above the minimum wage.

2.69 The Association of Licensed Multiple Retailers (ALMR) reported that their own surveys of members had shown that the minimum wage had become the average hourly wage for bar staff within the sector. In addition, fewer members were paying a different rate to other hourly paid staff from that paid to bar staff. ALMR saw this as evidence of an erosion of pay differentials at the lower pay levels. The British Apparel and Textile Confederation (BATC) said that, given the economic background of great pressures on suppliers' margins, employers in the textiles and clothing sector had negotiated below inflation pay increases, and that differentials would again be hit by any disproportionate rise in the minimum wage.

2.70 The British Retail Consortium (BRC) also maintained that the minimum wage was squeezing differentials in the retail trade. The BRC reported that in June 2006 the average wage for multiple retailers was 16 per cent above the minimum wage rate of £5.05 and almost 10 per cent above the future rate of £5.35. In June 2007, the average wage had fallen to 13.6 per cent above the minimum wage rate of £5.35 and 9.2 per cent above the future rate of £5.52. On the other hand, the Union of Shop Distributive and Allied Workers (Usdaw) reported that many retail employers had taken alternative approaches to the October 2007 upratings. Some had adopted the National Minimum Wage as their main sales assistant rate, while others had taken the decision to position their sales assistant rate at a specific distance above the minimum wage. Usdaw said that in its experience, as the minimum wage began to affect a company's wage structures, various measures were taken to accommodate this as best suited the company, and that this did not limit the ability to offer and improve non-wage related elements, such as staff discounts. Accordingly, Usdaw maintained, the Commission should not be unduly concerned that raising the minimum wage rate would present insurmountable obstacles for employers' pay structures.

2.71 In agriculture, the National Farmers' Union (NFU) pointed out the National Minimum Wage had a direct impact by dictating the lowest wage rate set by the Agricultural Wages Boards and it also affected indirectly rates payable to other grades where the Boards wanted to maintain the pay differentials for the minimum rates of the higher grades.

86 per cent of staff in our hospitality business are paid at the NMW. When the NMW was introduced the company aimed to maintain a differential with the minimum wage, but were only able to do so for the first two years... There is no scope to pay more to reward the most experienced or productive staff.

Hospitality sector employer. Commission visit to Cardiff

Although the minimum wage had led to some compression of differentials these were being managed by retailers, for example, by merging bottom grades.

Usdaw evidence

Summary of Research on Pay Structures and Composition

2.72   As in previous years, we commissioned work to assess the impact of the October 2006 upratings and employers' ongoing responses to the minimum wage. IDS (2007a) found that in some sectors the 2006 NMW uprating had an impact on relative pay levels, either through narrowed differentials, or by precipitating changes to pay structures in response to the narrowed differentials. This was particularly the case in retail and fast food companies where the supervisor/sales assistant distinction is important, but not substantial in pay terms.

2.73   Research by Holt, Kehil and White (2008) found some changes in the pay composition of the low-paid since the introduction of the minimum wage. Between 1997 and 2006, the incidence of additional payments among low-paid employees increased at the same time as it declined for better paid employees. However, low-paid employees were still less likely to be receiving shift premia, incentive payments or additional pay components such as car allowances or on call/stand-by allowances. By contrast, low-paid employees were as likely to be paid overtime as better paid employees. The sectors with the highest increases in the incidence of overtime among the low paid since 1997 were food processing, leisure, social care and agriculture.

Impact of the 2006 and 2007 Minimum Wage Upratings on Household Earnings

2.74   The National Minimum Wage is part of a wider Government strategy to make work pay and to improve the financial incentives for people to participate in the labour market. It is designed to interact with tax credits and benefits and these supplement the household income of many minimum wage earners. It is difficult to generalise about how the minimum wage affects household income, as the impact will depend on the household circumstances of the minimum wage worker. When the minimum wage was raised to £5.35 in October 2006, gross earned income for a 35-hour week would have been £187.25. HM Treasury estimates that this would result in a net income of £179 with the disregard[15] (up to April 2007) and £175 without the disregard (after April

---

[15]   The rules for claiming Tax Credit allow a household's income to increase by up to £25,000 in the financial year without penalty. The increased earnings are taken into account only in the next financial year.

2007) for a single individual over the age of 25 with no children, equivalent to £5.12 an hour initially and £5.01 an hour after April 2007. The tax and benefit system is more generous to those with children. If that same minimum wage earner was part of a couple with one child, HM Treasury estimate that net income would have been £273 with the disregard (up to April 2007) and £269 without (after April 2007), equivalent to £7.79 an hour before April 2007 and £7.68 thereafter.

2.75   Following the increase in the adult minimum wage in October 2007 to £5.52 per hour, a person working 35 hours would have a gross income of £193.20. The Pre-Budget Report (HM Treasury, 2007a) estimated that the net income for a family with one child and one earner would be £290 a week in April 2008. This would be equivalent to £8.29 per hour take home pay once tax credits and benefits are taken into account. For a single earner couple without children or a disability, the net income in April 2008 will be £187 a week (£5.34 an hour for a 35 hour week). In October 2007, the net income was £278 for a family with one child and one earner (£7.96 an hour) and £182 for a single person aged over 25 years old (£5.20 an hour).

Impact of the 2006 and 2007 National Minimum Wage Upratings on the Labour Market

2.76   Having established that the minimum wage has had an impact on earnings, we now look at a range of labour market indicators to discover whether employment, unemployment, hours, vacancies and redundancies have been affected. We first consider trends at aggregate, whole economy level before turning to those sectors and groups of workers more likely to be affected by the minimum wage.

Employment and Unemployment

2.77   In recent years there has been a substantial increase in labour supply in the UK. This has been driven by large numbers of migrants, especially those from Eastern Europe; a sizeable increase in workers over pension age returning to or remaining in employment; and an increase in participation from those previously inactive as a result of Government reforms to the benefit system for those on sickness and invalidity benefits. The UK labour market has so far proven robust and has been able to absorb these large increases in supply.

2.78 As Figure 2.12 shows, employment generally has risen steadily since the introduction of the minimum wage. Unemployment, on the other hand, fell at first then rose for a period from mid-2005 to mid-2006 before levelling out. Looking at developments over the past year, by November 2007 the UK labour market appeared to have fully recovered from the weak growth of the first quarter. There were 29.36 million people in employment in the UK in the three months to November 2007, 263,000 more than in the same period of the previous year.

Figure 2.12

Employment and ILO Unemployment Level for those Aged 16 and Over, UK, 1995–2007

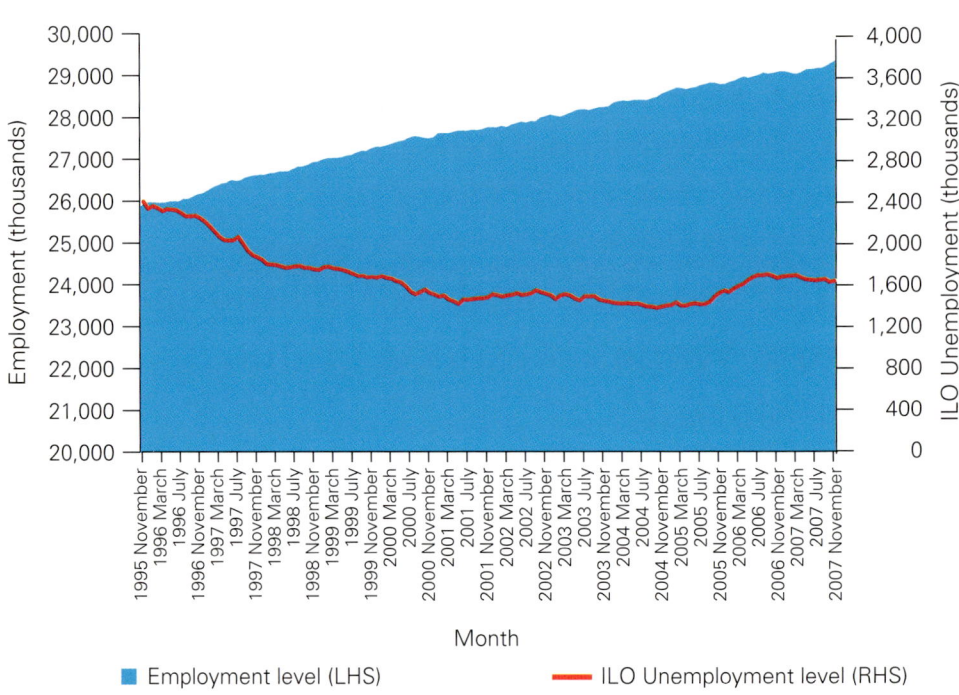

Source: ONS, LFS, employment level (ONS code MGRZ), ILO unemployment level (ONS code MGSC), monthly, seasonally adjusted, UK, 1995–2007.

2.79 The headline (or ILO) unemployment level measures the number of people actively seeking work and available to start. The number of people of working age who were unemployed in the three months to November 2007 was 1.63 million, 23,000 fewer than in the same period a year ago. The claimant count, which measures the number of people claiming Job Seeker's Allowance, fell for the fourteenth consecutive month in December 2007, declining to 807,700, down

131,400 compared with December 2006 and its lowest level since June 1975. That left the claimant count rate at 2.5 per cent, the lowest unemployment rate in the UK since April 1975.

2.80 Employment grew by 0.9 per cent over the year to November 2007. Table 2.7 shows that this increase has consisted mainly of permanent, full-time jobs in the private sector. The number of full-time employees accounted for nearly 95 per cent of this increase, growing by nearly a quarter of a million over the year to November 2007. In contrast, the number of part-time employees fell by 40,000. Further, the number of people in permanent employment increased by 0.9 per cent at the same time as the numbers in temporary employment fell by 0.7 per cent.

Self-employment

2.81 Prior to the introduction of the minimum wage there was some concern that a National Minimum Wage might lead to a growth in self-employment as a means of bypassing the requirements of the new legislation. The data suggest that this has not happened. Between 1998, shortly before the introduction of the minimum wage, and 2007, the number of self-employed in the low-paying sectors fell by 6 per cent compared with a growth in self-employment in the whole economy of 10 per cent.

Groups of Workers

2.82 Table 2.7 also shows that, over the last year, employment has increased for most age groups. Employment growth has been strongest for those aged over 50. However, the youngest age group, 16–17 year olds, have continued to fare badly in the labour market with employment falling by 13,000. Although there has been an increase of one per cent in the number of 18–24 year olds employed, the population of this age group has risen faster, resulting in a reduction of 0.7 percentage points in their employment rate. The labour market performance of those with no qualifications has mirrored that of young people with their employment rate falling, over the year to September 2007, by over one percentage point to 46.7. This is lower than when the minimum wage was introduced.

Table 2.7

Summary of Labour Market Data, UK, 2005–2007

Population Aged 16 and Over	Latest Data (November 2007) (thousands)	Change on November 2006 (thousands)	Change on November 2005 (thousands)
Employment	**29,355**	263	557
Employees	**25,286**	207	381
Self-employed	**3,856**	54	158
Others	**213**	2	19
Employment by Age			
16–17	**543**	−13	−29
18–24	**3,657**	35	132
25–34	**6,287**	20	−13
35–49	**11,043**	63	140
50–59/64	**6,558**	82	164
60/65+	**1,268**	77	163
Work Status			
Full-time Employees	**18,883**	248	312
Part-time Employees	**6,404**	−40	70
Contract Type			
Permanent Employees	**23,822**	218	317
Temporary Employees	**1,464**	−11	64
Sector[1]			
Private Sector	**23,521**	263	546
Public Sector	**5,770**	−37	−85
All	**29,291**	226	461

Source: ONS, LFS, Total employment (MGRZ); Total employees (MGRN); Total self-employed (MGRQ); Other employment includes unpaid family workers and Government supported training and employment programmes (MGRT + MGRW); Employment age 16–17 (YBTO); Employment age 18–24 (YBTR); Employment age 25–34 (YBTU); Employment age 35–49 (YBTX); Employment age 50–59/64 (MGUW); Employment age 59/64+ (MGUZ); Full-time employees (YCBK); Part-time employees (YCBN); Permanent employees (MGRN); Temporary employees (YCBZ); Public sector (G7AU); Private sector (G7K5); and Total employment (G7GO) three months to November, all seasonally adjusted, UK, 2005–2007.
Note: 1. Latest data for public or private sector are up to the third quarter of 2007.

2.83 The employment performance of other groups of workers – such as women, those with disabilities, those from ethnic minority groups and older workers – appears much better than younger workers, with employment rates only marginally lower in September 2007 than a year ago. The labour market performance of youths and other groups of workers are explored in more detail in Chapter 3.

Employee Jobs

2.84   Data on employee jobs form an important part of our analysis of the impact of the minimum wage, and are the main source for monitoring changes in employment for each low-paying industrial sector. At the time of our last report, we noted that there had been a slight decline in the overall number of employee jobs in the low-paying sectors for the first time since the introduction of the minimum wage, largely accounted for by job losses in hospitality. The official data showed year-on-year falls in jobs in the low-paying sectors for each quarter from December 2005 to September 2006. However, as explained earlier in this chapter, recent methodological changes by ONS mean that reliable data on annual changes in employee jobs between March 2006 and June 2007 are no longer available. As a result we are unable to estimate with any confidence what happened to employee jobs in this period. In looking at the employee jobs data for periods after December 2005, the only annual period available to us for which reliable comparisons can be made is that between September 2006 and September 2007.

The Minimum Wage and Jobs in Low-paying Sectors

2.85   Focusing on that period, we can see from Figure 2.13 that the growth in employee jobs in the low-paying sectors in the year to September 2007 was, at 0.85 per cent, marginally higher than the 0.77 per cent jobs growth in the whole economy. This contrasts with the slower growth seen in the low-paying sectors in 2005. This is not the first time that job growth in the low-paying sectors has exceeded that in the economy as a whole. For most of the period between December 2001 and March 2005, the low-paying sectors performed better than the whole economy in terms of employee job growth.

Figure 2.13

Change in Employee Jobs in Whole Economy and Low-paying Sectors, GB, 1999–2007

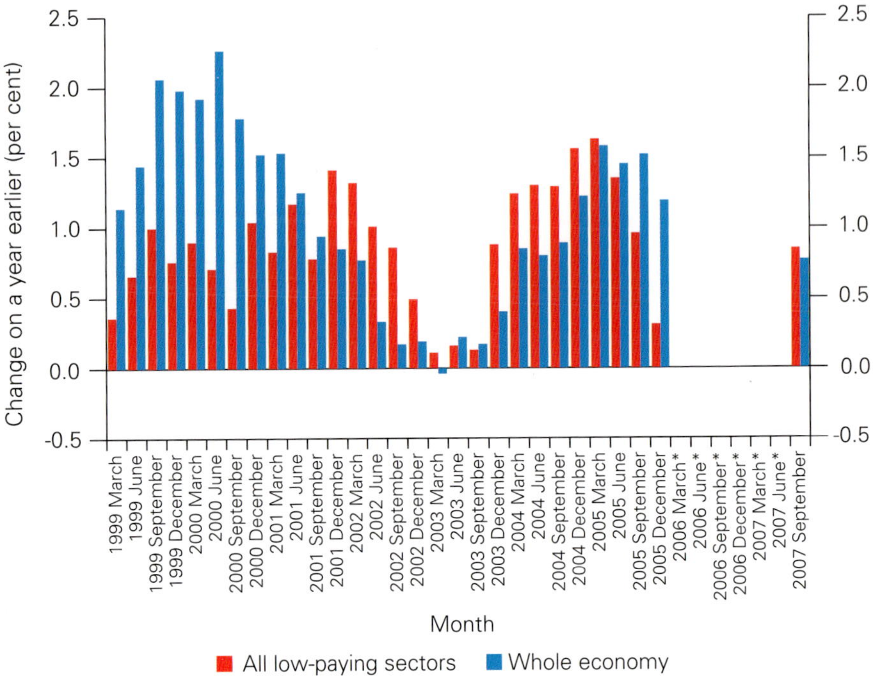

Source: ONS employee jobs series, not seasonally adjusted, GB, 1999–2007.
Note: * As a result of the break in the employee jobs series between December 2005 and September 2006, annual changes cannot be estimated for these periods (March 2006 to June 2007).

2.86 In September 2007, as shown in Table 2.8, there were over 8.4 million jobs in the ten low-paying industrial sectors, around 32 per cent of all jobs in the economy, and nearly 71,000 more jobs than in September 2006. The number of jobs in the low-paying sectors was 527,000 higher in December 2005 than it was in December 1998, an increase of nearly 7 per cent since the introduction of the National Minimum Wage. This compares with an increase of almost 8 per cent in the number of jobs in the economy as a whole over the same period.

2.87 However, the story as regards jobs varies for each low-paying sector. In some sectors there has been a substantial rise in the number of jobs since the introduction of the minimum wage (retail, hospitality, social care, leisure, hairdressing and security), while others have experienced a substantial decline (textiles and clothing, agriculture and food processing). Of course the reasons for growth or decline are many and various and it is difficult to know for sure what role, if any, the minimum wage has played. In textiles, for example, there was fierce competition from low-wage economies well before the advent of the minimum wage, and it is generally agreed that in agriculture the decline in employment goes back over a century and stems in large part from structural and technical developments. In the case of food processing, mechanisation, overseas competition and the consolidation of operations within the sector have all been important factors in the decline in the number of jobs.

Table 2.8
Change in Employee Jobs, Whole Economy and Low-paying Sectors, GB, 1998–2007

(thousands)	September 2007	Change on September 2006	Change between December 1998 and December 2005
Whole Economy	26,388	201	1,857
All low-paying	8,412	71	527
of which:			
Retail	3,351	37	294
Hospitality	1,805	19	217
Social care	1,156	19	149
Cleaning	494	2	−27
Agriculture	229	−1	−64
Security	171	5	37
Textiles and clothing	94	−4	−187
Food processing	352	−4	−66
Leisure, travel and sport	640	0	152
Hairdressing	120	−3	22

Source: ONS employee jobs, not seasonally adjusted, GB, 1998–2007.

2.88   To understand better the changes that have occurred in employment in the low-paying sectors, we focus on official data for those industrial sectors which account for the largest number of minimum wage jobs (retail, hospitality, social care and cleaning), together with the childcare occupational sector. However, as explained earlier, recent changes by ONS to the employee jobs data limit our ability to analyse changes over time for these sectors. We also set out the views of stakeholders, and the evidence they have submitted, on the impact of the minimum wage on jobs and hours.

Retail

2.89   As noted earlier in the chapter, household spending proved robust throughout 2007 with consumers funding their purchases by drawing on savings and increasing borrowing. Consequently, official statistics show that retail sales were also healthy. The value of retail sales grew by 3.6 per cent in 2007, with growth strongest in the first half of the year. This represented a strong recovery from the downturn in 2005 when the value of retail sales growth was just one per cent. Growth in 2006 was 2.8 per cent. However, consumers appeared to be feeling the effects of the financial market turmoil, with growth slowing to 2.3 per cent in the fourth quarter of 2007. Further evidence of a slowdown in the retail sector is provided by the BRC-KPMG Retail Sales Monitor (BRC-KPMG, 2008), which indicated that total sales in December 2007 rose by 2.3 per cent compared to December 2006. The three-month trend rate of growth to December 2007 also increased, up by 2.8 per cent compared to the same period in 2006. However, these growth rates were much lower than those observed earlier in the year.

Figure 2.14

Employee Jobs in the Retail Sector and Annual Change, Thousands, GB, 1999–2007

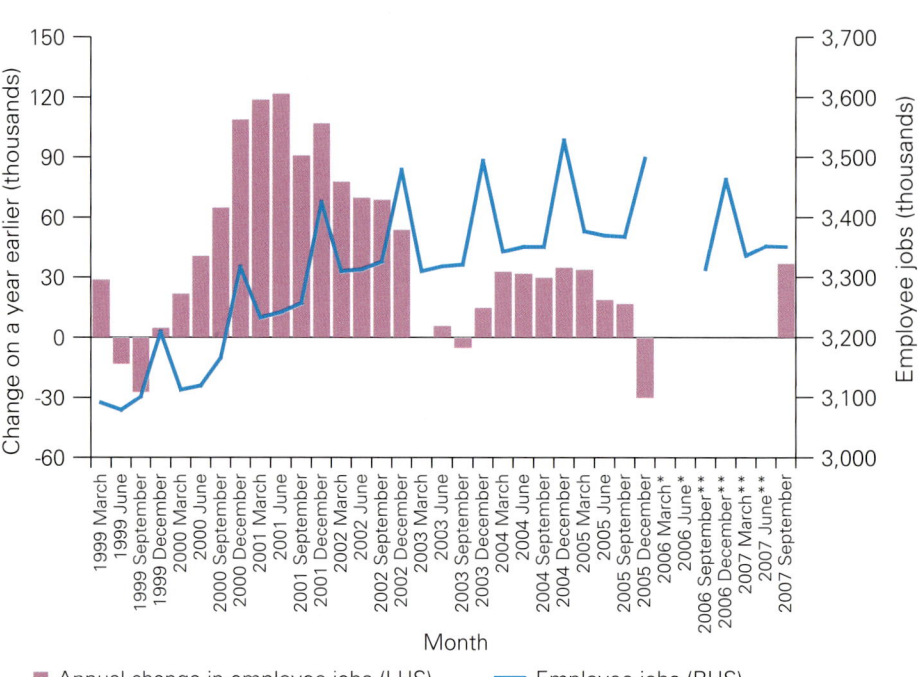

Source: ONS employee jobs series, not seasonally adjusted, GB, 1999–2007.
Notes:
1. * As a result of the break in the employee jobs series between December 2005 and September 2006, employment levels and annual changes cannot be estimated for these periods (March 2006 and June 2006).
2. ** The break mentioned in Note 1 also means that annual changes cannot be estimated for these periods (September 2006 to June 2007).

2.90   As a result of the robust growth in retail sales earlier in 2007, employment growth in the retail sector has been strong. Figure 2.14 shows that jobs in the sector rose by over 37,000 (1 per cent) to nearly 3.4 million in the year to September 2007, accounting for around 40 per cent of all jobs in the low-paying sectors (13 per cent of jobs in the economy as a whole). The growth in jobs was relatively evenly spread between full-time and part-time work. According to the LFS microdata[16], there was an increase in employment in low-paying retail occupations of around 35,000 to 2.14 million between the third quarter of 2006 and the same period in 2007.

Hospitality

2.91   The hospitality sector, also boosted by the robustness of consumer spending, has experienced strong growth in output (gross value added) since the beginning of 2006, peaking at over 7 per cent in the third quarter of that year before slowing to just over 4 per cent in the third quarter of 2007. Consequently, in the year to September 2007, there was a rise of over 19,000 hospitality jobs to 1.8 million, as shown in Figure 2.15. All bar one of the sub-sectors of hospitality experienced an increase in jobs over this period (restaurants by over 16,000, hotels by over 8,000, canteens and catering by over 4,000, and camp sites by over 1,000). The exception was the pubs and bars sector where jobs fell by over 11,000, perhaps as a result of the smoking ban.

2.92   We have also looked at employment change in the low-paying occupations in the hospitality sector using the LFS microdata. There was a fall of over 52,000 in the year to the third quarter of 2007, to just under 1.01 million. However, this total was still over 38,000 higher than employment in these occupations in the same period in 2005.

---

[16]   LFS microdata are weighted to the UK population in March 2003. Employment data derived from this source is likely to underestimate the actual totals as the population has grown since then.

Figure 2.15

Employee Jobs in the Hospitality Sector and Annual Change, Thousands, GB, 1999–2007

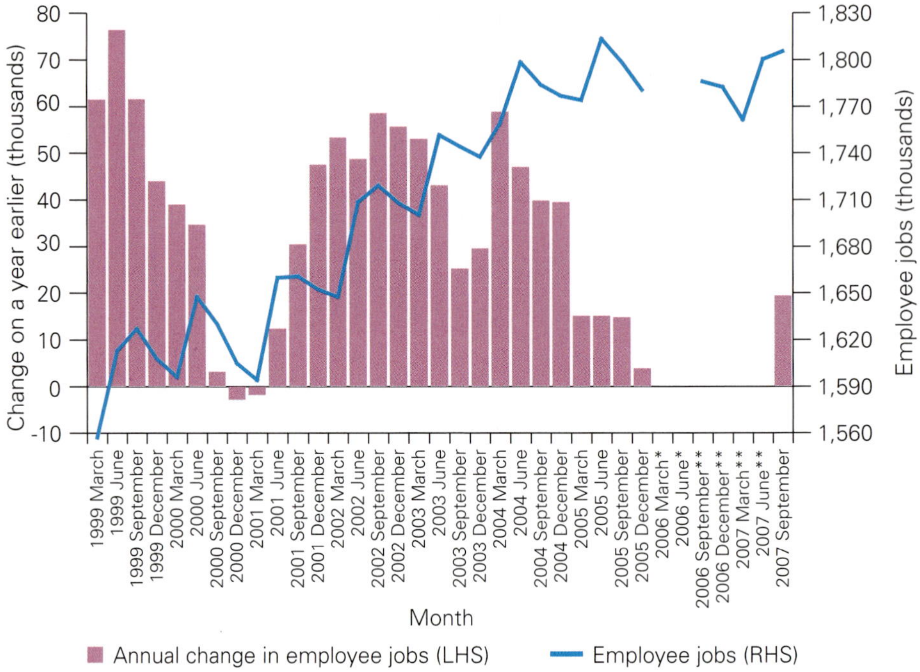

Annual change in employee jobs (LHS)   Employee jobs (RHS)

Source: ONS employee jobs series, not seasonally adjusted, GB, 1999–2007.

Notes:

1. * As a result of the break in the employee jobs series between December 2005 and September 2006, employment levels and annual changes cannot be estimated for these periods (March 2006 and June 2006).

2. ** The break mentioned in Note 1 also means that annual changes cannot be estimated for these periods (September 2006 to June 2007).

Social Care

2.93   The number of jobs in social care has grown strongly since December 2003. In September 2007 there were nearly 1.2 million jobs in social care, an increase of nearly 19,000 on September 2006. Figure 2.16 also shows that this increase in jobs was at a lower rate than in some preceding periods. According to the LFS microdata, employment in low-paying social care occupations was over 646,000 in the third quarter of 2007, a fall of nearly 3,000 on the same period in 2006. This was still some 38,000 higher than the employment level in the third quarter of 2005.

Figure 2.16

Employee Jobs in the Social Care Sector and Annual Change, Thousands, GB, 1999–2007

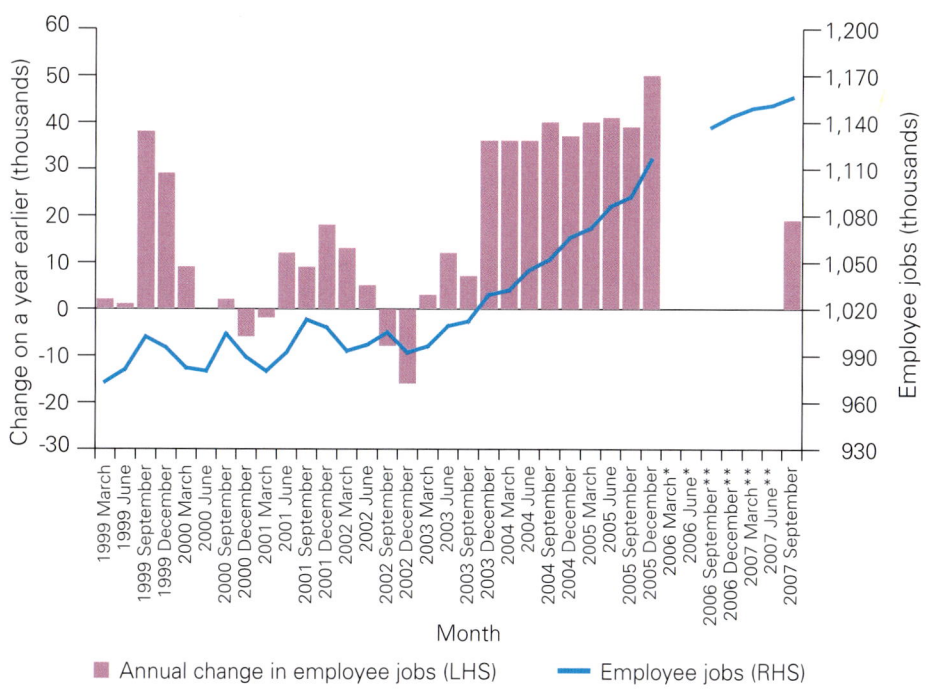

Source: ONS employee jobs series, not seasonally adjusted, GB, 1999–2007.
Notes:
1. * As a result of the break in the employee jobs series between December 2005 and September 2006, employment levels and annual changes cannot be estimated for these periods (March 2006 and June 2006).
2. ** The break mentioned in Note 1 also means that annual changes cannot be estimated for these periods (September 2006 to June 2007).

Childcare

2.94 According to the Childcare and Early Years Providers Survey (DCSF, 2007), conducted in mid-2006, there were over 822,000 places in full day and sessional[17] childcare in England, a rise of 9 per cent on 2003 and 6 per cent on 2005. The substantial overall increase in the 2003 to 2006 period masked some significant variation, with sessional care places falling by 14 per cent, while full day care places increased by 26 per cent. From 2003 to 2006, places in after-school clubs grew by 58 per cent (to over 260,000) and in holiday clubs by 117 per cent (to nearly 264,000). The same survey found there were over 306,000 paid

[17] 'Full day care' is defined as facilities that provide day care for children under eight for a continuous period of four hours or more in any day in premises which are not domestic premises. 'Sessional care' is defined as facilities where children under eight attend day care for no more than five sessions a week, each session being less than a continuous period of four hours in any day. Where two sessions are offered in any one day, there is a break between sessions with no children in the care of the provider.

staff working for childcare providers in England, up from over 228,000 in 2003[18]. This rise was across all provision except sessional care. Figure 2.17 shows that employment in low-paying childcare occupations was broadly stable between the third quarter of 2006 and the third quarter of 2007, at over 346,000. There was a rise of over 10,000 in full-time employment, and a fall of a similar magnitude in part-time work. Employment of nursery nurses also remained fairly steady during this period, with only a marginal fall of around 1,000.

Figure 2.17

Employment in Low-paying Childcare Occupations, UK, 2002–2007

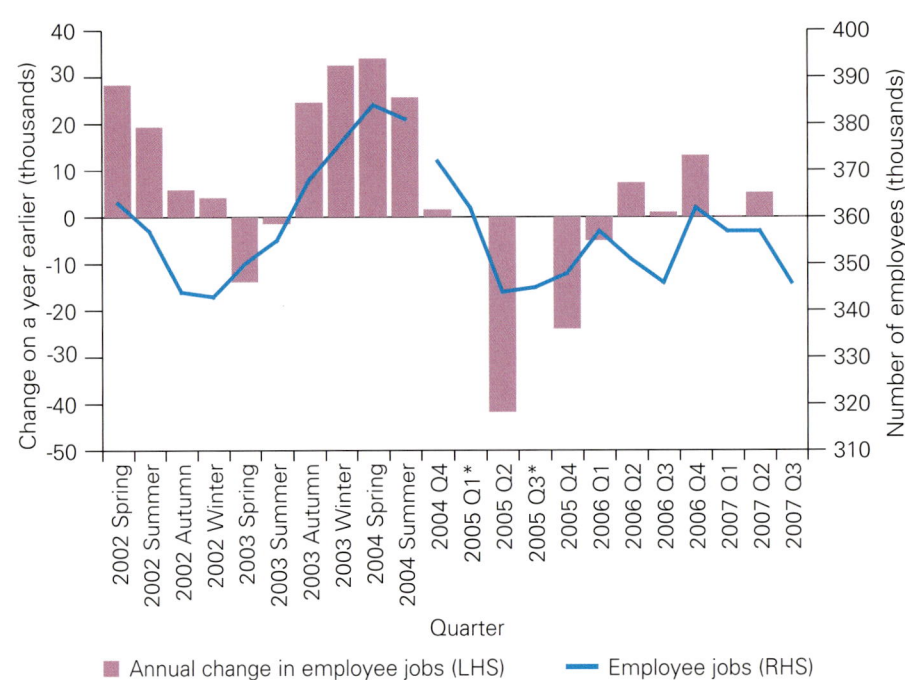

Source: LPC estimates based on LFS microdata, seasonal / calendar quarters, not seasonally adjusted, UK, 2002 to 2007.

Notes:

1. The move from seasonal quarters to calendar quarters has led to a discontinuity in the LFS microdata series between Summer 2004 and 2004 Q4; thus comparisons across these periods should be made with care.

2. * Indicate periods where annual changes cannot be shown due to a lack of comparable calendar quarter data.

---

18 Totals for each year derived by adding together number of paid staff for each type of childcare provider. Caution should be exercised with these totals as some double counting may have taken place because members of staff may have worked for more than one childcare provider.

2.95 IDS research (IDS, 2007a) focused on independent sector (private and voluntary) nurseries, which are estimated to provide around four-fifths of all childcare places (DCSF, 2007). IDS found that, unlike in other low-paying sectors, the October 2006 upratings of the minimum wage had led to a reduction in staffing levels in about 10 per cent of nurseries. In addition, 14 per cent of these independent nurseries said they had reduced hours worked. One explanation offered for the reduction in staffing numbers and hours worked is that the increase in the minimum wage resulted, in a majority of instances, in increased fees, leading in some cases to fewer children being placed at nurseries, and as consequence fewer staff being required. Fifty eight per cent of those independent sector nurseries said they had increased fees as a result of the October 2006 minimum wage upratings (up from 45 per cent in 2005).

> A nursery said it had to increase charges to parents, causing some to leave the nursery and as a consequence the nursery requires fewer employees.
>
> **IDS Research, 2007**

Cleaning

2.96 The employee jobs series shows that there has been an upturn in jobs in the cleaning sector since June 2004 (Figure 2.18), following a long-term decline which began prior to the introduction of the minimum wage. There was a further small increase of over 2,000 jobs between September 2006 and September 2007. Although the majority of jobs continue to be part-time, the shift towards full-time employment in the sector continued. It is likely, however, that the actual number of people employed in a cleaning capacity is greater than suggested as the employment data for the cleaning industrial sector will not include those employed directly by firms categorised within another industry. Moreover, a number of cleaners may be self-employed or working informally in a domestic setting. LFS microdata shows that, with 726,000 jobs in the third quarter of 2007, employment in low-paying cleaning occupations was considerably higher than the numbers in the cleaning industry suggested by the employee jobs series data. This was an increase of more than 6 per cent on a year ago.

Figure 2.18
Employee Jobs in the Cleaning Sector and Annual Change,
Thousands, GB, 1999–2007

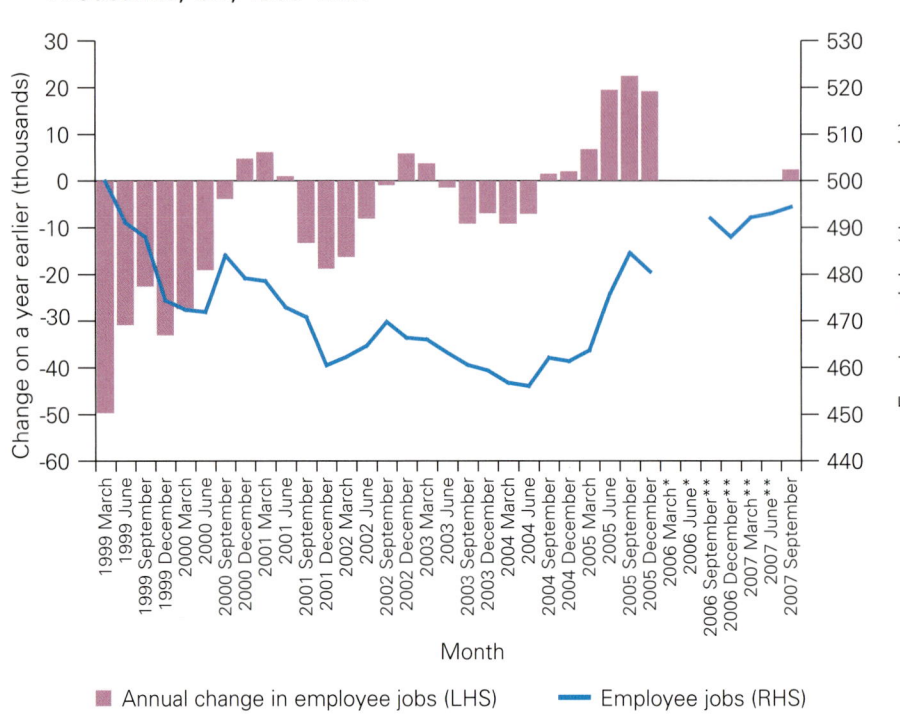

Source: ONS employee jobs series, not seasonally adjusted, GB, 1999–2007
Notes:
1. * As a result of the break in the employee jobs series between December 2005 and September 2006, employment levels and annual changes cannot be estimated for these periods (March 2006 and June 2006).
2. ** The break mentioned in Note 1 also means that annual changes cannot be estimated for these periods (September 2006 to June 2007).

Other Low-paying Sectors

2.97   Employment in agriculture and textiles has been in long-term decline. Between September 2006 and September 2007 agriculture and textiles again experienced falls in jobs, but at a more moderate rate than in the past. Jobs in food-processing have also continued on a downward trend, with a further fall of 4,000. Two of the sectors that had generally experienced an upward trend in jobs, hairdressing and leisure, saw no growth in the year to September 2007. There was a small fall of 3,000 jobs in hairdressing, whereas in leisure, travel and sport, a sector which has seen a substantial increase in jobs since the introduction of the minimum wage, the number of jobs remained unchanged. Conversely the security sector saw a rise of over 5,000 jobs in the year to September 2007 but the sector contains only 2 per cent of the jobs in the low-paying sectors. LFS microdata suggests that in the third quarter of 2007, there were over 301,000 employees in low-paying office work jobs, a fall of nearly 23,000 on the total for the same period in 2006.

Other Labour Market Indicators

2.98 Jobs are an important indicator of the strength of the labour market but there are other indicators of labour supply and demand which might adjust to changes in the National Minimum Wage. One of these is the number of hours worked. Employers might react to an increase in the minimum wage by maintaining the same number of employees but reducing their hours. Official statistics reveal that the number of hours worked has increased over the past year more or less in line with the increase in the number of jobs. The number of hours worked per week in the UK has risen by 1.3 per cent, from 927.7 million in the three months to November 2006 to 939.5 million in the three months to November 2007. Over the same period the average number of hours worked per employee per week increased from 31.9 to 32.1, reflecting the increase in full-time employment.

2.99 Redundancy and vacancy figures are indicators of the demand for labour in the economy. Analysis reveals a mixed picture. The number of advertised vacancies rose in the three months to December 2007 compared with both the previous three months and the same period of the previous year (by 7,100 and 75,200 respectively). The sectoral breakdown of the data shows that the number of vacancies in the distribution sector (which includes retail and hospitality) increased by 21,300 (a rise of 12.5 per cent) over the year to December 2007. However, in the three months to November 2007, the number of redundancies in the UK rose by 3,000 over the quarter, but remained 12,000 below that seen in the same period of the previous year. The increase in redundancies was confined to the financial and business services sector, perhaps, as a result of the credit crunch.

Stakeholders' Views and Evidence on the Impact of the National Minimum Wage on Jobs and Hours

2.100 A number of respondents to our written consultation reported that the minimum wage was having an impact on jobs, either directly or in conjunction with other costs. The BHA, BISL and BBPA pointed out that, although employment in hospitality and leisure had increased

... last year, employment in sectors with a high concentration of low pay also saw a slight increase of 37,000 extra jobs. This suggests that these sectors have, as a whole, been robust enough to cope with the most recent NMW increases.

TUC evidence

The National Minimum Wage has had an adverse impact on the staffing levels within our retail stores. The stores are operating on less hours than they were several years ago in order to absorb the impact of the hefty increases. This has largely been achieved by way of natural wastage, but nevertheless, the significance of the staffing cover should not be underestimated. Nearly all staff are now employed on a part-time basis (less than 30 hours) with the average being for 16 hours a week.

The Peacock Group Ltd. Low Pay Commission Visit to Cardiff.

since the introduction of the minimum wage, it had stalled in the past two years. A BHA survey of members indicated continuing upward pressure on payroll as a proportion of turnover leading in some cases to a cut in jobs. ALMR said that for the first time its survey showed that a majority of respondents said they had to let staff go as a result of increases in the minimum wage.

2.101   In the cleaning sector, CSSA reported that clients were cutting the hours worked and changing the specifications of contracts to absorb the effect of minimum wage increases. The Association of Convenience Stores (ACS) said that many retailers had been forced to reduce the hours worked by employees, with some trying to offset National Minimum Wage costs by employing staff for less than 16 hours to reduce National Insurance costs. Although some had laid off staff, most had not yet done so, though a number had this under review. These changes have meant that supervisors and managers have faced an increased workload and longer working hours.

2.102   The CBI pointed to an increasing number of firms and sectors now affected by the minimum wage. More CBI members in retail were affected than before and similar trends were discernable in construction, communication and transport. It said that the minimum wage was having a negative impact on employment and investment in affected firms. In a CBI survey, over a quarter of the firms affected by the October 2007 upratings said they would curb growth plans or reduce investment in other areas, while a fifth said they would have to reduce staffing levels. The CBI interpreted this as evidence that the labour market had been increasingly affected as minimum wage coverage has increased.

2.103   On the other hand, trade unions made the point that employment had been rising in the low-paying sectors. Usdaw pointed out that employment in retailing, the largest of the low-paying sectors, had grown and had done so primarily at a time of rapid increases in the minimum wage. It referred to ONS data showing employment increasing by over 20,000 (almost one per cent) over the last year, which it described as a very creditable performance after five increases in interest rates. Usdaw also reminded us that the National Minimum Wage was not mentioned as one of the top 65 reasons for business failures listed by the UK Insolvency Helpline.

Impact of the National Minimum Wage on Small Firms

2.104 As the minimum wage is likely to have relatively greater impact on small firms than on larger businesses, we next look at how changes to employment levels and employee earnings in small firms compare to those in larger organisations. We also set out stakeholder views on the impact of the minimum wage on small firms.

Earnings

2.105 Figure 2.19 below shows how the minimum wage[19] has a greater impact on small firms (by which we mean firms with between 1 and 49 employees) than on larger businesses. Over 4 per cent of jobs in small firms were paid at the adult rate of the minimum wage in April 2007, whereas in medium-size firms (50–249 employees) just over 3 per cent of jobs were paid at this level, and in large firms (250+ employees) it was just over 2 per cent.

Figure 2.19
Hourly Earnings Distribution for Small, Medium and Large Firms, Employees Aged 18 and Over, UK, 2007

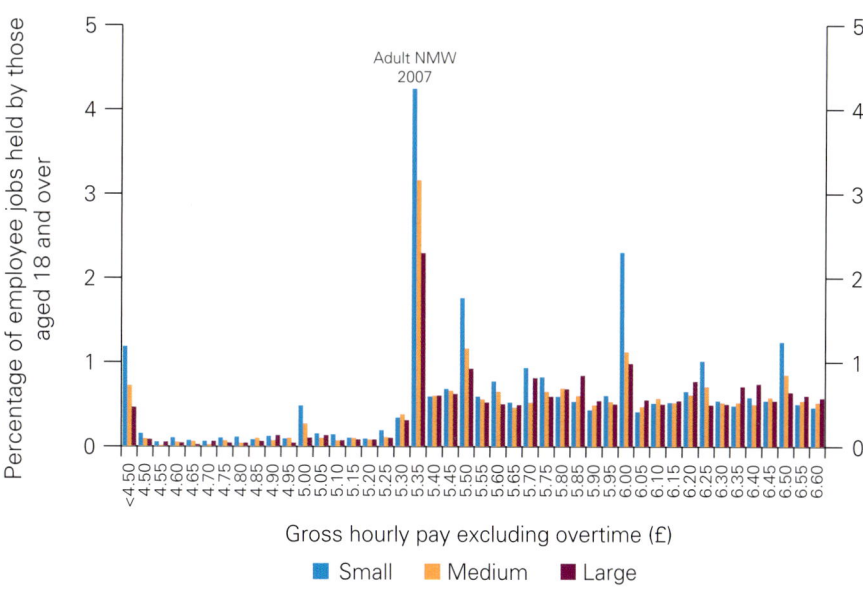

Source: LPC estimates based on ASHE 2007 methodology, low-pay weights, UK, April 2007.
Note: NMW label shows the adult minimum wage rate in April of the given year.

---

[19] The minimum wage is defined here as the actual minimum wage in the April of that year.

2.106 The proportion of jobs paid at the minimum wage rose marginally for all firm sizes between April 2006 and April 2007; however the largest rise of over 0.5 percentage points was experienced by both medium-sized and large firms.

Employment

2.107 According to the latest data[20], small firms accounted for 97 per cent of the 1.2 million private sector enterprises in the UK with one or more employees in 2006. They accounted for just over 37 per cent of employment and around 32 per cent of all turnover. These figures showed little change from 2005.

Figure 2.20
Change in Number of Employees by Firm Size, UK, 2005–2007

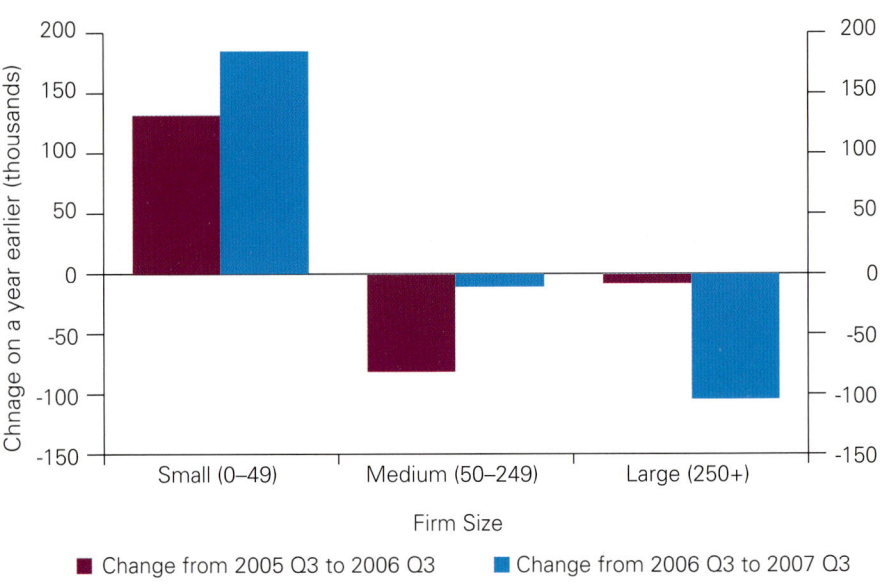

Source: LPC estimates based on LFS microdata, calendar quarters, not seasonally adjusted, UK, Q3 2005–Q3 2007.

2.108 LFS microdata for employees by firm size[21] in Figure 2.20 show that in the third quarter of 2007 there were 185,000 more employees in small firms than in the same period in 2006, reaching a total of nearly 11.8 million employees. Over the same period, there was a fall of

---

[20] BERR Enterprise Directorate, Analytical Unit, August 2007.
[21] There are differences between the estimates of the share of employment by firm size from LFS and BERR data in paragraph 2.107 and paragraph 2.108 / Figure 2.20. BERR data estimate 'employment' by firm size and are mainly derived from the Annual Business Inquiry (ABI), a survey of businesses. LFS microdata estimate 'employees' by firm size and are derived from a household survey of individuals, operating on a self-reporting basis. While the LFS data is more timely, estimates by firm size from the BERR data are likely to be more accurate.

nearly 11,000 to about 6.3 million employees for medium-size firms (firms with 50 to 249 employees). Large firms (250 workers or more) also experienced a fall in employees, down nearly 104,000 on the third quarter of 2006, to stand at over 6.4 million employees in the third quarter of 2007. A corresponding rise in employees in small firms, and falls in employees in medium-size and large firms, also occurred between the third quarter of 2005 and the same period in 2006.

Stakeholders' Views and Evidence on the Impact of the National Minimum Wage on Small Firms

2.109   We heard again this year how small businesses are particularly affected by the National Minimum Wage. The Federation of Small Businesses (FSB) said that increases since 2004/05 were starting to have a more significant impact. The FSB's 2006 Employment Survey of members had found that, for affected businesses, the main impact of the minimum wage had been to reduce profit margins (72 per cent), increase prices (56 per cent) and reduce employment (36 per cent). One third of respondents said that they had to uprate workers' pay as a result of the October 2006 minimum wage increase. The National Hairdressers' Federation (NHF) said that the margins of small employers had been squeezed by the minimum wage, and that further cost increases would not be easily absorbed.

We generally support the NMW, but find it an increasing struggle to meet pay costs. Pay would not have risen so quickly in the absence of a minimum wage.

Hartley Dyke Farm Shop. Commission Visit to Kent.

2.110   The British Chambers of Commerce (BCC) argued that the economic situation looked uncertain for small firms, which already faced an onerous burden from Government regulations. The October 2007 increase in the minimum wage followed a period of large increases in the minimum wage at well above average earnings growth. The BCC said it had previously warned these could have adverse affects on employment prospects in key areas of the UK labour market, with small and medium-sized businesses particularly vulnerable. The problems facing small businesses could be exacerbated by domestic credit becoming costlier and less easily available, together with a slowdown in economic activity. The Forum of Private Business referred to research carried out at the end of 2006 in which 27 per cent of the small businesses surveyed reported that the increases in the minimum wage had reduced their ability to employ more people over the previous 12 months.

2.111   The Rural Shops Alliance said that the minimum wage had a significant impact on micro retail businesses, with a high proportion of staff paid at this rate and the pay of others directly linked through maintenance of differentials. However, the trade union Unite pointed out that the supermarkets dominated the food retail sector with 88 per cent of grocery sales, and argued that it was this market consolidation that had adversely affected small retailers, not the National Minimum Wage. The TUC noted that according to the latest data, the rate of start-ups and the increase in the total number of businesses had been greater for the low-paying sectors than for the whole economy.

Impact of the National Minimum Wage on Prices, Profits, Productivity, Investment and Business Start-ups and Failures

2.112   In this section we consider the impact of the minimum wage on prices, profits, productivity and investment, in many ways the determinants of the longer-term sustainability of businesses. If profitability is the ultimate determinant of sustainability, prices, productivity and investment are mechanisms through which to achieve this. Here we scrutinise the data to determine how these variables have been affected by the minimum wage. Upratings of the minimum wage may result in a rise in prices, a fall in profits, an increase in productivity, a reduction in investment, a reduction in business start-ups or an upsurge in business failures. We investigate each in turn.

Prices

2.113   Firms who employ minimum wage workers could have passed on higher labour costs in the form of higher prices. We discussed some measures of inflation earlier in the chapter in our review of the economy. Here, we first look at measures of inflation for the whole economy before investigating price rises in low-paying sectors.

2.114 Figure 2.21 shows that while price inflation rose through 2006, it has been relatively contained in 2007. On all three consumer price measures – CPI, RPI and RPIX – inflation fell back after peaking in the first quarter of 2007. However, there are signs that, led by increases in the prices of energy, fuel and food, it has picked up again in the last quarter of 2007. This pick-up in prices can also be seen in the factory output price series which shows sharp increases towards the end of 2007. Business services prices have yet to show similar signs.

Figure 2.21

Whole Economy Price Inflation, UK, 1998–2007

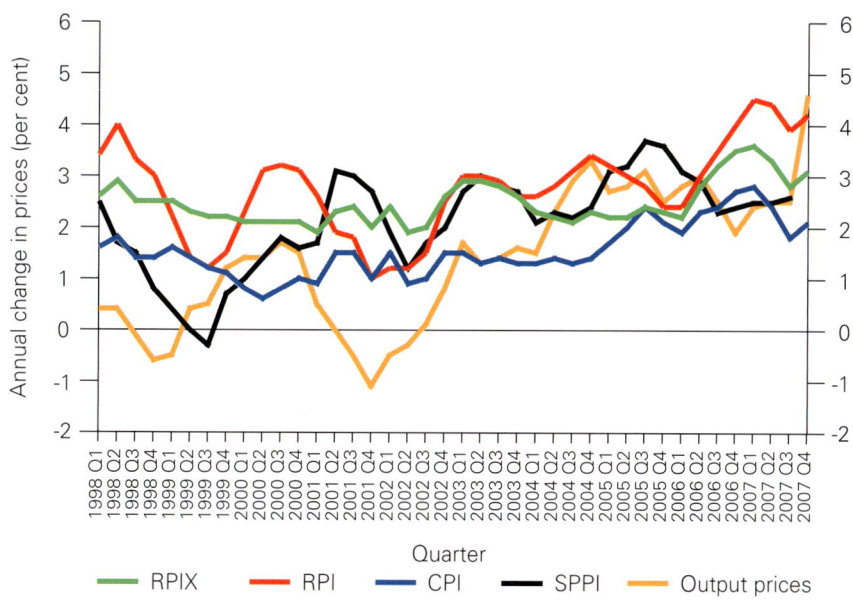

Source: ONS, CPI (ONS code D7G7), RPI (ONS code CZBH), RPIX (ONS code CDKQ), SPPI (ONS code DZZ8) and Output prices (based on ONS code PLLU), quarterly, not seasonally adjusted, UK, 1998–2007.

2.115 Looking in more detail at the low-paying sectors, we can see from Figure 2.22 that the ONS experimental business-to-business price series, SPPI, suggests that firms in many low-paying sectors have not been able to raise prices by as much as the RPI. In sectors such as commercial cleaning, industrial cleaning and hotels, price inflation has been below RPI though the price of security services has increased much faster. There is some evidence of an energy effect on prices in some low-paying sectors.

Figure 2.22
Price Inflation in Selected Low-paying Sectors, UK, 1996–2007

Source: ONS, SPPI experimental sector series (ONS code DZZ8), Security services (ONS code PWJQ), Industrial cleaning (ONS code PWKD) and Commercial washing and dry cleaning (ONS code E23D), quarterly, not seasonally adjusted, UK, 1996–2007.

2.116 An initial study by Wadsworth (2007) suggested that the introduction and subsequent uprating of the minimum wage may have led certain industries and services to raise prices. Those industries in which the workforce contained a high proportion of minimum wage workers may have raised prices more rapidly than other industries. However, the findings from this research were tentative, due to data limitations, data availability and time constraints which precluded a more in-depth analysis of these issues.

2.117 In a subsequent study, Wadsworth (2008) concludes that, while it is hard to detect much evidence of a significant change in prices in the month in which the minimum wage changed, prices in several minimum wage industries appear to have risen relatively faster than prices in non-minimum wage sectors in the period after the minimum wage was introduced. These inflation effects were particularly significant in the four years immediately after the introduction of the minimum wage.

Profits

2.118 Firms might try and absorb the costs of minimum wage increases by accepting a squeeze on their profit margins. If these firms are earning excessive profits this need not have an adverse economic effect, but where firms are earning normal profits, this position cannot be sustained in the long-run. For the economy as a whole, there is little evidence of any impact on profits, measured in a number of ways, in the last year. Corporate financial balances are currently looking healthy. Gross and net rates of return on capital, even after excluding the oil sector, are at record levels and have been driven by services. The overall profitability of UK private non-financial corporations in the third quarter of 2007 was 16 per cent, which was higher than the 14.3 per cent observed in the third quarter of 2006. Excluding the oil and gas extraction corporations, the annual net rate of return for private non-financial corporations was 15.4 per cent, an increase of 2 percentage points on the equivalent period in 2006.

2.119 An alternative way of measuring the profitability of companies is to look at the corporate gross operating surplus. Excluding the volatile oil sector, Figure 2.23 shows the non-oil private sector profits on this measure as a percentage of GDP. It shows that the profit share has picked up since the beginning of 2006 after falling in the second half of 2005. In the third quarter of 2007, it was back to its average level (since 1980). In contrast, the wage share of GDP has been falling over the same period.

2.120 Long-run share prices can also shed some light on the expected future profit performance of companies. The FTSE All-Share Index at the end of December 2007 was up by 80 points over the year, although it closed the year 200 points below its May 2007 peak. The FTSE All-Share Index fell sharply in early January 2008 following disappointing economic news from the US.

2.121 For data on low-paying industries, we rely on the most recent information from the ABI. The latest data, for 2006, suggest that profits increased in retail, hospitality, social care and hairdressing. However, these data also indicate that profits may have fallen in agriculture, textiles, leisure, security and cleaning.

Figure 2.23

Non-oil Private Sector Profit Share and Whole Economy Wage Share, UK, 1989–2007

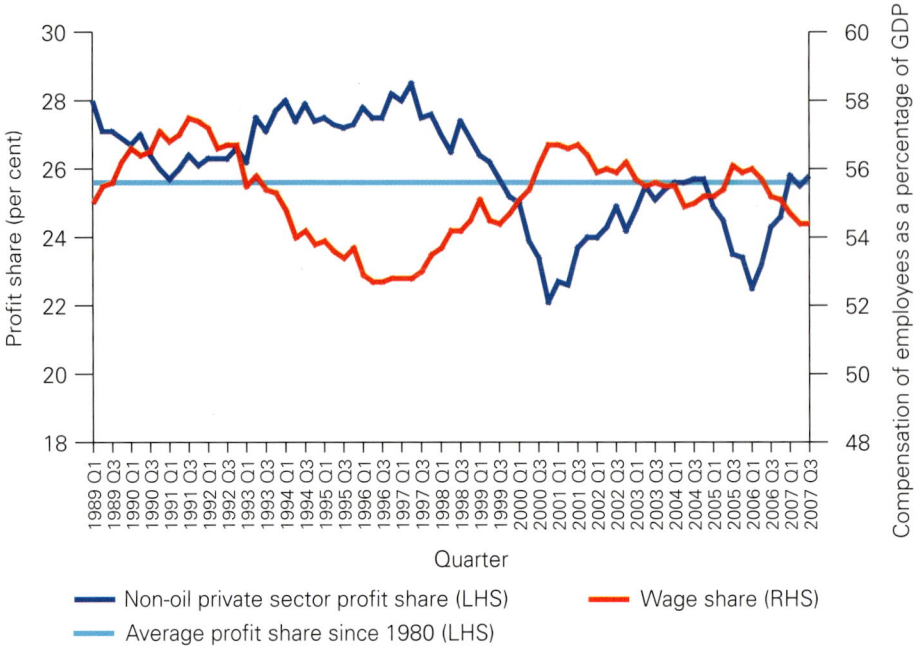

Source: Bank of England estimates of the non-oil profit share defined as non-oil private sector profits divided by non-oil private sector final output, and ONS Compensation of employees as percentage of Gross Domestic Product (ONS code IHXP), current prices, quarterly, seasonally adjusted, UK, 1989–2007.

Productivity

2.122 Firms can also adjust to the impact of the minimum wage by increasing labour productivity. There are many ways this might occur, including firms monitoring employees more closely; motivating them to put in extra effort as a result of higher pay; substituting capital for labour; or trying to improve the quality of their capital (new technology) and workforce (training). We go on to look at investment in the following section.

Figure 2.24

Growth in Productivity for the Whole Economy, Total Services and Distribution (including Retail and Hospitality), UK, 1998–2007

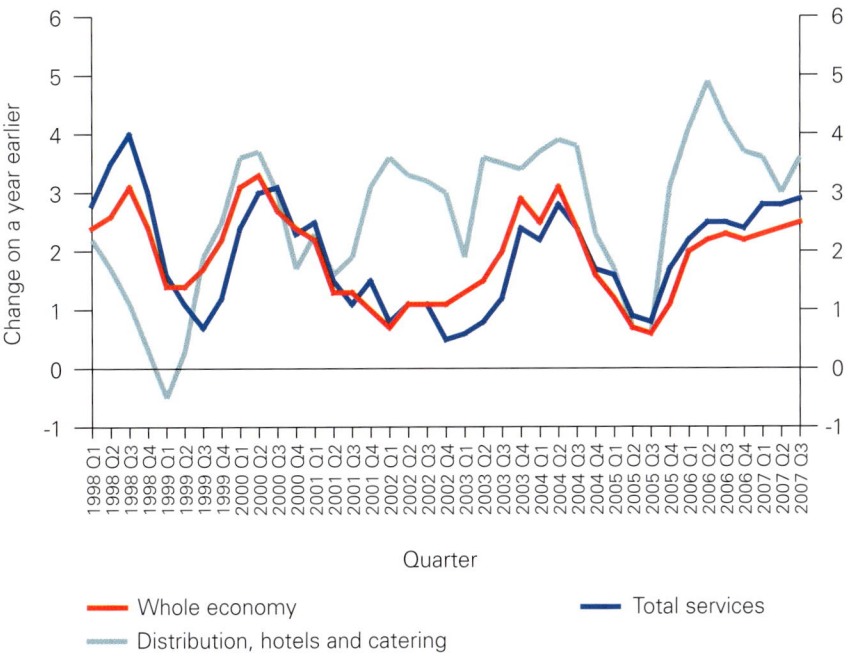

Quarter

— Whole economy   — Total services
— Distribution, hotels and catering

Source: ONS, output per job for the whole economy (ONS code LNNP) and experimental series for total services (ONS code GGSJ) and distribution, hotels and catering (ONS code GGSM), quarterly, seasonally adjusted, UK, 1998–2007.

2.123   Official data from ONS show that productivity has been increasing in the economy as a whole since the third quarter of 2005. Figure 2.24 shows that productivity in the service sector increased at a slightly faster pace than for the economy as a whole. Although this series is not available for the low-paying sectors, it is available for the distribution sector, of which retail and hospitality are large components. We can see that productivity in the distribution sector has risen even faster than in the service sector throughout 2006 and 2007.

2.124   This picture of increasing productivity in the retail and hospitality sector is also supported by evidence from the ABI[22]. Using gross value added data, and adjusting for employment and hours, the figures suggest that productivity growth was sluggish in 2005 but rose sharply in 2006 in both retail and hospitality, whether measured in terms of per worker employed or per hour. In contrast, productivity growth in the leisure sector in 2006 was sluggish on both measures.

---

[22]   The ABI is conducted annually. The latest available is September 2006.

Business Investment

2.125 Minimum wages might also have an impact on business investment as any squeeze on profits is likely to impair the ability of businesses to invest. We investigate this issue by comparing business investment in the economy as a whole with that in an important low-paying sector, hospitality, for which relevant data are available. We can see from Figure 2.25 that, since the second quarter of 2006, business investment in the whole economy has been stronger than it has been for some time. Over the last year, business investment in the hospitality sector has shown even stronger growth than in the economy as a whole.

Figure 2.25

Annual Change in Business Investment for Whole Economy and Hospitality Sector, UK, 1997–2007

Source: ONS Business investment for Whole economy (based on ONS code NPEL) and Hotels and restaurants (based on ONS code YGRP), chained volume measures, quarterly, seasonally adjusted, UK, 1997–2007.

Entrepreneurship – Births and Deaths of Firms

2.126 The National Minimum Wage might also have an effect on the number of business start-ups and failures. An increase in the minimum wage that adds to payroll costs might deter entrepreneurs from starting a business. If the increase was sufficiently large, the profits of existing firms might be squeezed leading to a rise in the number of business failures. In this section, we consider the number of business start-ups and failures in the whole economy and make comparisons between the whole economy and the low-paying sectors, focusing in particular on retail and hospitality. We then look more specifically at company insolvencies.

Business Start-ups and Failures

2.127 Looking at the net change in business start-ups and closures using data on the number of businesses registering and de-registering for VAT and focusing on the economy as a whole, Figure 2.26 demonstrates that the stock of VAT-registered enterprises has increased in every year since 1995. In the latest year available, 2006, there were some 182,000 registrations and 143,000 de-registrations resulting in a net increase of more than 39,000 in the stock of VAT-registered enterprises.

2.128 Since 2002, the number of business start-ups in the low-paying sectors has outstripped the number of business closures, suggesting that the minimum wage upratings that have taken place since 2003 have not had an adverse impact on entrepreneurial activity. In 2006, about 55,000 new firms registered in the low-paying sectors with around 47,000 de-registering, a net change of nearly 8,000. The largest net increases in the stock of VAT-registered businesses in the low-paying sectors were in retail (around 4,700) and hospitality (about 5,300). The largest net fall was in the agriculture sector (2,000).

Figure 2.26

Net Change in the Stock of VAT-registered Enterprises in the UK, 1994–2006

Source: BERR Enterprise Directorate Analytical Unit, business start-ups and closures: VAT registrations and de-registrations, annual, UK, 1994–2006

Insolvencies

2.129 The number of insolvencies in the economy represents another indicator of business closures. The number of insolvencies hit record levels during the course of 2007, peaking in the first quarter. However, the recent increases in the number of insolvencies have been driven almost entirely by increases in individual insolvencies as a result of increases in both bankruptcy orders and Individual Voluntary Agreements. Company liquidations, on the other hand, have remained relatively stable. In the year to the third quarter of 2007, they decreased by 2.8 per cent from 3,172 to 3,082 in England and Wales. They also fell in Scotland but rose in Northern Ireland.

Stakeholders' Views and Evidence on Affordability and Funding of Minimum Wage Increases

2.130 A number of employer organisations told us of the many rising costs they face, including the minimum wage, and of the difficulty they were having in finding the financial resource to fund increases. On the other hand, a number of trade unions provided contrary evidence suggesting businesses were well able to fund increases in the minimum wage.

2.131 For example, in retail, the BRC told us that their 2007 survey results suggested that the rise in the minimum wage to £5.35 had cost the retail industry over £1.7 billion, 13 per cent more than predicted in 2006. The BRC maintained that the 6 per cent increase to £5.35 had caused many retailers severe difficulties and they would have to continue to absorb the impact of past heavy increases for some time to come. The Independent Retailers Confederation (IRC) also reported that independent retailers were finding it increasingly difficult to accommodate minimum wage increases.

2.132 A number of respondents said that the minimum wage had affected margins. The Association of Convenience Stores (ACS) told us that convenience stores operated on tight margins and, due to the National Minimum Wage, labour costs had increased well ahead of possible increases in turnover. For many retailers, they claimed, continued increases in the minimum wage had been a key reason for reduced profits and decreased competitiveness. The BRC reported that, although productivity in retail had increased, the additional revenue being generated by employees had been heavily outweighed by increased cost pressures, including wage inflation.

2.133 There were cost pressures in other low-paying industries. In the baking industry the Scottish Association of Master Bakers said that bakeries were experiencing an unprecedented increase in raw material costs, due to global economic factors and further increases were expected as the balance of supply and demand for basic agricultural produce adjusts. The National Day Nurseries Association reported that the sector had sustainability problems: many businesses were operating on low margins, with just half breaking even and a fifth making a loss. It said that recent experience showed that minimum wage increases usually resulted in a rise in fees to parents.

2.134   Against this, trade unions maintained that most businesses could easily afford increases in the minimum wage. They pointed to the strength of business profitability. The TUC noted that the current rate of profitability in UK private non-financial corporations was 15.5 per cent. Profitability in non-financial service sector corporations was higher at 21.1 per cent – the highest since records began nearly 20 years ago. The Government's evidence stated that corporate profitability continued to be strong. Unite said that retailers were doing well, with 22 UK retailers ranked within the top 250 companies of the world in Deloitte's Global Powers of Retailing, and argued that they were undoubtedly able to afford further increases in the minimum wage. Unite also referred to the American Express 2007 Hospitality Monitor survey, which it said showed that the UK hospitality sector was positive about future profits. Unite reported that when the sector was asked in this survey about the most significant challenge in the future it cited direct competition (50 per cent), followed by the cost of goods (18 per cent) and customer preferences (12 per cent) – not minimum wage increases.

2.135   Other stakeholders told us that some difficulties arise from an inability to increase pay sufficiently. Using the example of social care, Unison argued that low pay generated costs, by inducing high staff turnover. The United Kingdom Home Care Association (UKHCA) pointed to a turnover rate of 25 per cent in the domiciliary care sector. With the cost of training a new care worker at around £980, and averaging costs and turnover across the whole of social care, UKHCA estimated an annual loss to the sector of £78 million arising from the failure to retain trained workers, part of which could be ascribed to the sector's inability to afford higher wages.

2.136   The National Care Association (NCA) and the English Community Care Association (ECCA) told us that fee increases paid by local authorities to providers of social care were not matching increases in the minimum wage and other costs. UKHCA reported that initial findings from its survey of local authorities in August 2007 found the average contract price increase by local authorities was 1.77 per cent, with no price increase in 38 per cent of council contracts.

2.137 In our last report we again recommended that the commissioning policies of local authorities should reflect the cost of providing care. We also emphasised the need for Government to monitor how far practice matched policy, examining reasons for any uneven provision and, if appropriate, to give further guidance. The Government has once more advised us of the substantial increase it has provided in funds for social care in recent years, together with guidance to local authorities when they commission services. The latest commissioning guidance was issued for consultation in March 2007, with the Government's response published in early 2008.

2.138 Although the Government does not set fee levels from the centre, it does expect councils to use fair commissioning practice and continues to stress the need for councils to reflect the legitimate costs of providers when agreeing fee levels for care home placements. It is disappointing that the Government has not produced any evidence to demonstrate that it has undertaken the type of monitoring work we proposed, despite having apparently accepted our recommendation. At the same time we see continued evidence of a geographical variation in the level of fee increases paid by local authorities, with some providers facing very low or zero rises (reported to us by social care providers, sector representatives and in the Laing & Buisson (2007) market survey). We will continue to monitor developments in this area and reiterate the need for fees to reflect the costs of care including the cost of the minimum wage.

Conclusion

2.139 In this chapter we have reviewed the impact of the minimum wage using the best available information. Our review suggests that the UK economy performed rather better than anticipated when we recommended the October 2007 upratings last year. The 3.2 per cent wage increase introduced in October 2007 is now estimated to have covered around 0.8–1.0 million jobs held by adults (about 4.5 per cent). It is too early to assess fully the impact of this latest increase on the economy but we have been able to look at the impact of the 2006 increase.

2.140 Our review of the impact of the large 2006 upratings noted that the 'bite', on various measures, was at its highest in October 2006. Research found evidence that pay structures had been changed as a result of the minimum wage and that differentials had been squeezed but we still found little impact on employment. Indeed, employment in the UK was at record levels with unemployment falling. Moreover, the number of employee jobs in the low-paying sectors grew marginally faster than in the economy as a whole. There was some research evidence that firms may have passed on the costs of the minimum wage to their customers in the form of higher prices. Profits, however, appeared to increase across the economy and productivity had increased faster in retail and hospitality than in the whole economy. The evidence also suggested that the minimum wage had not affected business creation or failure.

2.141 In the next chapter we examine the effect of the minimum wage on groups of workers.

Groups of Workers

Introduction

3.1   As in previous years, we were asked in our terms of reference to consider the impact of the minimum wage on different groups of workers, including different age groups, ethnic minorities, women, people with disabilities and, for the first time, migrant workers. When the minimum wage was first introduced, there were concerns that it would adversely affect the employment prospects of some groups of workers more than others as they were more likely to be low-paid. In our reports we have carefully monitored the position of women, ethnic minority groups and those with work-limiting disabilities. Earlier reports have shown that both their employment prospects and relative earnings have improved in recent years. In this chapter we review the labour market outcomes of these groups of workers. We also consider the labour market prospects of young people and the situation of other groups of workers who, by the nature of their work and its organisation, face particular issues in respect of the operation of the minimum wage.

Women, Ethnic Minorities and People with Work-limiting Disabilities

Women

3.2   A growing number of women have entered the labour market in the last 40 years. Figure 3.1 shows that the employment rate of women has been steadily rising since the 1970s and does not seem to have been affected by the introduction of the minimum wage in April 1999. Although women's employment rate remains lower than that of men, it has been following the same trend in the last ten years. Likewise,

> *While ... women have been the main beneficiaries of the National Minimum Wage, ... it has not transformed the conditions underpinning the evaluation of their work.*
>
> **EOC evidence**

the unemployment rate of both groups have followed a similar pattern. In 2005 and 2006, both men and women experienced a slight rise in unemployment. However, the growth in unemployment has eased in the last year. The female unemployment rate stood at 5.3 per cent in the third quarter of 2007 compared to 4.4 per cent in the same quarter of 2005, while the male unemployment rate increased from 5.3 per cent to 5.8 per cent over the same period.

3.3   Despite their increased participation in the labour market, women remain disproportionately represented in low-paying sectors. According to the Labour Force Survey (LFS), in the third quarter of 2007 55 per cent of employees working in low-paying sectors were female, compared to 57 per cent in Autumn 1998. The incidence of female employees in the low-paid occupations is even more pronounced as they are less likely to hold supervisory or management positions. In the third quarter of 2007, around 67 per cent of employees in these occupations were women with some occupations such as nursery nurses, care assistants, office workers and hairdressers being particularly female-dominated. Women are also much more likely to be working part-time. According to the LFS, in the third quarter of 2007 78 per cent of part-time employees were women. Both these factors, the preponderance of women in low-paid occupations and their high propensity to be working part-time, will have an impact on their earnings. As we saw in Chapter 2, around two-thirds of jobs covered by the October 2007 upratings in the National Minimum Wage were held by women.

Figure 3.1

Working Age Employment and Unemployment Rates by Gender, UK, 1971–2007

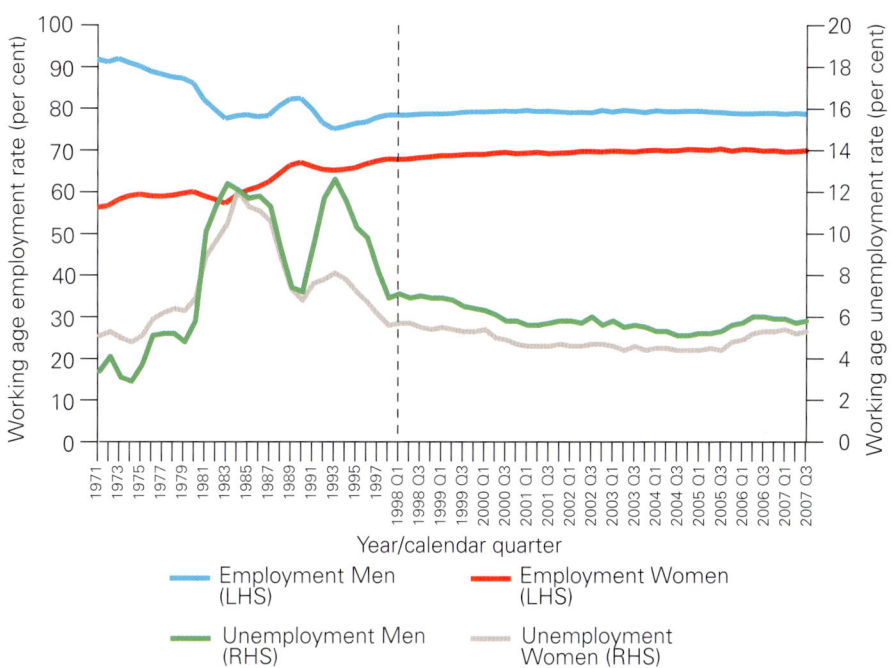

Year/calendar quarter

———— Employment Men (LHS) ———— Employment Women (LHS)

———— Unemployment Men (RHS) ———— Unemployment Women (RHS)

Source: ONS LFS working age employment rate (MGSV, MGSW) and working age unemployment rate (YBTJ, YBTK), seasonally adjusted, UK, 1971–1997 and Q1 1998–Q3 2007.

Note: The dashed line indicates a break between data for whole years and quarters.

3.4 We have said in previous reports that there is evidence to demonstrate that the introduction and subsequent upratings of the minimum wage have contributed to a narrowing of the pay gap at the bottom of the earnings distribution. Figure 3.2 shows that in the last ten years, the gender pay gap for full-time employees aged 18 and over has been steadily narrowing at the lower end of the earnings distribution, and up to the 85th percentile, while it marginally increased at the top end of the distribution. The gender pay gap in the middle of the earnings distribution has been narrowing for some time and is therefore to a large extent independent of the influence of the minimum wage. However, the reduction in the pay gap has been most pronounced at the very bottom of the distribution since 1997 (declining from 10.5 per cent in 1998 to 3.8 per cent in 2007 at the fifth percentile) than at the median (down from 16.8 to 11.2 per cent), which suggests that the minimum wage has had a major impact on closing the gender pay gap among the low-paid. Little progress, however, has been made at the upper end of the earnings distribution where the pay gap has widened and the minimum wage has no influence.

Figure 3.2

Gender Pay Gap for Full-time Employees Aged 18 and Over, UK, 1998–2007

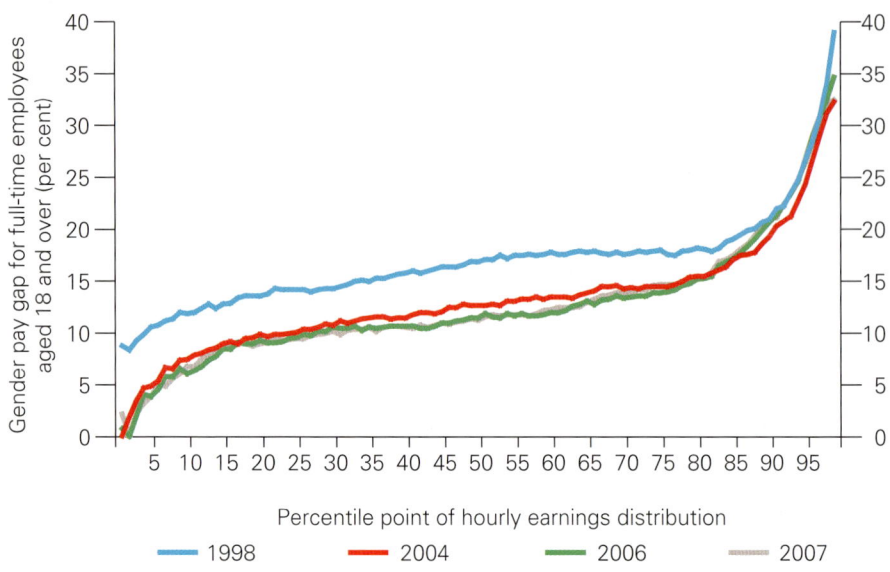

Source: LPC estimates based on ASHE without supplementary information, 1998, ASHE with supplementary information, 2004 and ASHE 2007 methodology, 2006–2007, standard weights, UK.
Note: The gender pay gap is the difference between 100 per cent and the ratio of women's hourly earnings to male hourly earnings.

People with Work-limiting Disabilities

3.5   According to the LFS, 5.3 million people, or up to 16 per cent of the working age population, had work-limiting disabilities in the year to the third quarter of 2007. This group is much less likely to be participating in the labour market than other employees. In the third-quarter of 2007, the inactivity rate of people with work-limiting disabilities was 54.2 per cent compared to 15 per cent among those without such disabilities. Overall, employees with work-limiting disabilities were only slightly more likely to be working in low-paying sectors and occupations than other employees, although their incidence was higher in particular occupations such as cleaning, agriculture and textiles. In these three occupations the latest LFS data show well over one in ten employees with work-limiting disabilities. Research by Rigg (2005) on labour market disadvantage among disabled people found that people with disabilities were significantly more likely to enter low-paid work and significantly less likely to exit low pay than people with no disabilities.

3.6. The employment rate of those with work-limiting disabilities has historically been much lower than for other groups, but has been slowly increasing over the last ten years. In the third quarter of 2007, 40.3 per cent of employees with work-limiting disabilities were employed compared to 37.8 per cent in Autumn 1998, while the employment rate for other employees increased by 0.3 percentage points to 80.7 per cent over the same period. Unemployment for those with disabilities also declined at a much faster rate than for other employees between 1998 and 2004 as illustrated in Figure 3.3. Since 2004, however, unemployment has been increasing slightly more rapidly than for other groups. In the third quarter of 2007, the unemployment rate of those with work-limiting disabilities was 12 per cent compared to 9.8 per cent in the second quarter 2005. This rise in unemployment coincides with a sharp decline in the number of incapacity benefit claimants following moves by the Government to encourage this group back into work through welfare reforms.

Figure 3.3

Working Age Unemployment Rate of People with Work-limiting Disabilities, UK, 1998–2007

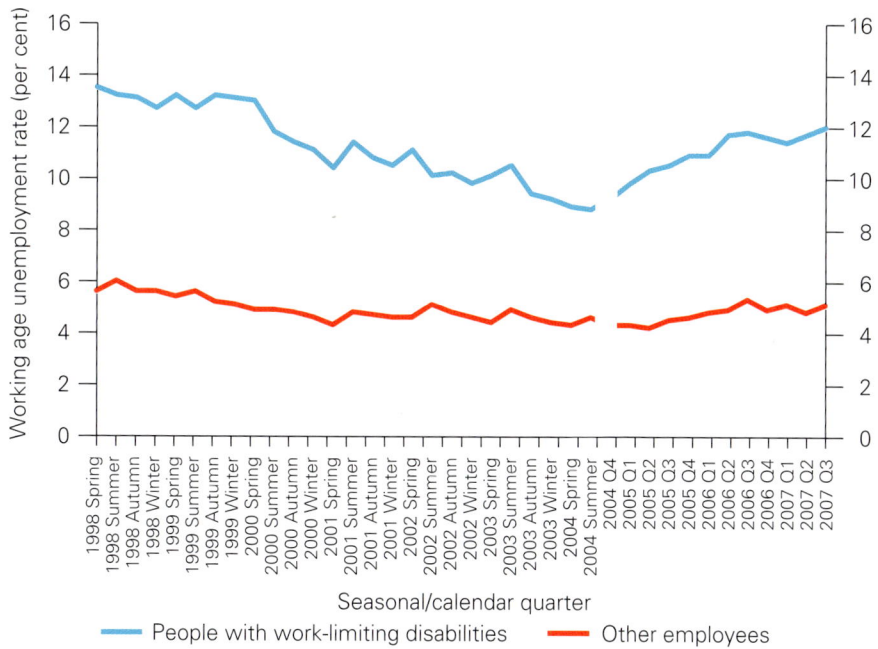

Source: LPC estimates based on LFS microdata, seasonal/calendar quarters, not seasonally adjusted, UK, 1998–2007.

Note: The break between Summer 2004 and Q4 2004 is a result of a discontinuity in the series as the LFS moved from seasonal to calendar quarters; thus comparisons should be made with care.

3.7   We reported in our 2007 Report that, since the introduction of the National Minimum Wage, the pay gap between the hourly earnings of employees with a work-limiting disability and those of other workers seems to have narrowed at the lower end of the distribution. Moreover, a higher proportion of workers with work-limiting disabilities continues to benefit from increases in the minimum wage as is illustrated in Figure 3.4. We estimate that, in April 2007, 8.7 per cent of employees with work-limiting disabilities were covered by the October 2007 minimum wage upratings, compared to 5.2 per cent of workers without such disabilities. The proportion of those covered rises to 10.2 per cent when we consider those workers who have both a disability as defined under the Disability Discrimination Act (DDA) and who also have a work-limiting disability.

Figure 3.4

Estimated Coverage of the 2007 Upratings of the National Minimum Wage by Disability for Employees Aged 16 and Over, UK, 2007

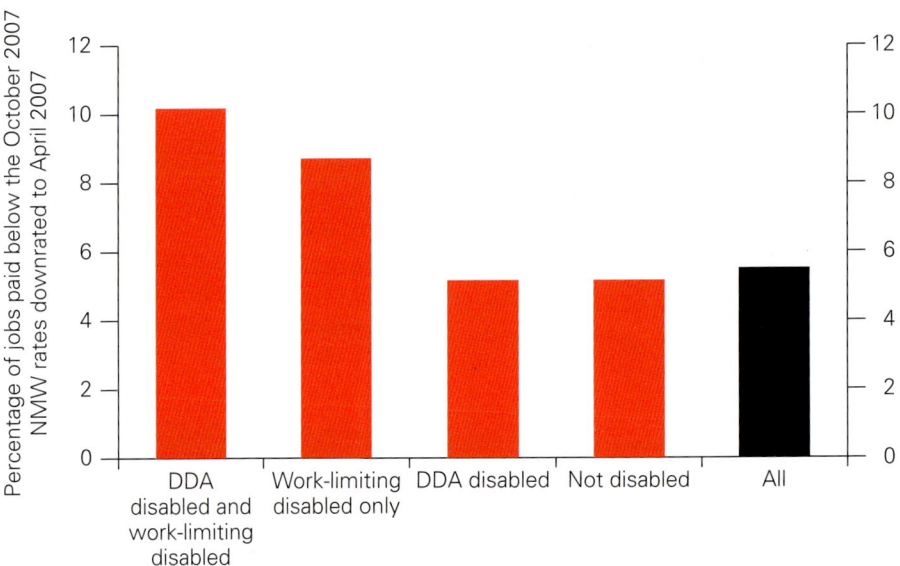

Source: ONS estimates based on LFS microdata, not seasonally adjusted, UK, Q2 2007.
Note: Covered employees defined as adults (aged 22 and over) earning less than £5.40, youths (aged 18–21) earning less than £4.50 and 16–17 year olds earning less than £3.32 in April 2007.

Ethnic Minority Groups

3.8 Our terms of reference ask us to monitor the impact of the minimum wage on people from ethnic minorities. The definition of an ethnic minority is not a simple one and no system of classification can be entirely free of arbitrary delineations. In the analysis that follows we have used the LFS self-reported classification of ethnicity as adopted by the 2001 Census[1] but we recognise that this does not take into consideration the additional dimension resulting from the recent arrival of migrant workers principally from central and eastern Europe. Migrant workers are considered in a separate section later in this chapter.

3.9 Workers from ethnic minorities are more likely to be working in low-paying sectors than white workers. In the third quarter of 2007, 12.2 per cent of employees working in low-paying occupations were from ethnic minority groups compared to 8.3 per cent in other occupations. In the textiles and security low-paying occupations, around a quarter of the workforce was from a ethnic minority group.

3.10 Employees from ethnic minority groups generally have lower employment rates than white employees but, as shown in Figure 3.5, they have seen an increase in employment at a generally faster pace than that of white employees in recent years. Around 60.7 per cent of ethnic minority employees were employed in the third quarter of 2007 compared with 56.9 per cent in Autumn 1998. In 2007, their employment rate increased by 0.3 percentage points in contrast to white employees who experienced a very small decline in their employment rate from 76.3 to 76.2 per cent. Similarly, although the unemployment rate of ethnic minority workers is higher than that of white workers, it has been declining since the introduction of the minimum wage. However, the recent increase in unemployment was slightly more pronounced among those from ethnic minorities. It rose from 10.2 per cent in the third quarter of 2005 to 11.7 per cent in the fourth quarter of 2006, but has since then reduced to 11.3 per cent in the third quarter of 2007. However, these figures mask significant differences between the various ethnic minority groups and, within these, between men and women. Pakistani and Bangladeshi women have by far the lowest employment

---

[1] 2001 Census questions distinguished between the following ethnic groups: White; Mixed; Asian or Asian British; Black or Black British; Chinese or Other Ethnic Group. More detailed distinctions were made within these ethnic groups.

rate and the highest unemployment rate among ethnic minority groups, despite improvements in the last ten years.

Figure 3.5

Working Age Employment Rates By Ethnic Group, UK, 1998–2007

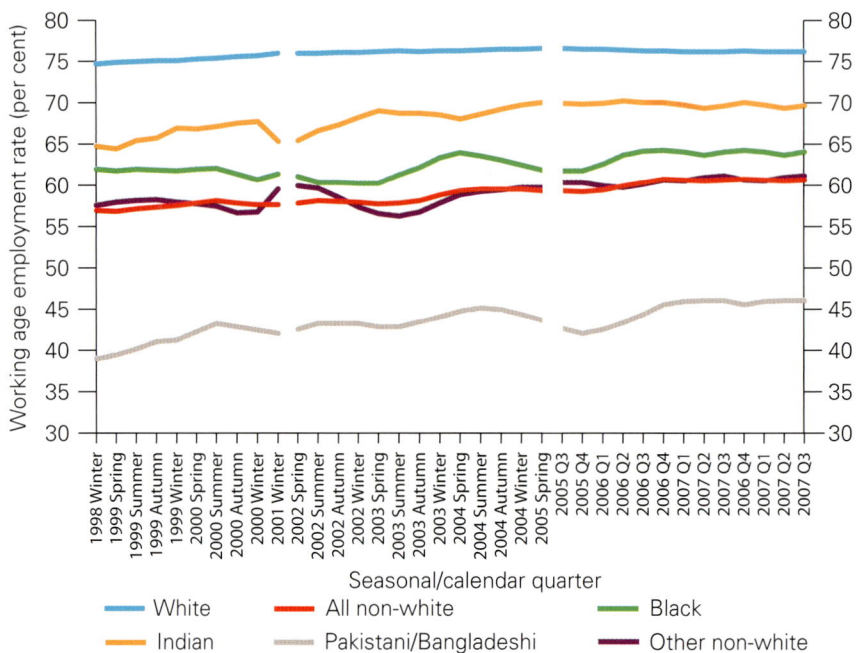

Source: LPC estimates based on LFS microdata, seasonal/calendar quarters, four-quarter moving average, UK, 1998–2007.

Notes:

1. The definition of ethnic groups in the LFS changed in Spring 2001 to be consistent with the 2001 Census classifications; thus comparisons between the periods before and after should not be made.

2. The break between Spring 2005 and Q3 2005 is a result of a discontinuity in the series as the LFS moved from seasonal to calendar quarters; thus comparisons should be made with care.

3.11.   There is evidence that since the introduction of the minimum wage, the earnings position of ethnic minorities has improved at the lower end of the distribution. The difference between the earnings of ethnic minorities and whites is slightly less than the pay gaps experienced by employees with work-limiting disabilities or women. We estimate that overall 7.7 per cent of employees from minority ethnic groups were covered by the October 2007 upratings in the minimum wage compared to 5.3 per cent of white employees. However, this masks large differences between specific minority ethnic groups as seen in Figure 3.6. Asian/Asian British origin employees or those from other ethnic groups or of mixed origin were more likely to be covered by the upratings in the minimum wage than Black/Black British or Chinese employees. However, Heath and Cheung (2006) found that even after controlling for age, education and other personal characteristics, there were still significant net disadvantages for

Black Africans, Black Caribbeans, Pakistanis and Bangladeshis with respect to unemployment, earnings and occupational attainment.

Figure 3.6

Estimated Coverage of the 2007 Upratings of the National Minimum Wage by Ethnic Group for Employees Aged 16 and Over, UK, 2007

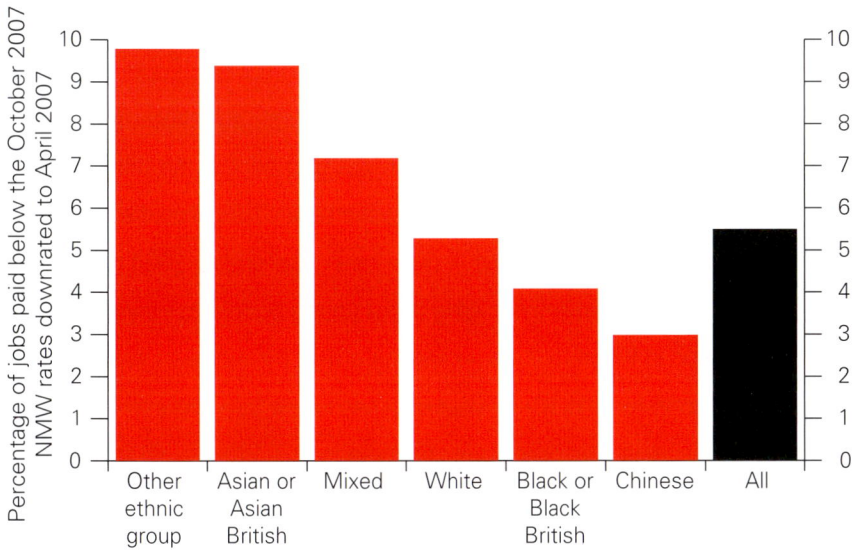

Source: ONS estimates based on LFS microdata, not seasonally adjusted, UK, Q2 2007.
Note: Covered employees defined as adults (aged 22 and over) earning less than £5.40, youths (aged 18–21) earning less than £4.50 and 16–17 year olds earning less than £3.32 in April 2007.

Conclusions

3.12 The labour market participation of women, ethnic minority groups and people with work-limiting disabilities has improved in the last ten years. There is no evidence that the minimum wage has had an adverse impact on employment. All three groups, especially women, are more likely to be working in low-paying sectors and occupations and as a result are more likely to have benefited from the upratings in the National Minimum Wage. The minimum wage appears to have helped improve the earnings position of those groups of workers at the lower end of the earnings distribution. It has little effect on inequalities higher up the earnings distribution or those arising from occupational segregation.

Young People and Apprentices

Economic Activity and Participation in Education

3.13   From the outset, the Commission has been concerned that the National Minimum Wage should not provide a disincentive for young people to enter or remain in education. So far there has not been any evidence of a detrimental impact of the minimum wage on young people's participation in education. Most 16–17 year olds are in full-time education (FTE). The proportion of full-time students was 76.7 per cent in the third quarter of 2007 (Figure 3.7). There is evidence (Battistin *et al,* 2005) that the introduction of the Education Maintenance Allowance in September 2004 has been an important factor in encouraging more young people to stay in FTE. However, as shown in Figure 3.7, there are signs that the increase in the participation rate among female 16–17 year olds has come to a halt in the last eighteen months, while participation is still rising for 16–17 year old males. At age 18 and over, many young people are still in FTE though participation decreases with age. Around 52.3 per cent of 18 year olds were in FTE in the third quarter of 2007, and participation in FTE fell to 27.2 per cent by the age of 21.

Figure 3.7

Proportion of 16–17 and 18–21 Year Olds in Full-time Education by Gender, UK, 1998–2007

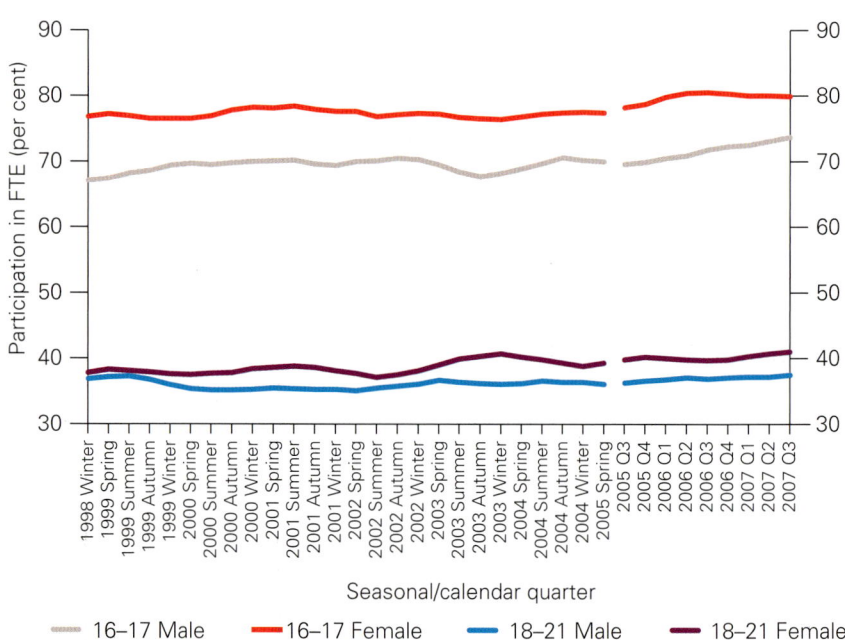

Source: LPC estimates based on LFS microdata, seasonal/calendar quarters, four-quarter moving average, UK, 1998–2007.

Note: The break between Spring 2005 and Q3 2005 is a result of a discontinuity in the series as the LFS moved from seasonal to calendar quarters; thus comparisons should be made with care.

3.14 The labour market prospects of the decreasing number of 16–17 year olds who are not in FTE have been worsening since the end of the 1990s as shown in Figure 3.8. However, in the last year, the decline in employment and increase in inactivity and unemployment have shown signs of reversing. In the third quarter of 2007, the employment rate of 16–17 year olds not in FTE was 52.1 per cent, compared to 49.9 per cent a year ago, while the proportion of inactive 16–17 year olds not in FTE declined by 1.9 percentage points to 24.7 per cent over the same period. The unemployment rate remained stable at around 30.8 per cent.

Figure 3.8

Economic Activity of 16–17 Year Olds Not in Full-time Education, UK, 1998–2007

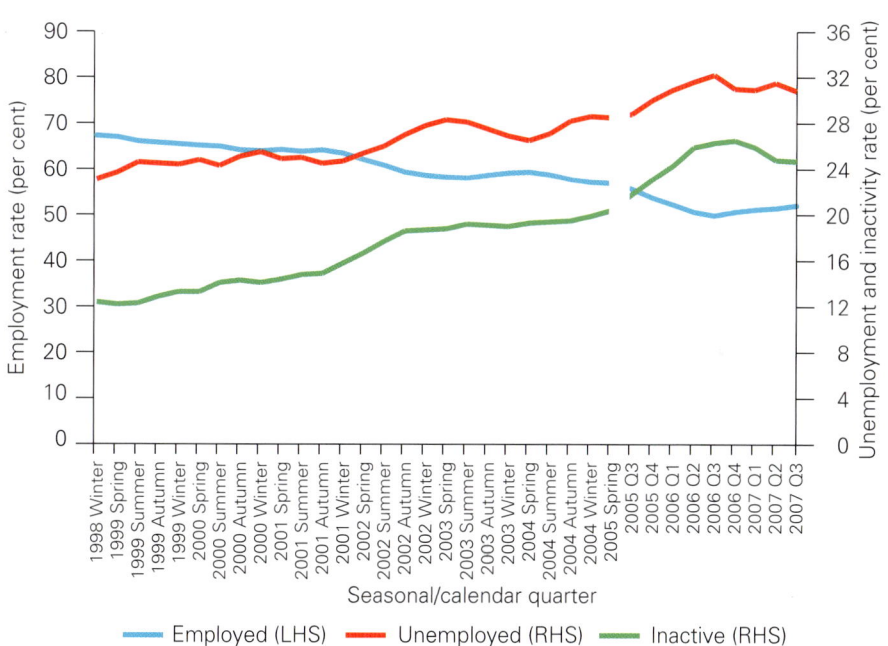

Source: LPC estimates based on LFS microdata, seasonal/calendar quarters, four-quarter moving average, UK, 1998–2007.
Note: The break between Spring 2005 and Q3 2005 is a result of a discontinuity in the series as the LFS moved from seasonal to calendar quarters; thus comparisons should be made with care.

3.15   Despite this improvement in the labour market position of 16–17 year olds not in FTE, just under half of this group (173,000 people) were either inactive or unemployed in 2007. While it is true that those young people not in FTE could be engaged in some form of part-time education, DfES figures (DfES, 2007) on participation in education and training show that most of the increase in inactive 16–17 year olds has occurred among those not in education or training. Those Not in Education, Employment or Training (NEET) have been of particular concern to the Government in recent years. DfES estimated that 10 per cent of 16–18 year olds were NEET in 2006, an increase of one percentage point since 1998. The increase was more pronounced for men and among 17 and 18 year olds, that is, for young people more likely to be active in the labour market than those who have just left school. The Prince's Trust (2007) reported that the number of 16–24 year old NEETs had increased by 15 per cent from 1.08 million in 1997 to 1.24 million in 2006. However, there is a considerable degree of churn among NEETs. Research by the Learning And Skills Council (LSC, 2006) found that only one per cent of the 16–18 year-old cohort was NEET throughout the three year period it covered.

3.16   We now turn to consider 18–21 year olds. Figure 3.9 shows that in the third quarter of 2007 over 70 per cent of the 1.87 million 18–21 year olds not in FTE were employed. However, there has been a continuous decline in their employment rate since 2000, accompanied by a steady increase in their inactivity rate and, since 2004, a sharp rise in their unemployment rate. Overall, 554,000 or 32.2 per cent of 18–21 year olds not in FTE were unemployed or inactive, compared to 26.3 per cent in 2000.

3.17   Looking at individual ages, it is the labour market position of 18 year olds, and to a lesser extent that of 19 year olds, which seems to have deteriorated the most. Eighteen year olds not in FTE went from having the lowest inactivity rate of the cohort in 1998 to the highest in 2007. It has been hypothesised that the growing popularity of taking a gap year before entering higher education might be a factor. However, data from the Universities and Colleges Admissions Service show that the proportion of accepted applicants deferring entry to higher education for a year decreased from 7.9 per cent in 2002/2003 to 7.3 per cent in 2006/2007.

Figure 3.9

Economic Activity of 18–21 Year Olds Not in Full-time Education, UK, 1998–2007

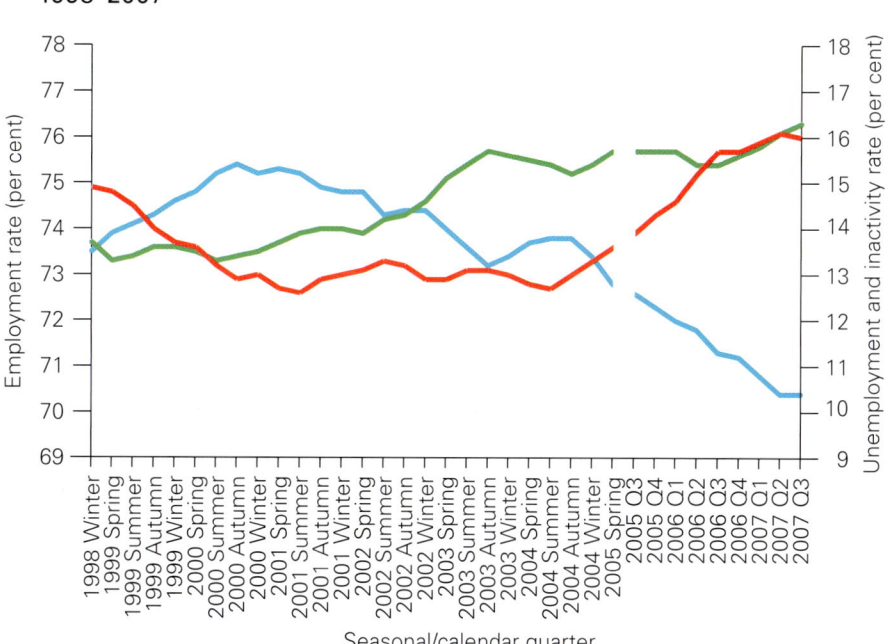

Source: LPC estimates based on LFS microdata, seasonal/calendar quarters, four-quarter moving average, UK, 1998–2007.

Note: The break between Spring 2005 and Q3 2005 is a result of a discontinuity in the series as the LFS moved from seasonal to calendar quarters; thus comparisons should be made with care.

3.18   The decline in the labour market position of young people has been general across the UK. The proportion of young people not in FTE aged 16–21 who were in employment fell in almost all regions between 1998 and 2007, unlike those aged 22 and over who saw their employment share increase in all areas of the UK except London. However, by European standards, young people's labour market position in the UK is relatively strong. According to Eurostat (2007), in the second quarter of 2006, Britain had the fourth highest employment rate overall and also the fourth highest rate for those aged 15–24 among the 27 European countries. However, its position with regard to unemployment was less good.

3.19   Given that employment in the UK has been at record levels, it is difficult to explain why young people have not done better in the labour market. Two significant developments in the labour market in recent years have been the increase in the number of people of pension age becoming economically active and the arrival of predominantly young migrant workers from the European Union accession countries.

However, little evidence is available to substantiate the hypothesis that some young people might be substituted by older workers or migrants beyond anecdotal evidence given by some of our stakeholders. Employment vacancies information produced by Connexions Services in 2006 indicated that some employers prefer to recruit migrant workers who were perceived as having more developed interpersonal and technical skills. This is a point that has been frequently made to us during Commission visits, although it is worth noting that the decline of young people in the labour market started before this recent wave of immigration. We intend to continue to engage with other interested stakeholders and to encourage further research in this area so that we can reach a better understanding of the developments in this part of the labour market.

Earnings

3.20   Table 3.1 shows the proportion of jobs held by 16–17 year olds which paid below the 16–17 year old rate, the Youth Development Rate (YDR) and the adult rate applicable in April of the relevant year. In April 2007, 4.1 per cent of jobs held by 16–17 year olds were paying below the 16–17 year olds rate, a small increase from 3.8 per cent in 2006. Overall, the proportion of jobs held by 16–17 year olds at or above the 16–17 year old rate and below the Youth Development Rate increased from 24.5 per cent in 2004 to 27.5 per cent in 2007 while the proportion of jobs paying at or above the Youth Development Rate but below the adult rate remained stable. Of note is the decline in the proportion of jobs held by 16–17 year olds which paid at or above the adult rate, from 42.3 per cent in 2004 to 37 per cent in 2007. Among those, however, there was a sharp increase in the proportion of jobs paid at the adult rate from 3.8 per cent (13,600) in 2006 to 7.3 per cent (28,400) in 2007. In the same period, there were also noticeable peaks in the distribution at £4.00 (although that peak was much smaller than in 2006), £4.50, £4.85 and £5.00.

Table 3.1

Proportion of Jobs Held by 16–17 Year Olds at the National Minimum
Wage Rates, UK, 2004–2007

Per cent	16–17 Year Old Rate	Youth Development rate (in April)	Adult rate (in April)	Below 16–17 Year Old Rate	At 16–17 Year Old Rate	Above 16–17 Year Old Rate and Below YDR	At YDR	Above YDR and Below Adult Rate	At Adult Rate	Above Adult Rate
2004	–	£3.80	£4.50	–	–	25.0	5.7	27.0	4.9	37.4
2005	£3.00	£4.10	£4.85	4.0	1.8	22.8	2.8	28.3	4.3	36.1
2006	£3.00	£4.25	£5.05	4.0	1.6	25.5	3.8	25.4	3.8	36.0
2006	£3.00	£4.25	£5.05	3.8	1.5	25.5	3.9	25.6	3.8	35.9
2007	£3.30	£4.45	£5.35	4.1	2.8	24.7	2.9	28.5	7.3	29.7

Source: LPC estimates based on ASHE with supplementary information 2004–2006 and ASHE 2007
methodology 2006–2007, low-pay weights, UK.
Note: Direct comparisons between the 2004–2006 and 2006–2007 series should be made with care due to
changes in the methodology.

3.21 Table 3.2 shows that there has been a similar decline in the proportion of
jobs held by 18–21 year olds which paid at or above the adult rate from
86 per cent in 2004 to 81 per cent in 2007, but with the actual proportion
of jobs paying at the adult rate increasing only slightly. Around 2.5 per
cent of jobs held by that age group paid below the Youth Development
Rate in 2007, a small increase from 2.3 per cent in 2004. There were
also two noticeable peaks in the 2007 earnings distribution at £5.50 and
£6.00.

Table 3.2

Proportion of Jobs Held by 18–21 Year Olds at the National Minimum
Wage Rates, UK, 2004–2007

Per cent	Youth Development rate (in April)	Adult rate (in April)	Below YDR	At YDR	Above YDR and below Adult Rate	At Adult Rate	Above Adult Rate
2004	£3.80	£4.50	2.3	1.7	10.3	5.7	80.0
2005	£4.10	£4.85	3.0	2.6	10.2	5.2	79.0
2006	£4.25	£5.05	2.3	3.0	12.3	6.1	76.3
2006	£4.25	£5.05	2.3	3.0	12.1	6.1	76.4
2007	£4.45	£5.35	2.5	2.9	13.6	7.2	73.7

Source: LPC estimates based on ASHE with supplementary information 2004–2006 and ASHE 2007
methodology 2006–2007, low-pay weights, UK.
Note: Direct comparisons between the 2004–2006 and 2006–2007 series should be made with care due to
changes in the methodology.

Age-related Pay

3.22 For the 16–22 age group, there is a clear relationship between age and earnings as illustrated by Table 3.3. In all years shown, gross hourly earnings progressively increase with every year of age. Over the last three years, the lower decile earnings of 18 year olds and 21 year olds have equalled the Youth Development Rate and the adult rate of the minimum wage respectively. The differential in decile earnings between 21 year olds and those aged 22 had considerably reduced in the last three years and to a much greater extent than for 20 year olds. In 2007, the bottom decile earnings of 21 year olds were nearly 100 per cent of those of 22 year olds, compared to 97 per cent in 2005.

Table 3.3

Gross Hourly Earnings for Young People by Age, UK, 2005–2007

Age	Lowest decile			Lowest quartile			Median		
	2005	2006	2007	2005	2006	2007	2005	2006	2007
16	£3.22	£3.24	£3.35	£3.91	£4.00	£4.09	£4.38	£4.55	£4.64
17	£3.55	£3.57	£3.75	£4.07	£4.17	£4.31	£4.70	£4.80	£5.00
18	£4.10	£4.25	£4.45	£4.70	£4.90	£5.00	£5.15	£5.34	£5.50
19	£4.46	£4.57	£4.73	£4.95	£5.05	£5.35	£5.50	£5.63	£5.94
20	£4.72	£4.98	£5.04	£5.00	£5.23	£5.49	£5.75	£6.00	£6.17
21	£4.85	£5.05	£5.35	£5.25	£5.45	£5.64	£6.15	£6.33	£6.60
22	£5.00	£5.14	£5.37	£5.51	£5.73	£5.91	£6.70	£6.96	£7.05

Source: LPC estimates based on ASHE with supplementary information, 2005, and ASHE 2007 methodology 2006–2007, standard weights, UK.
Note: Direct comparisons between 2005 and 2006–2007 should be made with care due to changes in the methodology.

3.23 We have seen earlier that there has been a progressive decline in the proportion of 16–21 year olds paid at or above the adult rate of the National Minimum Wage. This increase in the use of age-related pay has been experienced mainly by 16–18 year olds. In April 2007, around 66 per cent of 18 year olds were paid at or above the adult rate, rising to 78 per cent of 19 year olds, 85 per cent of 20 year olds and 90 per cent of 21 year olds.

3.24 Evidence from our consultation and the research we commissioned provides a mixed picture on the use of age-related pay. Income Data Services (IDS, 2007a) have found that there has been a continuing divergence in the use of youth rates, with some companies moving away from age-related pay while others have increased their use of it.

This has been most clearly an issue in the retail and fast food sectors. In retail, there has been a continuing trend to lower the age at which the adult rate is paid and a number of retailers have ended the practice of age-related pay completely. Other companies have narrowed the differentials between under–18 rates and pay rates for adults aged 18 and over. By contrast, some have introduced new youth rates to their pay structures. Overall, however, an increasing majority of retailers seem to be paying the adult rate from 18. This is confirmed by data from the Annual Survey of Hours and Earnings (ASHE) which show that 90 per cent of 18–21 years olds working in retail were paid at least the adult rate in April 2007 compared to 83 per cent in 2004. In their written evidence, the British Retail Consortium noted that none of the multiple retailers they surveyed in 2007 were using the Youth Development Rate, compared to 89 per cent not using it in 2006. The proportion of retailers that said they were unlikely to start using the Youth Development Rate also increased from 82 to 100 per cent. It could be that this pattern is more evident among large retailers. In their evidence to the Commission, the Independent Retailers Confederation reported that independent retailers, which tend to be smaller, were finding it increasingly difficult to accommodate increases to the minimum wage particularly in relation to the lower wage bandings. However, the ASHE data show that although micro and small firms are slightly less likely to pay young people at the adult rate than larger firms, the small decline in the use of age-related pay has occurred across firms of all sizes.

3.25 In the fast food sector, IDS found that larger traditional fast food chains have introduced the use of youth rates over the last four to five years, while newer, smaller establishments have pay structures solely based on experience. A similar pattern was observed in pubs. In the hospitality sector, the adult rate is typically paid from the age of 22. ASHE data show that 68 per cent of 18–21 year olds were paid at or above the adult rate in April 2007. According to ASHE, 92 per cent of 18–21 year olds employed in the social care sector were paid at or above the adult rate in April 2007, an increase of 10 per cent since 2004.

3.26 IDS also found, as in previous years, that youth rates were not widely used in the social care sector (a sector where there are restrictions on the use of under 18s in direct caring roles) and that those organisations which differentiated pay by age tended to pay the adult rate from the age of 18. In the nurseries sector, 37 per cent of respondents to the IDS survey said that they used age-related pay, up from just over a third in the previous survey. Of those using age-related pay, 69 per cent said that the threshold was age 22 and 10 per cent said that the threshold was age 21.

3.27   We came across similar issues during our visits across the UK to meet employers and workers, with some employers paying 16–21 year olds above the youth rates and others having age-related pay in their wage structures. During a Commission visit in London, McDonald's explained that 16–17 year olds were paid above the Youth Rate but that a differential was maintained with 18–21 year olds to reflect the fact that there are some legal restrictions on 16–17 year olds such as the ability to do late shifts.

Stakeholders' Views

The adult rate minimum wage should be paid from age 18 rather than 22. This would reflect the social norm that adulthood starts at 18 and be consistent with the trend back towards paying the adult rates at the age of 18.

TUC evidence

3.28   Respondents to our consultation from trade unions invariably argued that the adult rate of the minimum wage should be paid from the age of 18 rather than from 22. The TUC argued that the existence of lower National Minimum Rates for young workers was inconsistent with the Government's strategy to 'make work pay'. It was concerned that low wages would provide a disincentive for 18–21 year olds to seek employment and that inequitable treatment in the work place would have a demoralising effect. Unite reported that there had been no evidence of a decrease in youth employment where youth rates had been abolished through negotiation.

3.29   Trade unions also advocated that the increases in the 16–17 year old rate should be higher than the increase in the adult rate. In its evidence, the TUC noted that the decline in the employment of 16–17 year olds had abated and that there was sufficient headroom in the labour market for an increase in the 16–17 year old rate that outstripped the growth in average earnings. UNISON called for 16–17 year olds to be entitled to the Youth Development Rate with a view to harmonising it with the adult rate over time.

3.30 These views were largely mirrored by youth organisations which consistently called for the abolition of youth rates altogether on the grounds that an age-tiered National Minimum Wage was discriminatory and was inconsistent with other Government policies to tackle prejudice and inequalities. The British Youth Council (BYC) presented the Commission with a petition signed by 600 young people expressing their dissatisfaction with the current minimum wage system and calling for an equal National Minimum Wage. In their evidence, the BYC contended that the reason for higher unemployment among young people without post–16 qualifications was an effect of multiple deprivation factors, including poverty and a low sense of self-esteem and that an equal minimum wage would increase labour market activity for them. The Children's Rights Alliance for England argued that unequal wage rates for young people posed a serious barrier to young people's entering and staying in education as low wages pushed many of the youths in full-time education who needed to support themselves to work longer hours and spend less time on their studies.

3.31 In their responses, some employers were more cautious and continued to emphasise the importance of the youth rates. The CBI noted that unemployment among the young remained high and strongly supported maintaining the youth rates to protect the employment prospects of young people. The CBI also argued that the uprating of the adult rate of the National Minimum Wage needed to be modest as many firms paid youths at this rate. This would also allow the youth rates to rise proportionately and help young people maintain their standards of living without affecting firms' marginal decisions to hire. The Association of Licensed Multiple Retailers (ALMR) argued that the youth rates provided their members with an incentive to provide in-house training rather than simply recruiting employees with existing skills. The Institute of Directors argued that the Commission should bear in mind the impact on employers of the proposed changes to participation in education for under-18s when considering the level of the 16–17 year old rate.

> *I have worked in a supermarket for just less than 5 years and I did a similar job throughout my time. My pay did increase when I hit 18 but not to the same level as older people I worked with, even though I was as well trained and did a very similar job. This seems unfair, just because we were different ages why should the pay be different, as an 18 year old or even 16 year old, we can be faced with the same out payments as a 21 year old, such as car, or house or even kids.*
>
> *Joe, 20*
>
> **BYC evidence**

> *The youth rates must be retained – abolition would further undermine the labour market position of younger workers.*
>
> **CBI evidence**

The Role of Youth Rates

3.32   The evidence we have examined in this chapter indicates that young people have continued to do less well in the labour market than older workers, although there have been signs that the decline in employment has abated in the last year for 16–17 year olds not in full-time education and in the last six months for 18–21 year olds not in full-time education. We nevertheless believe that lower National Minimum Wage rates for young people continue to be justified to protect their position in the labour market.

21 Year Olds

3.33   Since our First Report (1998), we have consistently recommended that 21 year olds should be entitled to the adult rate of the National Minimum Wage. Our view has always been that, on balance, the 21st birthday is the appropriate cut-off point for the adult rate and that the employment prospects of 21 year olds does not need to be protected by the Youth Development Rate.

3.34   The Government has consistently rejected our recommendations, urging caution and arguing that the labour market position of 21 year olds was closer to that of 20 year olds than 22 year olds. In their latest economic evidence (BERR, 2007a), the Government argued that the employment rate of 21 year olds not in FTE generally moved more in line with the 19–20 year old rate. We do not agree. Figure 3.10, which is taken from the Government's own economic evidence to us for this report, clearly shows that 21 year olds not in FTE have not fared as badly in the labour market as 19–20 year olds in recent years and their employment rate is now clearly more aligned to that of 22–23 year olds. In the third quarter of 2007, 73.6 per cent of 21 year olds – excluding those in FTE and graduates – were employed compared to 70.5 per cent of 19–20 year olds and 74.9 per cent of 22–23 year olds. In the same period, the unemployment rate of 21 year olds was 9.7 per cent, closer to the unemployment rate of 22–23 year olds (at 7.8 per cent) than 19–20 year olds (at 13.4 per cent).

Figure 3.10

Comparison of Employment Rate of 21 Year Olds with 19–20 and 22–23 Year Olds, Excluding Full-time Students and Graduates, UK, 1998–2007

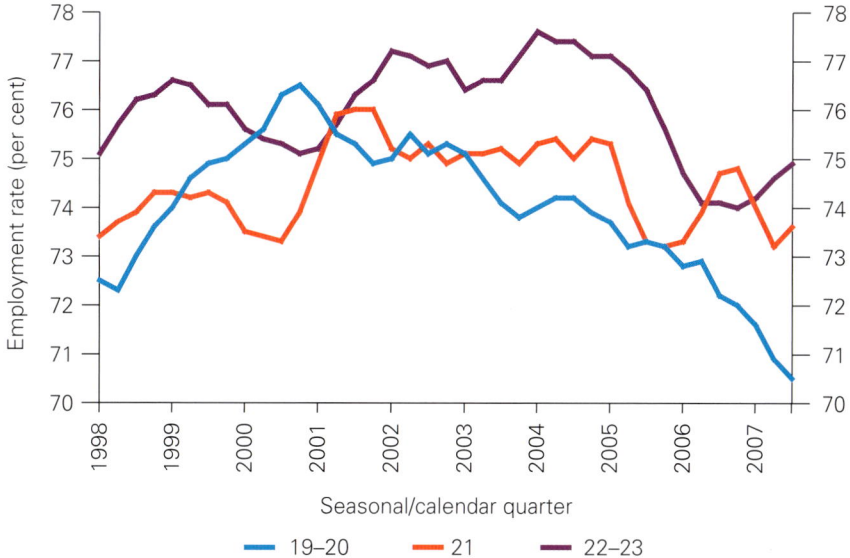

Seasonal/calendar quarter

—— 19–20   —— 21   —— 22–23

Source: Government economic evidence. LFS microdata, seasonal/calendar quarters, four quarter moving average, UK, 1998–2007
Note: Results for Q3 2005 and earlier are calculated from seasonal LFS microdata.

3.35   The evidence on earnings is equally strong and suggests that employers overwhelmingly pay 21 year olds at least the adult rate. Earnings data show that fewer than 10 per cent of jobs (around 52,000) held by 21 year olds were paying below the adult rate of the minimum wage in April 2007. The slight increase in the use of age-related pay which we have observed in the last four years has mainly taken place among 16–19 year olds. Moreover, as shown in Table 3.3, the differential in the decile hourly earnings of 21 and 22 year olds seem to have substantially narrowed over time to the point where the bottom decile hourly earnings of these two age groups were practically the same in April 2007. Thus a move to lower the age at which the adult rate should be paid from 22 to 21 is likely to have little impact on employers. In the evidence we received no stakeholders argued that the cut off point for the adult rate should be maintained at the 22nd birthday.

3.36   We believe that the latest evidence reinforces our view that lowering the entitlement to the adult rate to the age of 21 will not have a detrimental impact on their employment prospects and therefore **recommend again that 21 year olds should be entitled to the adult rate of the National Minimum Wage. Should the Government maintain its opposition to this proposal, we would welcome an indication of the exact nature of its opposition and a specification of what would need to change for the Government to adopt a positive approach to this recommendation.**

Apprentices

3.37   In our 2006 and 2007 Reports we recommended that the Government invite us to review the minimum wage exemptions for apprentices and report in 2008. We believed a thorough review of the apprenticeship exemptions was necessary to assess how they have worked in practice given the number of developments which have taken place since the minimum wage was introduced and which may have had an impact on apprentices and the use of the exemptions. In particular, we felt it was necessary to understand the impact of the extension of the minimum wage to 16–17 year olds in 2004, changes to the financial support models for trainees, and the opening up of apprenticeships to older workers. We were therefore disappointed that the Government confirmed in this year's remit that it did not want us to undertake such a review for this report.

3.38   Although we did not seek comment on apprentices this year, a number of stakeholders continued to raise concerns that the apprentice exemptions were being abused by some employers who offered little or low quality training and that low pay had been contributing to high non-completion rates. Several trade unions and other organisations representing workers again called for a review of the treatment of apprentices, with many seeking the removal of the minimum wage exemptions. Some argued that the Government's proposals to extend the school leaving age and to increase the number of apprenticeship opportunities made a review at this time even more pertinent. The key allegations made were that exploitative rates were being paid to some apprentices and the quality of some training was sub-standard. There was a view that this could discourage young people from undertaking training and could be a significant reason for the high non-completion rate for apprenticeships. Some organisations also highlighted the pay gap between male and female apprentices. The Equal Opportunities Commission registered concern about the negative impact of the apprenticeship exemption on pay, particularly for female apprentices.

3.39 We also received a small number of consultation responses from employer bodies on the topic of apprentices, particularly in relation to the hairdressing sector. The National Hairdressers' Federation advised that, although there was an increased interest in careers in the industry, most small salons were reluctant to take on trainees, in part due to the £80 per week minimum pay requirement. It suggested that the minimum wage exemption for apprentices should apply for the whole period of training, which in hairdressing might be up to three years.

3.40 Our belief that there is a strong case for a review of the minimum wage treatment of apprentices has been reinforced by the evidence we have received from stakeholders. Moreover, it will be some time before the Government's proposals in the Education and Training Post-16 Green Paper (which applies to England alone) are implemented while apprenticeship schemes and the minimum wage cover the UK as a whole. We were therefore pleased that the Prime Minister announced in the House of Commons on 28 November 2007 that the Commission would be asked to undertake a review of apprenticeships and we look forward to carrying out this task in the coming year.

Migrant Workers

3.41 This year our remit asked us to report on the effects of the National Minimum Wage on migrant workers. We noted in our 2006 Report the substantial increase in the number of migrant workers in the UK over a number of years. This was particularly pronounced following enlargement of the European Union (EU) on 1 May 2004 and represented the most significant change to the labour market since the introduction of the minimum wage. The two key areas of interest for us regarding migrant workers are the effects they have on unemployment and wage inflation at the lower end of the labour market and the specific issues that arise in respect of minimum wage compliance and enforcement.

3.42   The UK has experienced high levels of both inward and outward migration[2] since the mid-1990s, with in-migration rising at a faster rate than out-migration. Migrant workers have been an important element of the UK labour market for many years. While many migrant workers are highly skilled and paid well in excess of the minimum wage, a further group are concentrated at the low skill end of the labour market. It is this group we focus on, and in particular, migrant workers from the eight central and eastern European accession countries (the A8)[3]. It is workers from these countries who have had an important impact on the lower end of the labour market in recent years and for whom our consultation indicated there is particular concern in respect of the minimum wage. We also consider whether the migrant worker dynamic in the UK has changed further as a result of Romania and Bulgaria (the A2) joining the EU on 1 January 2007.

3.43   There are currently limited and imperfect data to help to understand the number of low-skilled migrant workers in the UK, the sectors in which they work and their country of origin. The ONS is developing a strategy to address this problem which will see modest improvements made to international migration statistics by 2008, although more substantial improvements will not be in place for a number of years. In October 2007, the House of Commons Trade and Industry Committee, in its report on the impact of the new EU Member States on UK business, recommended that the Government gave urgent consideration to how it could improve the information it collected on A8/A2 immigration before the next census in 2011. We welcome and endorse this recommendation and trust that it will be taken forward by the Government. However, at this time we can only draw on the statistics that are available and the information presented to us during our visits throughout the UK and our consultation to form our general understanding of migrant workers.

---

[2]   A migrant is defined as someone who changes his or her country of usual residence for a period of at least a year, so that the country of destination effectively becomes the country of usual residence.

[3]   The Czech Republic, Estonia, Hungary, Latvia, Lithuania, Poland, Slovakia and Slovenia.

Migrant Workers from the Central and Eastern European Accession Countries

3.44   Migrant workers from the A8 countries were granted free access to the UK labour market from May 2004, but were required to register under the Worker Registration Scheme (WRS) if employed for a month or more[4]. The WRS shows that a total of 715,000 applicants from the A8 countries were approved to work in the UK between 1 May 2004 and 30 September 2007 (Border and Immigration Agency *et al*, 2007d)[5]. The composition of these workers has been fairly consistent since the scheme began, with the majority (66 per cent) of approved applicants coming from Poland. The vast majority were aged between 18 and 34 and were working full-time (more than 16 hours a week). However, the limitations of the WRS data mean that there continues to be much speculation on the number of A8 workers in the UK at any given time. Some evidence suggests that the number is substantially greater than indicated by the WRS, other evidence suggests it may be lower.

3.45   Workers from the A8 countries were concentrated in the low-paying sectors. Figure 3.11 below shows the top ten occupations in which A8 workers were registered under the WRS, accounting for 70 per cent of all registered. The occupations have remained largely consistent, with just over three-quarters earning[6] between £4.50 and £5.99 an hour. This data is consistent with what we have been told during our visits and during consultation with stakeholders over the last couple of years, although we have begun to receive anecdotal evidence to suggest that some migrant workers may now be graduating to better paid jobs that more closely reflect their qualifications.

---

[4]   Those registered on the WRS working legally in the UK for 12 months without a break are eligible to apply for a residence permit.

[5]   The number of applicants to the WRS scheme does not represent a measurement of net migration from the A8 to the UK; it is a gross (cumulative) figure for the number of applicants that have been approved to work in the UK.

[6]   These data are derived from responses to answers in the WRS application form and are not verified by the Home Office.

Figure 3.11

Worker Registration Scheme Applicants by Occupation, UK, 2004–2007

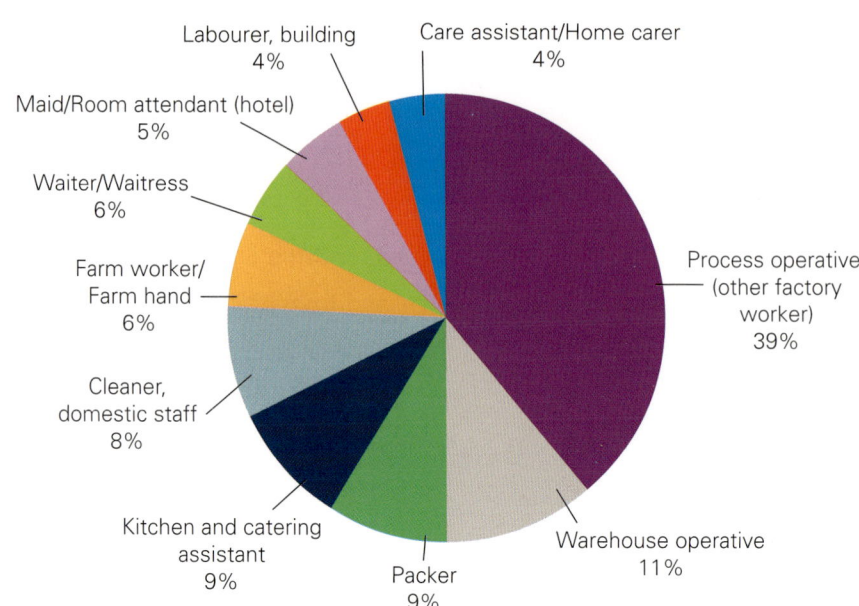

Source: Home Office Accession Monitoring Report A8 Countries, UK, May 2004–June 2007.
Notes:
1. May/June 2004 data not available.
2. Percentages indicate percentage of all workers registered, July 2004–June 2007.

3.46 There has been little change in the geographical distribution of A8 migrant workers since the WRS was introduced. Anglia remains the most popular destination, with 15 per cent of the total who have registered; followed by the Midlands and London, with 13 per cent and 12 per cent of the total respectively. Northern Ireland and Wales continue to attract the fewest A8 workers (4 per cent and 3 per cent of the total respectively).

Workers from Romania and Bulgaria

3.47 Nationals from the A2 countries were not given the same right to access the UK labour market as those from the A8 and their entry to work in the UK is by means of the work permit schemes operated by the Government. Changes to the work permit schemes will give priority to workers from the A2 countries and this will restrict the opportunities for other groups of migrant workers to access the UK labour market. We will monitor the impact of this new group of workers carefully over the coming year.

3.48 Below we look at the impact of migrant workers on the labour market and some specific compliance and enforcement issues that relate to these workers.

Impact on the Labour Market

3.49 In our 2007 Report we concluded that the evidence available indicated that workers from the A8 countries were contributing to the success of the UK economy by filling gaps in the labour market. The evidence also suggested that the increase in A8 workers had not displaced UK nationals in the workplace. This year, there was little evidence to suggest that the position has changed, although there was some limited evidence that A8 workers were being substituted for other groups of migrant workers.

3.50 Other reports on this topic appear to support the view that migrant workers have had little or no negative impact on employment. The Bank of England Quarterly Bulletin (Bank of England, 2007a) found concerns that native workers would be displaced by migrant workers, especially following the accession of new member states in 2004, were ill-founded, as migrant workers appear to have complementary skills to the native workforce. A cross-departmental submission to the House of Lords Select Committee on Economic Affairs in October 2007 stated, "So far, both theoretical and empirical analysis suggests that migration has had no impact on the employment prospects of UK natives". In its evidence to us, the Government referred to research conducted by the Department for Work and Pensions (DWP) in 2006 which found no discernible statistical evidence to suggest that A8 migration has had a negative impact on employment.

3.51 The effect of migrant workers on wage inflation is slightly less clear, although most indications are that if there has been an impact, it has been minimal. The study we commissioned for the 2007 Report by Dustmann, Frattini and Preston (2007) to assess the impact of migrant workers on wages found some evidence that there had been a small negative effect on wages at the bottom end of the earnings distribution, while native workers in the middle of the earnings distribution appeared to have gained as a result of the increasing number of migrant workers. The study, however, used data that largely pre-dated the arrival of significant numbers of A8 workers in 2004.

3.52 We have looked at other sources of information to help assess whether migrant workers had an impact on wage inflation. Research by Gilpin, Henty, Lemos, Portes and Bullen (2006) and Blanchflower and Shadforth (2007) found no evidence that the increased flow of migrant workers into the UK has exerted downward pressure on wages.

3.53 In evidence this year, a few stakeholders referred to the impact migrant workers were having on employment and pay. A joint submission from the British Hospitality Association, the British Beer and Pub Association and Business in Sport and Leisure noted that the availability of A8 workers had made a favourable impact on labour shortages in the sector. However, their joint submission also expressed concern that the continued inflow of A8 workers to the sector might not be sustained as the tourism industry in the A8 countries was beginning to develop. It was thought that the westbound flow of hospitality workers could be reversed over the coming years. The submission also noted that migrant workers might have had an impact on average wage levels. The ALMR advised that, in a survey of its members, 35 per cent had employed migrant workers this year to curb costs.

3.54 During our visits throughout the UK, there was some evidence that A8 workers were willing to take on jobs with greater levels of responsibility for only a slight increase in pay, work which UK nationals were unwilling to do for a similarly low rate of remuneration.

3.55 In their evidence to us, Unite expressed the view that migrant workers (both those with and without documentation) were often recruited because employers knew they would be able to get away with paying lower wages, sometimes significantly less than the minimum wage. The union believed that this had exerted a downward pressure on the wages of indigenous workers at the lower end of the earnings distribution.

Compliance and Enforcement

3.56 The vulnerability of some low-paid migrant workers is a concern for worker and employer representative organisations and not-for-profit groups alike. A number of responses to our consultation raised concerns about the exploitation of migrant workers. A similar picture emerged from our visits throughout the UK.

3.57 The Scottish Low Pay Unit reported a high number of calls from young migrant workers from Eastern Europe, particularly from Poland, and primarily working in the hospitality and agricultural sectors. The issues raised ranged from blatant underpayment of the minimum wage to a wide range of excessive deductions from pay.

3.58 The Government in its evidence recognised that migrant workers were a group at particular risk of being underpaid the minimum wage, as well as at risk of missing out on other basic employment entitlements. It referred to the emphasis which it had put on ensuring there was information available to inform migrant workers about UK employment laws, including the Know Your Rights leaflets, the National Minimum Wage migrant workers campaign and the Vulnerable Workers Pilots which were set up this year in Birmingham and London. We consider the compliance and enforcement issues relating to migrant workers further in Chapter 4.

Voluntary Workers

3.59 Voluntary workers are a group given a particular meaning in the National Minimum Wage Act. When working for specific organisations (a charity, voluntary organisation, associated fund-raising body, or a statutory body), and receiving only very specific payments and benefits-in-kind (such as necessary expenses incurred, reasonable subsistence or training required to perform the work) they are excluded from minimum wage coverage. The objective of this arrangement is to ensure that genuine 'volunteers' may continue to work (and receive necessary expenses) without minimum wage liability, while 'workers' in the voluntary sector retain their right to be paid at least the National Minimum Wage. Our experience is that the minimum wage law has worked well in this area, and when problems have arisen they have generally been organisation specific and have been resolved through improved guidance and understanding. The Commission regards good guidance as particularly important for the voluntary sector, and in recent reports we have called for the existing guidance to be updated, consolidated and made more accessible.

3.60 During the summer of 2007 the Government consulted on a proposal, arising from its review of the *National Minimum Wage and Voluntary Workers* (DTI, 2007e), to exclude from National Minimum Wage coverage participants on schemes that are supported by the Russell Commission's national framework for youth action and engagement. It also sought views on whether a similar exclusion should apply to Ministry of Defence (MOD) Cadet Force Adult Volunteers. In addition, it confirmed its intention to act on the Commission's recommendation to update guidance to the voluntary sector. We welcomed confirmation of the Government's intention to update the existing guidance. While fully supporting the Government's intention to encourage more volunteering activities for young people, we raised a number of concerns about how the proposed new exclusion for national framework participants would operate and the possible implications for the minimum wage. We argued for a clearer statement of the benefits for the young people involved, and a precise account of the quality standards and systems which will ensure that they are delivered. There was potential for exploitation of those participating under the framework, with their use in substitution for workers. We called for greater clarity on the parameters of the proposed exclusion in order to ensure organisations did not use it opportunistically to avoid paying the minimum wage. We were not convinced of the case for an exemption from the minimum wage for MOD Cadet Force Adult Volunteers. Our full response can be viewed on our website (www.lowpay.gov.uk).

3.61 In evidence to us, trade unions expressed concern at the Government's proposal regarding schemes supported by the national framework. The TUC said that the change would undermine the minimum wage settlement that was painstakingly negotiated for the voluntary sector by generating pressure to extend exclusions further. UNISON said the proposed new exemption would take thousands of job opportunities for young people outside minimum wage coverage and create a loophole whereby there would be an incentive to replace paid positions with voluntary posts.

3.62 In its response to the public consultation (BERR, 2007b), the Government re-confirmed its intention to prepare new guidance. It also made clear that it intends to legislate to exclude MOD Cadet Force Adult Volunteers from coverage by the minimum wage. In addition, the Government response indicated that there were continuing discussions, involving the devolved administrations and the Office of the Third Sector, about the conditions under which an exclusion from National Minimum Wage coverage for participants on schemes that are supported by the Russell Commission's national framework would apply. We are pleased to note that the Government recognises the importance of clearly defined criteria for any exclusion, which avoids loopholes that might be exploited by unscrupulous employers. However, the Commission remains concerned about how this proposed exclusion would work in practice, and we will continue to monitor and report on any change the Government eventually introduces.

Unpaid Work Experience

3.63   There are specific types of work experience placements for which the minimum wage does not need to be paid, such as students on certain higher education courses undertaking a work placement as part of their studies. The Government has recently revised the regulations in this area so that the exemption for higher education is now for 'undertaking' rather than 'attending' a course (and will now cover distance learning), and the exemption has been extended to cover further education courses as well. There may also be other situations where the minimum wage does not apply, such as where the individual does not have an obligation to perform work and is therefore not a worker. However, sometimes labels such as 'volunteer', 'intern' or 'work experience' are applied to activities which are clearly work and for which at least the minimum wage should be paid. We expressed concern at evidence we received for the 2007 Report which suggested that it was becoming increasingly commonplace in certain sectors, particularly the media sector, for employers to demand a period of unpaid work as a price of entry into the industry. Guidance had been published by the Department of Trade and Industry (DTI, 2007b) for the television industry which we regarded as useful in helping improve employers' understanding of their obligations, both in that sector and more widely. We said we would monitor how the development and dissemination of this guidance affected employer practice.

3.64   We have again received evidence on unpaid work experience from trade unions, the TUC and workers in the media industry suggesting continued non-compliance with the minimum wage with regard to work experience. The TUC noted that some progress had been made (new guidance in the Houses of Parliament and the broadcast industry) but that it was not clear whether this was sufficient. It called for action to stamp out the use of unpaid work experience as a 'toll' for entering a desirable career and it asked us to review the rules on work experience to ensure that they were sufficiently rigorous to rule out exploitation. The National Union of Students thought that students on work placements as part of a further education course should qualify to be paid at least the minimum wage. It had concerns regarding the welfare of such students as well as believing non-entitlement created a significant barrier to education.

3.65   We believe that work experience is an area where wider dissemination of guidance and more effective enforcement, rather than any change to the rules themselves, is needed. **We recommend that the material concerning work experience placements in the official guide to the minimum wage should be updated in order to help raise awareness of this issue, including the recent extensions to the types of work experience which are exempt from the minimum wage**. We therefore fully support the Department for Business, Enterprise and Regulatory Reform's (BERR) decision to revise the existing official guidance in this area at the same time that it updates guidance on voluntary workers.

Homeworkers and Fair Piece Rates

3.66   Although homeworkers are given a specific definition in the National Minimum Wage Act 1998, with the intention of removing any possible ambiguity about who they are and the circumstances in which they are entitled to the minimum wage, we have repeatedly noted the particular difficulties such workers may face in ensuring they receive at least the minimum wage. Many low-paid homeworkers are rewarded through an output based payment method (piece rate), typically undertaking packing, sewing or assembly work. In October 2004 the Government introduced a new system of 'fair piece rates' as there were difficulties with the original arrangement for paying the minimum wage for output work (through 'fair estimate agreements'). The intention was that this would make arrangements simpler and more easily understood (DTI, 2004a). The Government also hoped that the change in regulations would significantly improve compliance and that there would be an increase in the coverage of the minimum wage among homeworkers.

3.67 We received evidence from the National Group on Homeworking (NGH) that in a small survey of 67 homeworkers only half were aware of the current rate of the minimum wage and, based on the available evidence, NGH estimated that probably around half were receiving less than this. Of the 44 who were paid by piece rate it was only possible to estimate the hourly rate of 28, but, of those, 19 were found to be earning less than the minimum wage (£5.35 at the time of the survey), with some earning as little as £1 per hour. The average for the 28 workers was £4.41 per hour. While NGH had welcomed the introduction of the fair piece rates system in 2004, its experience suggested that it was rarely applied. Its survey results showed only a minority of the 28 workers on piece rates were being paid in accordance with the fair piece rates system: most were not aware of any change to the way they were paid, and had not received the required written notice setting out such matters as their rate of pay.

3.68 Other evidence we received included that from the National Centre for Social Research, which reported the complexities it faced in applying a system of payment by assignment for its fieldforce of freelance interviewers, in order to ensure that at least the minimum wage was paid in each pay reference period. UNISON advised that the underpayment of the minimum wage to housekeeping staff paid at a 'room rate' by agencies, which it highlighted in 2006, had in many cases continued. Employment Information Services (EIS) supplied evidence on the problems faced in applying fair piece rates in the door-to-door distribution sector, together with a heightened potential for exploitation of the workforce. EIS claimed that workers were reluctant to complain for various reasons, including the often temporary nature of their employment.

3.69 We continue to receive evidence that homeworkers and those paid through fair piece rates face difficulties in enforcing their right to be paid at least the minimum wage. The fair piece rates system has been in place for around three years, but it is difficult to obtain hard evidence on how it is working in practice. However, the evidence put to us suggests that awareness and proper use of the new arrangements may be low. **We recommend that the Government takes stock and evaluates whether the fair piece rates arrangement is meeting its objectives.**

Seafarers

3.70   Seafarers are covered by the National Minimum Wage while employed to work on UK registered ships working in the UK or its internal waters (that is estuaries and the sea between the UK mainland and many islands). When working on board a ship registered in the UK, seafarers must be paid at least the minimum wage wherever in the world that ship may be, unless all their work takes place outside the UK and its internal waters, or they are not normally resident in the UK and the ship is outside the UK (and its internal waters). In its evidence, the TUC raised concern that the current exemptions from the minimum wage exclude many seafarers who do not live in the UK but who work for UK companies and whose work regularly brings them into UK ports. Over the coming year we will monitor carefully the application of the minimum wage in respect of seafarers.

Tips

3.71   One form of income which employers may use to make up minimum wage pay is tips – although only tips, gratuities or service charges paid by the employer to workers through the payroll may count towards the minimum wage. In our last report we said we would monitor the new guidance from Her Majesty's Revenue and Customs (HMRC) on the treatment of National Insurance Contributions (NICs) payments on tips to see if it led to any change of employer practice. We have received only limited evidence on tips this year, and little official data is available. ALMR advised us that, since the revised HMRC guidance, there was anecdotal evidence that some businesses in hospitality, in particular food-led operations, had sought to benefit from the revised NIC position by re-instating 'tronc' arrangements[7] to help make up some of the minimum wage. For these businesses, this had assisted in cushioning the effect of the recent upratings in the minimum wage.

---

[7]   A member of staff with responsibility for managing and allocating tips on behalf of other staff members.

In a further development in the treatment of tips, a decision in a recent employment tribunal (ET) case found that the payroll could consist of two parts – one for basic wages and one for tronc payments – with both elements counting towards the minimum wage. This decision could perhaps have wider implications for the payment of the minimum wage if the tronc was to be accepted as part of the employer's payroll. We understand that HMRC is appealing the ET judgement and we will again monitor developments.

Sleepovers

3.72 Sleepover arrangements concern payments made to workers when they are provided with facilities to sleep at or near their place of work and be available to deal with emergencies, but would not necessarily expect to be woken otherwise. The National Minimum Wage Regulations provide that the minimum wage does not apply when a worker is permitted to sleep, but that time spent awake and working is time for which the minimum wage must be paid. The official guidance on the minimum wage (DTI, 2004b) emphasises the need for the employment contract to set out clearly the period the worker is permitted to sleep, and for suitable sleeping facilities to be provided. In cases where the contract does not specify sleeping time, the guidance suggests tribunals are likely to conclude that the minimum wage should be paid for the full time when the worker is at work.

3.73 However, the evidence we received this year referred to a number of court and employment tribunal judgements which have created uncertainty about the obligations to pay the minimum wage during sleepovers. UNISON told us that a growing number of tribunal and court decisions are finding that workers are in fact 'working' during the entire sleepover period, by virtue of the fact that their work requires them to be in a particular place at a particular time and to be ready to react when a situation arises. It called for clarification of the guidance as it relates to sleepover payments to ensure that the National Minimum Wage is paid for all hours worked. The English Community Care Association (ECCA) said that sleepovers are now classed as working time and that this had a significant effect on its use by employers in the care sector. To be sure there was no breach of the regulations, ECCA considered that it was advisable for care providers to pay all sleepover hours at the minimum wage; however, it said employers could not afford to pay at this level because of the underfunding of care by local authorities. During our visits and in oral evidence we heard from social care employers that payment for sleepovers – especially in domiciliary care – was a significant issue. There was an increasing concern regarding what payments should be made to these staff.

3.74   The tribunal and court judgements have often been complex, involving decisions both on working time under the Working Time Regulations, and the minimum wage under the Minimum Wage Regulations. It appears that a situation has developed where some stakeholders believe there has been a change to requirements under the minimum wage, and that that the existing official guidance is not sufficient for employers to be sure what their minimum wage responsibilities are when asking staff to undertake a sleepover period. **In the light of the uncertainty created by these tribunal and court decisions we recommend that the Government reviews the existing official guidance on sleepovers as soon as practicable.** Following the outcome of such a review this is an area we may wish to return to in a future report.

Therapeutic Activity

3.75   Therapeutic work or activity are terms used to describe arrangements whereby people who have problems functioning in the normal labour market, because of a mental or physical impairment, are given the opportunity to undertake some form of work-like activity, for which they may receive some type of payment. If they are not workers the minimum wage will not apply. However, if these activities are carried out under an arrangement that is a worker's contract, they must be paid at least the minimum wage.

3.76   We recognise this is a complex area. In our last report we were concerned at continued claims of non-compliance with the minimum wage and possible exploitation of vulnerable people. We were also concerned that misplaced fears or misunderstandings regarding the minimum wage should not inhibit the provision of services of benefit to people with a disability or mental heath problem. We emphasised the need to raise awareness and for effective dissemination of guidance and therefore welcomed the publication by the DTI of an updated version of its guidance note on the minimum wage and therapeutic work (DTI, 2007a), which was widely distributed to appropriate organisations.

3.77   Citizens Advice Northern Ireland said there is a growing concern that arrangements used by many organisations, placement employers and disabled clients may be breaching the minimum wage legislation. It reported continued confusion regarding entitlement to the minimum wage when clients move from a supported placement with employers to become workers. Moreover, some employers may not be willing to pay the minimum wage to clients they regard as less productive than other workers. The minimum wage was not the main cause of the issues faced by the sector, but it has acted as a catalyst to highlight what was regarded as inflexibility in the benefits system and time restraints placed by their funding bodies, with the result that the client group were put at risk of exploitation and some were not receiving the minimum wage when it was due. We heard from another organisation that the minimum wage was having a strong and often detrimental impact on the availability of opportunities with employers providing therapeutic activities. These opportunities were 'carved out', not advertised vacancies, and the service users were additional to a staffing quota. Enforcement of the minimum wage was, they said, at risk of discouraging employers from offering such opportunities.

3.78   Our attention was also drawn to the fact that service users were on Incapacity Benefit, and most were also on other means-tested benefits. Under regulations governing permitted work[8], the weekly earnings disregard for Incapacity Benefit is £88.50, and has risen in line with upratings of the minimum wage. However, for income related benefits, the weekly earnings disregard is set at £20. This limits the hours that can be undertaken without loss of benefit to under four if service users must be paid at least the minimum wage. In addition, as the earnings disregard for income related benefits has not risen annually in line with the minimum wage, then each year service users have been able to

---

[8]   One of the qualifying conditions for Incapacity Benefit and related benefits is that a person is incapable of work, although permitted work can be undertaken within limits to encourage people to return to work or to encourage social contact (DWP 2007).

work fewer hours without loss of benefits (this fell from 3.7 to 3.6 hours on 1 October 2007).

3.79 In our past reports we have highlighted the need for better guidance and awareness raising to address problems relating to therapeutic activity. The DTI issued new guidance in January 2007, and while we understand this generated little further comment from stakeholders, it is too early to assess fully its impact. We acknowledge that the structure of the benefits system is outside of our remit, but we do want to draw the Government's attention to the difficulties which arise when the earnings disregard for income related benefits is not increased in line with the minimum wage. We have been advised of this issue in previous consultations and we have been told again that it can have the effect of reducing the opportunities for therapeutic activity in terms of the number of hours per week those with a disability or health problem can work.

Compliance and Enforcement

Introduction

4.1 Compliance is essential to the success of the minimum wage. When non-compliance arises it is in the best interests of employers and workers alike that enforcement action is swift and effective. We have paid close attention to the work of the Government as it has developed and enhanced its enforcement role, and have made recommendations in the areas where evidence suggested it was less effective. We continue to monitor closely how well the minimum wage is being enforced.

Awareness

4.2 For the minimum wage to be effectively self-enforced, it is essential that awareness is high, both for workers and employers. We have made a number of recommendations on raising awareness since the minimum wage was introduced and we are pleased that these have been acted upon by the Government. The evidence we have received over the last few years indicates that good progress has been made in raising awareness of the existence of the minimum wage, although less so on awareness of the detail, such as of the minimum wage rates and the exemptions that can apply. Some groups of workers remain particularly difficult to reach.

4.3 We received evidence on the effectiveness of the Government's awareness campaigns. A Citizens Advice Bureau we visited in Dagenham advised us that the national advertising campaigns on the minimum wage rates had worked well and business people in Lincolnshire told us that all of their employees were well aware of the timing and scale of minimum wage upratings. However, some organisations continued to raise concern about low levels of

> The Scottish Low Pay Unit said that people are often aware of the existence of the minimum wage, but not necessarily the rates or what to do to get paid the correct amount.
>
> **Low Pay Commission Visit to Aviemore**

awareness. We were told by a group of young people in Scotland that there was little awareness among young people. It was suggested that schools should play a bigger role in informing young people of their employment rights by providing them with appropriate information while they are still within the school system.

4.4   A number of organisations told us that awareness of the minimum wage among migrant workers was low, particularly workers from central and eastern Europe (the A8)[1]. The Government explained to us how it had re-evaluated its minimum wage publicity to enable it to reach this group of workers. We received some evidence, albeit anecdotal, that A8 workers' awareness of the minimum wage and of other employment rights was increasing, although there was concern that many were still hesitant to enforce these rights. We look at the specific enforcement issues affecting migrant workers later in this chapter.

4.5   In our 2007 Report, we expressed some concern that the minimum wage publicity budget had been substantially reduced in 2006/07. The Department of Trade and Industry (now the Department for Business, Enterprise and Regulatory Reform (BERR)) told us that this did not signify a lowering of the priority being given to raising awareness, but reflected the more strategic approach being taken. BERR's publicity campaign for 2006/07 was based around the uprating of the minimum wage on 1 October 2007. Its main features were an online campaign targeting young workers; the distribution of short guides for workers, young people and employers, available in a number of languages; publicity tailored for the childcare sector – the sector chosen for targeted enforcement during 2006/07; and various media coverage projects, including the use of regional and ethnic minority press. In addition, BERR ran a campaign specifically targeted at migrant workers from Poland, Lithuania and Slovakia, whom statistics from the Worker Registration Scheme showed as making up 90 per cent of migrant workers from the A8 countries. The campaign consisted of advertising in UK-based foreign language titles, on relevant websites and through outreach work, including the distribution of a poster for display in a network of shops.

---

[1]   The Czech Republic, Estonia, Hungary, Latvia, Lithuania, Poland, Slovakia and Slovenia.

4.6   In our 2007 Report, while we recognised that an effective publicity programme was not necessarily dependent on the amount of money spent, we registered our concern that the cut in publicity funding could be detrimental to the effectiveness of enforcement. We see awareness as crucial to ensuring that the minimum wage benefits the most vulnerable workers. We were therefore very pleased when the Chancellor of the Exchequer announced a 50 per cent increase in the funding for monitoring and enforcement of the minimum wage in his pre-Budget speech in December 2006 (HM Treasury, 2006). BERR has since allocated a substantial increase to the funding for publicity in 2007/08, and has committed to maintaining this at an appropriate level going forward. We fully support this commitment to raising awareness of the minimum wage. We consider how the remaining additional funding is to be utilised later in this chapter.

4.7   BERR advised in its evidence that its current approach on publicity is to target key groups of workers, with the aim of raising awareness of the rate itself. Its 2007/08 publicity campaign seeks to maintain the momentum throughout the year, as opposed to being focused solely at the time of the minimum wage upratings. It will target publicity at worker audiences in particularly hard-to-reach groups, who would be unlikely to consume mainstream media, or to seek Government information from established channels. In its evidence, the Government advised that research it has commissioned to evaluate its latest targeted enforcement campaign will also evaluate the success of the 2007/08 National Minimum Wage publicity campaign. This qualitative research will look at how workers and employers received the 2007/08 campaign and how improvements could be made to the way messages are delivered in the future. We welcome this new approach and look forward to seeing the evaluation of its impact.

4.8   We noted in our 2007 Report that a number of organisations were working to raise awareness of the minimum wage and other employment rights among migrant workers, in some cases with Government support, but that there was little co-ordination between these groups, often leading to a duplication of effort. We recommended that the Government work more collaboratively in its efforts to raise awareness. It accepted this recommendation and in its evidence advised how it was being taken forward.

There should be a requirement for current NMW rates to be displayed in the workplace.

National Hairdressers' Federation evidence

4.9   BERR told us that it has sought ways to work collaboratively with stakeholders in taking forward its 2007/08 campaign, engaging with other Government departments, as well as employer and employee stakeholders, in developing publicity material for the 2007/08 targeted enforcement in the hotel sector. It also worked with stakeholders, including the TUC and sector unions, the National Union of Students, Citizens Advice, London Citizens, and migrant community organisations and churches, in distributing minimum wage leaflets. In addition, a leaflet about employment rights, including the minimum wage, is now included in a pack sent by the Home Office to every new worker from the A8 countries and Romania and Bulgaria (A2 countries) who registers with the Worker Registration Scheme.

To help to minimise delays in enforcement action, HMRC should work in partnership with Acas to draw on its employment rights expertise

Leicester City Council evidence

4.10   Other actions the Government is taking to address this recommendation include the work of the Vulnerable Workers Pilots which are operated on a partnership basis, bringing together unions, Acas, community groups, business organisations and enforcement agencies. BERR's Vulnerable Worker Enforcement Forum, chaired by the Employment Relations Minister, is also considering our recommendation as part of its programme of work. We are pleased to note the work under way and will continue to monitor progress with interest.

Non-compliance

4.11   It is generally accepted that the vast majority of employers comply with the National Minimum Wage. However, the extent of minimum wage non-compliance is an issue that we have grappled with for several years. The Office for National Statistics (ONS) estimates that 292,000 jobs paid below the minimum wage in April 2007. This amounts to around 1.2 per cent of all jobs. However, this figure should not be used as a measure of non-compliance as there are a number of legitimate reasons for paying below the minimum wage. For example: apprentices covered by the minimum wage exemptions, workers legitimately subject to the accommodation offset deductor and those on piece rates may all be legally paid below the adult rate of the minimum wage. Together with ONS, we have recently undertaken some analysis in order to understand better the characteristics of those workers ONS estimate as paid below the minimum wage and to determine the extent to which the recorded underpayment is legitimate. This work (details of which can be found in Appendix 2) has confirmed three things: it is not possible to arrive at definitive answers from the available data; some, maybe as many as half, of those shown as being underpaid may be accounted for by legitimate reasons such as exemptions and measurement errors; for the rest, other types of reporting errors might provide one explanation, but non-compliance cannot be ruled out.

4.12   There will also be workers who are not receiving the minimum wage and who do not show up in the official statistics, such as those working in the informal economy. It is likely to be the workers who do not show up on the official radar who are most vulnerable to underpayment and exploitation. We have no way to identify the extent of such non-compliance, and therefore, as in previous years, we have drawn on other information sources in our assessment, such as the work of Her Majesty's Revenue and Customs' (HMRC) minimum wage enforcement team and evidence from our consultation and research.

4.13   The statistics produced by HMRC on its enforcement activities (Table 4.1) show that over 51,000 enquiries were received by the HMRC Helpline during 2006/07, a fall of 16 per cent over 2005/06 and 11 per cent when compared to the number of calls received in 2004/05. However, there were 2,210 complaints about non-payment of the minimum wage in 2006/07, an increase of 3 per cent over 2005/06 and 14 per cent over 2004/05. HMRC completed 1,523 investigations into minimum wage underpayment in 2006/07. This was fewer than in the previous two years, but the drop may be explained by the increase in the complexity and technical nature of many of the investigations now arising.

Table 4.1

National Minimum Wage: Enquiries and Complaints to HMRC and Enforcement Action Taken, 2004–2007

	2004/05	2005/06	2006/07
Enquiries received by the Helpline	57,733	61,355	51,454
Complaints of underpayment	1,946	2,141	2,210
Enquiries completed	5,155	4,904	4,500
Cases of non-compliance	1,798	1,582	1,523
Strike rate	35%	32%	34%
Enforcement notices issued	32	81	71
Penalty notices issued	0	1	2
Value of underpayments identified	£3.8 million	£3.3 million	£3.0 million

Source: HMRC, UK, 2004–2007.
Notes:
1. Enquiries completed are the number of cases closed with an inspection having been made.
2. The strike rate is the percentage of the cases investigated where non-compliance was found.

4.14   Over the last few years, non-compliance was found in about a third of HMRC investigations, although this figure varies considerably by region. The level of total minimum wage arrears identified has fluctuated quite significantly between years. The average arrears per worker in 2006/07 was £214, up from £130 the year before.

4.15   Figure 4.1 shows the breakdown of complaints by sector over the last three years. The highest number of complaints came from the hospitality sector. We are therefore pleased that the hotel sector was chosen for targeted enforcement in 2007/08, to be followed by the wider hospitality sector in 2008/09. We look at the Government's programme of targeted enforcement later in this chapter.

Figure 4.1

Number of Complaints of Non-compliance to the NMW Helpline by Sector, UK, 2004–2007

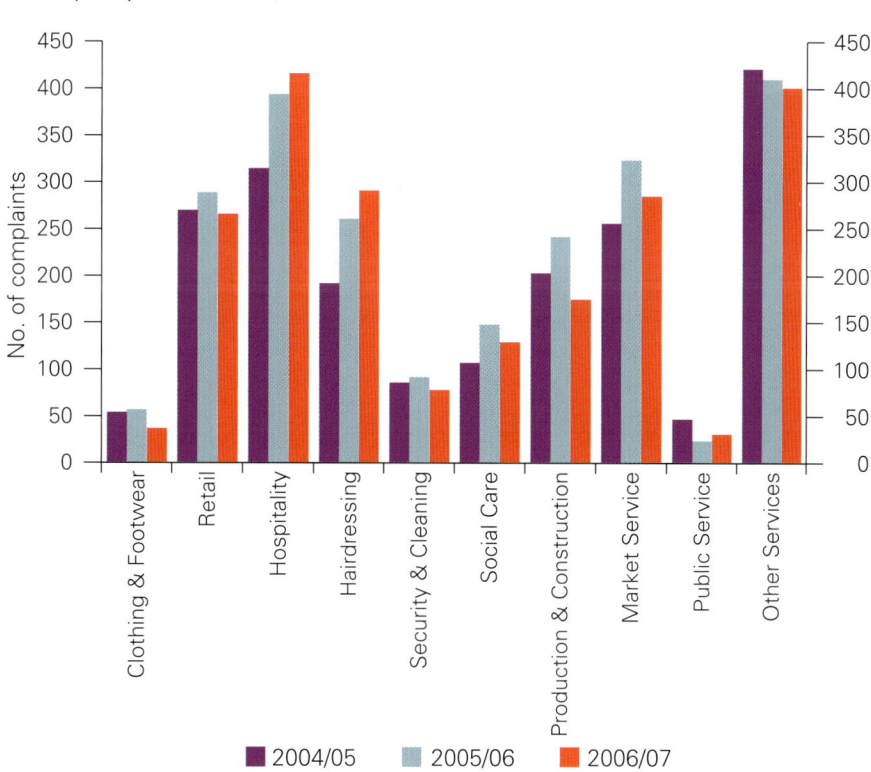

Source: HMRC, UK, 2004–2007.

4.16   We were told that many workers who were paid below the minimum wage were afraid to make a complaint for fear of victimisation or dismissal. During a visit to Northern Ireland we heard from trade unions that minimum wage non-compliance was a growing problem. Citizens Advice Northern Ireland reported that an unacceptable number of employers were failing to comply with the minimum wage and that some workers were too afraid to complain for fear of dismissal. Migrant workers were highlighted as being especially vulnerable.

4.17   In its written evidence, the GMB told us that workers who report underpayment to HMRC were often sacked or victimised. The Scottish Low Pay Unit also raised concern about the tendency for complainants to lose their jobs. It believed that BERR and HMRC should work together to publicise the illegality of dismissing workers for asserting their statutory rights. It recommended that compliance teams be given powers and resources to support workers who make a complaint and are dismissed as a result. Both the TUC and UNISON also recommended that HMRC should have a duty to pursue cases of detriment for workers claiming their minimum wage rights. The National Group on Homeworking raised concerns about the effectiveness of enforcement in tackling non-compliance in relation to homeworkers.

4.18   The TUC called for trade unions to be empowered to do more to help workers to enforce the minimum wage. One of the proposals it put forward, and which was echoed by a number of trade unions, was for HMRC's confidentiality rules to be amended to enable third parties to be informed of the outcome of complaints.

The Informal Economy

Employers are more tempted to fudge the books due to increasing costs. If an employer doesn't 'opt' into the formal economy, they are highly unlikely to be caught. It is the legitimate employer who tries to adhere to requirements that is penalised for any small error.

Evidence from a small retailer

4.19   The size of the informal economy and the extent to which current HMRC enforcement activities can effectively tackle the minimum wage underpayment arising continues to be an area for concern. Although the scale of non-compliance is difficult to determine, there continues to be a perception that the problem is becoming more substantial, particularly in respect of certain groups of workers. The evidence suggests that abuse of the minimum wage normally goes hand-in-hand with other violations of employment rights.

4.20   In our 2007 Report, we noted that reaching those in the informal sector was clearly difficult, particularly where there was collusion between a worker and their employer. Research commissioned for our 2005 Report (Ram, Edwards and Jones, 2004) suggested such collusion could be relatively common in some sectors. For example, a worker might be willing to accept pay below the minimum wage rate in order to remain eligible for working tax credits while receiving some wages on a 'cash in hand' basis. The Association of Labour Providers reported that the minimum wage was widely ignored throughout the informal economy, in a manner that seldom disadvantaged workers significantly, but which was at the expense of the taxpayer and legitimate business. It alleged that in many cases workers in the informal economy being paid below the minimum wage were as well off, if not more so, than many workers employed in the formal economy who were paid the minimum wage. It argued that enforcement was too often concentrated on the easy to reach employers, failing to pick up the areas of real abuse.

4.21   The CBI urged us to focus on improving the position of legal employers and workers by improving compliance. It was concerned that any increase in the minimum wage above average earnings would contribute to the 'pull' of the informal economy, especially bearing in mind the marginal tax rate that many minimum wage employees face. It reported a significant level of informal working in the hairdressing sector, with around 35,000 people self-employed; a rise of 20 per cent between 1999 and 2004. It was feared that this trend could be exacerbated by an increase in the minimum wage above average earnings.

4.22   A company in the hospitality sector reported that some employers were undoubtedly paying below the minimum wage and that there was a growing cash-in-hand culture, particularly in some small tenanted pubs.

Vulnerable Workers

4.23   In its evidence, the Government noted its commitment to helping vulnerable workers. In 2007 it launched the Vulnerable Worker Enforcement Forum and two Vulnerable Worker Pilots. It set up the forum to help it to ensure that all workers enjoyed their workplace rights in full, and to address enforcement issues where this was not the case. It advised us that its work was at an early stage, but that the enforcement challenges emerging included: what more could be done to raise awareness of enforcement bodies; how to overcome vulnerable workers' reluctance to complain and enforce their rights; how to improve local intelligence about bad employers and create conditions for more joined-up action by enforcement bodies; and how to create a stronger and more effective deterrent for non-compliant employers.

4.24   The Vulnerable Worker Pilots aim to identify practical ways of improving the advice and support available to vulnerable workers to help ensure they secure their full entitlement to employment rights and to provide opportunities for them to develop new skills. It aims to help employers to understand and comply with the law, as well as taking co-ordinated action against employers who fail to comply with legislation. The pilots operate on a partnership basis, drawing together organisations involved in providing services to vulnerable workers and to employers. One pilot is targeting the support services sector in the City of London and

CBI members reported growing competition from informal economy activities in some key sectors – including textiles, cleaning and hairdressing. Not surprisingly, the problem of informal work is most prevalent in sectors where the NMW is most likely to have an effect – labour intensive and cash-based, using migrant workers and other groups with low labour market attachment.

CBI evidence

Tower Hamlets and is led by the TUC; the other, led by Marketing Birmingham, is targeting the hospitality sector in Birmingham. The experiences of the pilots will be used to inform Government policy on vulnerable workers.

Migrant Workers

4.25   In Chapter 3 we noted the changes to the labour market as a result of the arrival of a substantial number of migrant workers from the A8 countries. This has given rise to some additional compliance and enforcement issues.

A group of Lithuanians were working on a building contract at a school for £15 a day cash in hand. In another case involving construction workers, they were 'hotbedding' in a garden shed.

John Cruddas MP, Low Pay Commission visit to Dagenham

4.26   In response to our consultation this year, we received both specific and anecdotal evidence of migrant workers being paid below the minimum wage and facing problems enforcing their rights. As we found last year, in some cases there appeared to be blatant underpayment of the minimum wage, but more often the problem arose through excessive deductions from pay for accommodation and other services, or because the worker was required to work in excess of their contractual hours which brought their hourly rate below the minimum wage. A number of organisations advised that workers from the A8 countries were particularly vulnerable to exploitation due to language barriers and because many were too afraid to complain for fear of losing their jobs or the threat of violence. Some were unclear about their employment status and this had been used against them.

4.27   Since November 2004, HMRC's National Minimum Wage team has carried out checks on a sample of employers who use migrant workers. Each month up to 15 employers are selected from around the UK on the basis of a risk assessment and information taken from the Workers Registration Scheme. Between November 2004 and January 2008, 28 per cent of the employers investigated were found to be non-compliant, with arrears of £385,112 identified for 2,742 workers.

4.28   In addition to the many groups of migrants that are entitled to work in the UK, there are others whose status is less clear. These individuals are particularly vulnerable as they fear any attempt to raise the issue of their employment rights could lead to them being deported. During a visit to Dagenham, we were advised that in recent years there had been a significant increase in problems relating to migrants with unclear work status who were subject to minimum wage abuses, as well as other exploitative practices. Unite was one of a number of unions and worker representative groups that also drew attention to the vulnerability of undocumented migrant workers. It argued that no worker should be exempt from basic employment rights and that employers should always face penalties for paying below the minimum wage whether their workers are documented or not.

4.29 To help tackle the problem of illegal migrant workers, in 2005 the Government introduced the Home Office-led Joint Workplace Enforcement Pilot (JWEP). It was launched in the West Midlands as a three-year pilot to explore the scope for closer co-ordinated working between Government workplace enforcement and compliance departments for the purpose of tackling both the use and exploitation of illegal migrant workers. Those involved include the UK Immigration Service, HMRC, BERR (formerly the DTI), the Department for Work and Pensions, the Health and Safety Executive and the Gangmasters Licensing Authority (GLA). This year the Government advised that an initial evaluation of the JWEP was completed during 2006 and the outcomes (based on anecdotal evidence) strengthened the hypothesis that businesses that use illegal migrant labour are likely to be in breach of other workplace regulation. The Government has indicated that, although all bodies involved in the project continue to support it, the pilot will need to be considered alongside existing resource commitments as extensive joint working teams, involving several departments, may not be the most effective strategy for the future. Current indications are that the future of successful joint workplace enforcement will emphasise the need for improved intelligence-sharing and data exchange between appropriate Government departments, to facilitate operations by individual or targeted combinations of workplace enforcement departments. A further report to evaluate the success and future of the JWEP is currently under way and is expected to be completed in early 2008.

4.30 The TUC argued that creating a robust system to help to protect vulnerable workers would need to involve removing the rules and incentives that inhibit closer working between enforcement agencies. It believed there were lessons to be learnt from the JWEP projects,

Restrictive visa requirements mean that many workers are frightened to complain of abuses for fear of losing the one job they are allowed to hold. … Ali works in conference banqueting. Every week he works for around 50 hours but gets paid for 39. He would like to get more money but is on a visa and cannot complain. He is often reminded that his work is dependent on the goodwill of his managers and that if he "doesn't like it he can get out and go back to Pakistan."

UNISON evidence

which were reinforced by the emerging finding of the TUC's Commission on Vulnerable Employment.

4.31   To promote effective intelligence-sharing between departments, the Border and Immigration Agency is considering producing a document setting out key indicators of non-compliance to provide workplace enforcement officers with a set of readily observable characteristics which may indicate workplace abuse. This guidance is to contain information on when and how to share intelligence between Government departments about these abuses of workplace regulations. We strongly welcome this initiative. Effective sharing of information will help to make the best use of finite resources and ensure that they are appropriately targeted on those employers who set out to exploit their workers.

4.32   A common theme of the evidence we received in respect of migrant workers was that those employed through employment agencies were more likely to be exploited. We consider this group next.

Agency Workers

4.33   Our consultation has provided evidence on the treatment of workers, particularly migrant workers, employed through employment agencies. A number of problems were brought to our attention. While most agencies comply fully with the minimum wage, the level of deductions made by some was a particular concern. In the worst cases deductions are used to bring down a worker's take-home pay to very low levels.

4.34   The TUC reported that the emerging findings of its Commission on Vulnerable Employment and the Government's Vulnerable Worker Enforcement Forum confirm that many of the problems experienced by migrant workers stem from abuse by unscrupulous employment agencies. Trade unions in Northern Ireland highlighted migrant agency workers as being particularly open to exploitation. We were told that the agency sector in Northern Ireland was highly competitive and this had led to undercutting by some agencies, largely funded through spurious deductions from the pay of migrant workers. Leicester City Council told us that a greater number of agency workers were affected by underpayments, with less likelihood of them receiving subsequent payment because of the transient nature of agency work. It reported a trend for agencies and labour providers to simply close down, sometimes to reappear a few weeks later under a different name.

4.35   Unite advised of an increase in the use of agency migrant labour in the low-paying sectors, with examples of minimum wage underpayment and other bad practices by employment agencies. Enforcement was made more difficult as the agencies often sub-contracted to labour providers further down the supply chain. It argued for the introduction of licensing for employment agencies. UNISON reported on evidence it had collected with London Citizens which showed that unscrupulous employers and employment agencies were continuing to take advantage of migrant workers despite the strengthening of enforcement measures in this area. Both UNISON and the TUC recommended that agency staff be given the same employment conditions as permanent staff and that employment agencies be made a priority target for enforcement.

4.36   The CBI made the point that reputable agencies recognised that the exploitation and abuse of workers by rogue agencies caused serious damage to the good reputation of the sector and fully accepted that non-compliance with the minimum wage, or any other employment right, was unacceptable. It told us that a number of reputable agencies were already working with the relevant enforcement agencies and within the industry itself to address these concerns.

4.37   The research we commissioned by French and Möhrke (2006) for our 2007 Report supports the concerns raised by stakeholders. It found that firms employing migrant workers directly were largely compliant with the minimum wage. However, it also reported, albeit based on a small sample, that where the worker was employed through an agency, there was more likely to be evidence of abuse, in particular under- or non-payment of wages and excessive deductions.

4.38   Last year we came to the conclusion that the introduction of new rules within the minimum wage legislation would not be an effective means to tackle the problem of excessive deductions from pay. Although we continue to be concerned by the evidence presented, we believe this remains the case. In our view, the problems arising are best tackled through effective enforcement.

4.39   In addition to HMRC's role in enforcing the minimum wage, two other Government bodies have specific responsibilities for enforcement in relation to the agency sector. We look at each in turn.

Employment Agency Standards Inspectorate

4.40   The activities of employment agencies and employment businesses are regulated by the Employment Agencies Act 1973 (as amended) and by the Conduct of Employment Agencies and Employment Business Regulations 2003. The Act is enforced by BERR's Employment Agency Standards (EAS) Inspectorate.

4.41   Action is being considered by the EAS which will strengthen its ability to enforce the law. The Conduct Regulations covering agencies clearly prohibit the take-up of services as a requirement of being offered work, but the right to withdraw from such services at a later date is less clear. As part of the follow up to the DTI's *Success at Work* policy statement (DTI, 2006), in February 2007 the EAS consulted on a range of issues which sought to tighten the regulation and provide greater protection for vulnerable agency workers. This included an amendment to tighten the Regulations to make explicit the worker's right of withdrawal from a service. BERR published the Government's response in December 2007 (BERR, 2007c) and Amendment Regulations were made in December and will come into force on 1 April 2008. Further steps are being taken to strengthen the penalty and enforcement regime for employment agencies in the Employment Bill currently going through Parliament. In addition, John Hutton, Secretary of State for BERR announced at the TUC conference in September 2007 that the number of EAS inspectors will be doubled to improve enforcement of employment agencies legislation.

4.42   We have offered our full support to the proposed changes and hope that they will go some way to address the problem of excessive deductions and enable the relevant Government bodies to take appropriate enforcement action when problems arise.

Gangmasters Licensing Authority

4.43   The GLA was set up in April 2005 and aims to curb the exploitation of labour within the agriculture, horticulture, fish processing and shellfish gathering industries, and in the packaging or processing of these products.

It became an offence for a gangmaster to operate without a licence in these sectors from October 2006. Since December 2006, it has also been an offence to use an unlicensed gangmaster. There are stiff penalties for operating without a licence – up to a maximum ten years imprisonment and/or a fine on conviction. A labour user engaging an unlicensed labour provider faces up to 51 weeks imprisonment and/or a fine on conviction.

4.44   The GLA's compliance team is responsible for carrying out compliance inspections on GLA licence holders. The GLA's Licensing Standards (GLA, 2006), against which licence applications and subsequent compliance inspections are assessed, include key areas of interest to us such as the payment of wages and improper deductions, and workers' accommodation. The Licensing Standards specifically state that the worker must be *'paid at least the national or agricultural minimum wage, taking into account the rules on the accommodation offset'* and this standard has been given a 'critical' category (the most serious category of non-compliance) by the GLA. In addition to its own compliance team, the GLA works closely with other Government departments and agencies to share intelligence to ensure legal requirements are met and enforced.

4.45   The GLA has been operating for a relatively short period but, according to the evidence we have gathered, it is already held in high regard and is seen to be making a difference. Research by Brindley et al (2007) on behalf of the GLA found that 40 per cent of labour providers felt the GLA had reduced business fraud, and that 45 per cent believed that the GLA had improved working conditions. However, the survey also highlighted perceptions that much work was still to be done, with only 6 per cent of gangmasters believing that worker exploitation was no longer an issue in the GLA sectors. The survey also revealed particular concerns related to 'Phoenix Gangmasters' re-emerging after prosecution or bankruptcy. Licensed operators were concerned that more needed to be done to tackle unlicensed gangmasters working under the Government radar.

4.46   UNISON advised that the stricter enforcement of employment legislation arising from the introduction of the GLA had driven gangmasters into other sectors not covered by the GLA, with many employment agencies now effectively acting as gangmasters. It called for the remit of the GLA be widened to include other sectors with a high proportion of migrant workers.

Other Developments in Enforcement

4.47   Over the last few years, there have been a number of positive developments that have sought to improve enforcement of the minimum wage. We look at these below.

Targeted Enforcement

4.48   In 2005 the Government announced a programme of targeted enforcement to tackle non-compliance in each of the low-paying sectors in turn. The initial sector chosen was hairdressing, followed by childcare in 2006/07. This year, the hotel sector is being targeted and the wider hospitality sector has been chosen for 2008/09. The choice of hotels and the hospitality sector addresses the recommendations in our 2006 and 2007 Reports that a low-paying sector employing a significant number of migrant workers be targeted as a priority.

4.49   In its evidence, the Government advised that its officials had met stakeholders representing hotel sector employers and workers to identify the issues relevant to the sector in order to inform the enabling stage of the campaign, including agreeing publicity materials in a variety of languages. In addition to the key messages on the minimum wage, the leaflets produced for the campaign covered wider employment law issues relevant to the sector, for example the increase in statutory annual leave entitlement. The Government advised us that it had taken into account research we commissioned by Croucher and White (2007) which evaluated the first targeted campaign of the hairdressing sector.

4.50   We have noted in the past the need for targeted enforcement to be effectively evaluated to ensure it justifies the extra resource. We are therefore pleased that the Government has allocated a portion of its additional funding for monitoring and enforcement to ensure that the various enforcement strands are properly evaluated.

Criminal Prosecutions

4.51   The National Minimum Wage Act 1998 provides for criminal prosecutions for six offences relating to the minimum wage. These include refusing or wilfully neglecting to pay the minimum wage and furnishing false records or information. The penalty is a fine of up to

£5,000 for each offence. The Government had not made use of this provision, but in December 2005 it announced that it would pursue criminal prosecutions in cases where lesser sanctions were not producing compliance. Two successful prosecutions were completed in 2007 and BERR advised that further prosecutions were being taken forward.

4.52 We welcome the progress that has been made, although we must again record our disappointment that only a handful of prosecutions are planned each year. We believe that a tough and systematic approach to prosecutions is required to act as an effective deterrent to employers who persistently flout the minimum wage rules. The TUC made a similar point in its evidence to us. It also argued that the current maximum penalty of £5,000 allowed by the minimum wage legislation is not commensurate with the worst offences uncovered by HMRC. It called for a substantial increase to the current penalties in the National Minimum Wage Act in order to redress this situation.

A sweatshop owner is likely to be treated far more harshly by the law for counterfeiting popular brands of shirts than for underpaying its workers.

TUC evidence

Penalty Notices

4.53 In January 2007, the Government announced a new policy to fine employers who ignore an official demand to pay the National Minimum Wage through the issue of Penalty Notices, as provided for in the minimum wage legislation. We welcomed this development. The Government advised us that the policy is helping to encourage employers to repay minimum wage arrears more quickly and less time is being spent by HRMC chasing overdue arrears.

A Penalty for Non-compliance and Fair Arrears

4.54 In our 2005 and 2007 Reports we said that a worker paid below the minimum wage could well suffer financial hardship even if arrears were eventually paid, since the worker would not receive any recompense to reflect the late payment, and that this situation needed to be rectified. We also recommended that, as a deterrent to non-compliance, the Government introduce a penalty to apply to any employer found to have underpaid the minimum wage. Early in 2007 the Government accepted our recommendations.

4.55   In May 2007 the Government launched the National Minimum Wage and Employment Agency Standards Enforcement consultation (DTI, 2007d). This proposed a new strategy to deal with cases of underpayment of the minimum wage based on a fairer way of dealing with arrears and a simpler, more effective penalty regime to deter non-compliance. During the consultation, the Government worked closely with us, employer bodies, trade sector representatives and trade unions on the proposals and the consultation document was sent to over 60 organisations. Although views differed as to how the end result could best be achieved, there was strong support for the changes from employer and worker representative organisations alike. The CBI fully supported the Government's proposals to ensure underpaid workers have better real terms payment. It also supported the introduction of an enhanced penalty regime which would provide employers with an incentive to comply with minimum wage legislation and which would help prevent arrears arising in the first place. The Forum for Private Business also gave its support to the fair arrears proposals and for a penalty that was proportional to the scale of underpayment. The TUC and all trade unions responding to the consultation gave their support to the introduction of a system to ensure fair arrears and a penalty for all non-compliant employers.

4.56   We were pleased to have the opportunity to respond to the consultation and submitted our response on 16 July 2007 (available on our website – www.lowpay.gov.uk). BERR published its response to the consultation in December 2007 (BERR, 2007c) and the new measures are being introduced through the Employment Bill currently going through the parliamentary process.

Employment Tribunals

4.57   The employment tribunal system provides an important means for workers to pursue claims for underpayment of the minimum wage. In 2006/07, there were 806 minimum wage applications registered by tribunals (Employment Tribunals Service, 2007). This is a significantly higher number than registered in the previous two years (440 in 2005/06 and 597 in 2004/05), but direct comparison cannot be made as the way in which data are collated by tribunals has changed.

Macdonald Hotels said it would support the introduction of a penalty for non-compliance if it were commensurate with the loss incurred by the employee, and which was able to distinguish between administrative error and systematic abuse.

Low Pay Commission visit to Aviemore

4.58 The effectiveness of the tribunal system was again raised by some organisations during our consultation. Although there continues to be general support for it, there are growing concerns about the number of employers failing to pay tribunal awards. A tribunal does not have the power to enforce the award and the worker must seek payment through the civil court system.

4.59 Leicester City Council again expressed its concern on this point, noting that awards often went unpaid and for a worker to take action through the civil courts to receive the payment due to them was costly, complex and offered no guarantee of return. No data were available to show the extent of non-payment of tribunal awards in respect of the minimum wage. This issue is not specific, however, to the minimum wage and could also apply to awards made under other jurisdictions. We reiterate our view that for the tribunal system is to be effective, there needs to be a means to tackle robustly and promptly those employers who show no regard to the awards made. We noted in our 2007 Report that proposals in the Tribunals, Courts and Enforcement Bill (Department for Constitutional Affairs, 2006) might help to address some of the problems highlighted. It is too early to say what the impact has been, but we will review this in the coming year.

4.60 The TUC and a number of trade unions called for trade unions to be able to bring cases to employment tribunals on behalf of groups of workers as a means of strengthening workers' ability to assert their rights to the minimum wage. They argued that the current system whereby a tribunal could only hear a case brought by an individual worker was a barrier to effective enforcement, as many workers with minimum wage problems were afraid to enforce their rights for fear that they would suffer some form of retribution from their employer. The CBI did not support this proposal, pointing out that Employment Tribunals could, under existing powers, choose to hear a number of cases together. The CBI accepted that this fell short of what the TUC was seeking, but was against any move to extend such arrangements so that a number of cases could be joined together under one name.

Resourcing Enforcement Activities

4.61   In December 2006, the Chancellor announced that funding for monitoring and enforcement of the minimum wage would be increased by 50 per cent, an additional £2.9 million in each of the next four years. This is a very positive step forward and should provide the opportunity to increase considerably the impact of enforcement activities.

4.62   BERR has developed what we consider to be a coherent enforcement strategy to make best use of the additional funding, on which we were consulted. We welcomed the opportunity to offer advice. The plan to use the funds includes recruiting 20 new staff; improving communications (we noted earlier that significant additional funding was put into raising awareness of the minimum wage) and undertaking research and evaluation of enforcement work to ensure that effective use is made of the resources available and that these are appropriately focused on priority areas.

Conclusion

4.63   The action that has been taken by the Government to strengthen the enforcement regime has been welcomed by employer and employee alike. We too welcome these developments. We believe that the measures introduced and those in train should have a tangible positive impact. In terms of enforcement, we conclude that the focus in the coming year should be on consolidation to allow time for the initiatives under way to be developed, and for those in the pipeline to be implemented. We therefore do not make any recommendations on minimum wage enforcement in this report. We will monitor developments closely.

Setting the Rates

Introduction

5.1 When we met in mid-January 2008 to agree our recommendations for this report we had a range of data before us covering the economy up to the fourth quarter of 2007. We also had our analyses of the impact of previous upratings and the evidence from stakeholders, both of which played a major part in our thinking. We took account too of changes to the legislative framework, particularly the proposed increase in annual leave entitlement in April 2009. Finally, we considered a range of forecasts for the UK economy in 2008 and beyond. These assumed particular importance this year as, by early 2008, the economic outlook for 2008 and beyond was becoming more uncertain.

5.2 In this chapter we give an overview of these factors before setting out our recommendations for the rates of the National Minimum Wage for October 2008 and offering a broad indication of the likely level of upratings in October 2009.

Prospects for the Economy

5.3 In Chapter 2 we analysed the impact of the minimum wage on the UK economy. We concluded that, although the large uprating in October 2006 had increased the 'bite' of the minimum wage and had some impact on pay structures and earnings distributions, there was no evidence of any significant adverse effect on the economy as a whole or on the low-paying sectors. While research had found some evidence that the minimum wage had contributed to price increases in some sectors, these increases had no discernible impact on the general inflation level. We noted that there had been, as yet, no thorough review of the large minimum wage upratings between 2003 and 2006 and, accordingly, we commissioned a comprehensive research programme to carry out such a review. We expect that research to be completed in time to inform our next report.

5.4   As well as looking backwards at impact, it is also important to look forward to take account of likely future developments in the economy and Government regulation. We consider the latter in our discussions of increased holiday entitlement later in this chapter but we focus next on the prospects for the economy in 2008 and 2009, the period during which – if the Government agrees – our recommendations will take effect.

5.5   As we looked forward in January 2008, the economic outlook was uncertain. The upheaval caused by the financial crisis and credit concerns in the US was causing problems in financial markets across the world. The US economy had weakened with growth declining from 3.3 per cent in 2006 to about 2.2 per cent in 2007. It was expected to weaken further in 2008, although growth was forecast to recover slightly in 2009. In response to turmoil on the stock markets and disappointing data on the economy, at the start of 2008 the US Federal Reserve took the unusual step of reducing interest rates by 1.25 percentage points in just 9 days in order to stimulate the US economy.

5.6   In early 2008, other financial and stock markets were also volatile, particularly in Asia and Europe. Eurozone growth had been strong in 2006 and remained robust throughout 2007 at around 2.6 per cent. However, as the world economy and the US economy in particular weakened, growth in the Eurozone was forecast to fall to 1.9 per cent in 2008 and 2 per cent in 2009. Continued world growth was therefore considered likely to depend in large part on Asia, the Middle East and Eastern Europe. The new economic power-houses, China and India, were continuing to grow at a rapid pace and growth was expected to continue but at a slower pace than before.

5.7   In January 2008 the implications for the UK were still unclear. Although UK output had grown at or above trend over the last two years, the economy was feeling the impact of the global credit crunch. Consumer spending showed signs of slowing and, with a few notable exceptions, retail sales over Christmas 2007 had confirmed the slowdown. House prices were stagnating and shares on the FTSE fell sharply in January 2008. Producer input and output prices also rose sharply in the final quarter of 2007. Business investment was levelling off and growth in

Government spending slowed, leaving the economy dependent on trade to lead growth in 2008. A recent reduction in interest rates and the expectations of further cuts led to a depreciation of sterling. As a result, in January 2008 the pound hit its lowest ever rate against the Euro, although it remained strong against the weakened US dollar. Interest rate cuts were expected to boost UK exports unless parallel concerns about inflation (fuelled by rises in food, oil and energy prices) intervened to prevent further reductions.

5.8   One surprising development over the course of 2007 was the continuing moderation in wage growth which was maintained even though employment rose to record levels, unemployment continued to fall, firms were complaining of skill shortages and there was persistent inflationary pressure.

5.9   As we look ahead to 2008 and 2009 the main areas of concern for the UK economy may be summarised as:

• the magnitude and duration of the effects of the financial problems stemming from the US;

• access to credit and the cost of borrowing for businesses and households;

• the burden of household debt and the impact of falling house prices;

• the speed of slowdown in the US economy and its wider impact;

• UK economic growth if consumer spending falls (both the growth in government spending and business investment are slowing); and

• concern about the impact of volatile prices for food, transport, oil and energy on price inflation.

5.10   Despite the concerns noted above, as we surveyed UK economic prospects in January 2008 we noted some grounds for optimism. There had been continuous economic growth since 1993, employment was at record highs and the number of employee jobs in low-paying sectors was growing at a similar pace to the economy as a whole. CPI and business to business services price inflation, as measured by the Services Producer Price Index, was muted and corporate financial balances looked healthy. Consumer spending, while not as buoyant as it had been, seemed to be holding up and wage growth remained subdued. Further interest rate cuts were expected to give the economy a boost, in part as the resultant weaker pound boosted the UK's export performance.

Forecasts

5.11   We now consider how these factors have affected the latest forecasts for 2008 and 2009. Figure 5.1 shows that, at the time we made our recommendations for October 2007 (in January 2007), the independent forecasts we relied on were predicting growth of 2.5 per cent in both 2007 and 2008. A year later we can report that consumer spending held up better than expected leading to GDP growth outstripping expectations. In contrast, the increased uncertainty and the extent of the problems in international finance markets in the second half of 2007 have led to downward revisions to forecasts of growth in 2008. By January 2008, the consensus forecasts for GDP growth in 2008 had fallen to 1.8 per cent, from the 2.5 per cent forecast by the same panel of experts a year earlier. However, as of late January 2008, the consensus expert view was that growth over 2007 and 2008 combined would be similar to our original expectations.

5.12   Table 5.1 shows the consensus of latest forecasts for 2008 and 2009 for a range of variables that we took into account when making our recommendations. Actual data for 2007 is given for comparison. As discussed above, GDP growth is expected to weaken in 2008 but it is then expected to pick up in 2009. Inflation, as measured by the Consumer Price Index (CPI), is expected to remain marginally above the Bank of England's target of 2 per cent throughout 2008 and 2009. In contrast, the Retail Price Index (RPI) is forecast to fall back to 2.6 per cent by the end of 2008, from the 4.2 per cent recorded in the last quarter of 2007, although similar expectations were not realised last year.

Figure 5.1

Revisions to Forecasts of GDP Growth, UK, 2007 and 2008

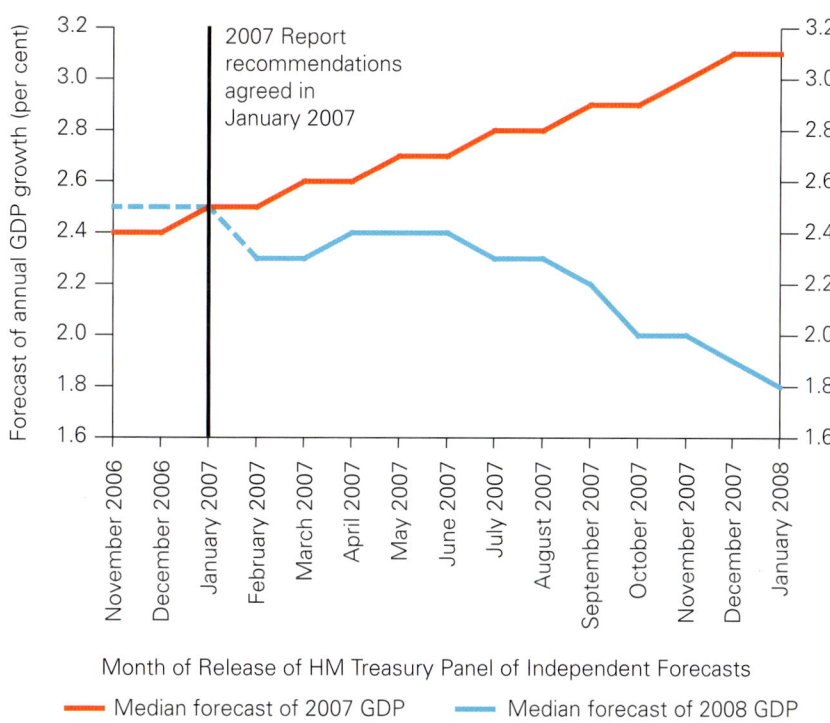

Month of Release of HM Treasury Panel of Independent Forecasts

—— Median forecast of 2007 GDP   —— Median forecast of 2008 GDP

Source: HM Treasury, UK, November 2006–January 2008.
Notes:
1. Forecasts for GDP 2007 are taken from the monthly panel (November 2006–January 2008).
2. Forecasts for GDP 2008 are taken from the monthly panel (November 2006, February 2007– January 2008).
3. Forecasts for GDP growth in 2008 were not available in December 2006 and January 2007. At the time of the last report, we used forecasts for 2008 from November 2006.

5.13   Average earnings growth is forecast to be about 4 per cent in 2008, similar to the growth recorded in the three months to November 2007. However, with RPI inflation still above 4 per cent, Industrial Relations Services is expecting the median pay settlement to increase in early 2008. Income Data Services (IDS) reported a rise in the median in January 2008 and noted that a third of settlements were at least 4 per cent. Despite the upward pressure on prices, pay settlements are expected to remain below 3.5 per cent, at least half a per cent below the growth in average earnings, as measured by the Average Earnings Index (AEI) including bonuses.

Table 5.1

Actual Outturn and Independent Forecasts of GDP Growth, Inflation and Average Earnings, UK, 2007–2009

Average percentage change over a year earlier (unless stated otherwise)	2007 (Actual) %	2008 (Forecast) %	2009 (Forecast) %
GDP growth	2.7	1.8	2.3
Average earnings[1]	4.0	4.0	–
CPI inflation	2.1	2.1	2.1
RPIX inflation	3.1	2.7	2.6
RPI inflation	4.2	2.6	–
Employment Growth	0.9	0.4	–
Claimant unemployment total (millions)	0.81	0.89	0.95

Source: ONS (actual data for 2007) and HM Treasury (January 2008 (forecast for 2008) and November 2007 (forecast for 2009)): GDP growth (ABMI); Total employment (DYDC); Claimant unemployed (BCJD); Average Earnings Index including bonuses (LNNC), all seasonally adjusted, RPI (CZBH); RPIX (CDKQ); CPI (D7G7), not seasonally adjusted, UK (GB for AEI), 2007–2009.
Note:
1. Average earnings figures are for Great Britain.
2. RPIX is the Retail Price Index excluding mortgage interest payments

5.14   The consensus forecast is that employment will continue to grow, although at a slower rate of 0.5 per cent (or fewer than 160,000 jobs) in 2008. This would be a sizeable reduction in the growth rate compared with 2007 when employment growth in the year to September was 0.9 per cent (or 287,000 jobs). Some commentators, such as the Chartered Institute of Personnel and Development, are even more pessimistic, predicting employment growth of just 0.25 per cent in 2008 (fewer than 80,000 jobs).

Implications of the Forecasts for Our Recommendations

5.15   The National Minimum Wage for adults increased in October 2007 to £5.52 per hour. If it was further increased in October 2008 by the anticipated growth in average earnings, it would rise to £5.74 per hour. If, instead, the adult minimum wage were to rise in line with the expected increase in prices, it would be somewhere between £5.64 and £5.67 an hour, depending on the price index used. If the adult minimum wage were to rise in line with median pay settlements in 2007, it would rise to about £5.70 per hour in October 2008.

International Comparisons

5.16   In addition to considering the macroeconomic position and the range of economic forecasts, we also looked again at the level of the UK National Minimum Wage as compared to those in other countries. The Government economic evidence (BERR, 2007a) indicated that the UK minimum wage was one of the highest in the OECD when adjusted for purchasing power parity, lying third behind Australia and Belgium. In their written submission, the CBI argued that, when adjusted for productivity, the UK minimum wage had grown faster than others since 2003 with the result that it was now the third highest. This is consistent with the evidence we gathered ourselves on international comparisons using both purchasing power parity and exchange rates. We found that the UK minimum wage was behind Australia and France using purchasing power and was also behind Ireland when using exchange rates. These findings are similar to last year, although recent increases in the Irish minimum wage now mean that the adult hourly rate of the Irish minimum wage is higher, using exchange rates, than the equivalent UK minimum wage.

5.17   However, the Government's evidence showed that the bite of the UK minimum wage (that is, its relative level when measured as a percentage of the average wage) was no greater than the OECD average. Using data from the OECD, our own enquiries confirmed that its bite relative to median earnings ranked no more than mid-table when compared to other EU and OECD countries. This suggests that the outcome of any international comparison depends on whether the focus is on an absolute monetary measure or whether it is upon the level of the minimum wage relative to the rest of the earnings distribution. In a high wage country like the UK the former measure will tend to result in a position near the top of the chart, but when taken in relation to the general level of wages as captured by the latter, the UK falls in the middle of the pack. These are headline comparisons and we must emphasise that comparisons of minimum wages in different countries are riddled with complexity. Further detail on the various comparisons can be found in Appendix 4.

Annual Leave Entitlement

5.18   In our remit, the Government asked us to take account of the impact of the second stage of the implementation of the legislation enhancing entitlement to statutory annual leave. The statutory entitlement to annual leave is currently being increased in two phases, from 4 to 5.6 weeks, pro-rata for part-timers, subject to a maximum entitlement of 28 days. The initial four day increase was introduced in October 2007 and we took this into account when we made our recommendations last year. The second increase, from 4.8 to 5.6 weeks, will be introduced from April 2009.

5.19   We estimate that the total increase (phase 1 and 2 combined) in annual leave entitlement is likely to affect 4.4 million employees (about 19 per cent of all employees), adding up to 0.5 per cent to the wage bill for the whole economy. Though there are, as yet, no hard data, estimates suggest that the increase in October 2007 has affected 3.4 million employees, adding up to 0.2 per cent to the wage bill for the whole economy. The impact is likely to have been more pronounced in low-paying sectors like hospitality, where about 43 per cent of employees are estimated to be affected.

5.20   Our estimates suggest that the second increase, in April 2009, will have a similar, albeit slightly bigger, impact. It is expected to affect around 4.4 million employees, adding up to 0.3 per cent to the wage bill for the whole economy. The impact is likely to be greater in low-paying sectors like hospitality, where around 49 per cent of employees are estimated to be affected, adding 0.9 per cent to the wage bill. These estimates are slightly below those in our 2007 Report due to the availability of improved data and a change in the method for estimating the impact. For those firms in which all employees will be entitled to the full four day increase, we estimate that the direct cost is likely to be equivalent to about 1.6 per cent on the wage bill.

5.21   Our calculations of the likely impact of these changes are based on estimates using data from before the time that the first increase in holiday entitlement was implemented. More recent information will become available when data referring to the fourth quarter of 2007 are released in the Labour Force Survey (LFS). These will be made available by ONS in mid-February 2008. These data will cover the three month period following the introduction of the first stage of the enhanced entitlement and should allow us to estimate more accurately the real impact of the increased holiday entitlement. When assessing impact, a number of other caveats should be borne in mind:

- the data available to estimate the impact are not robust;

- the estimates are for employees (not workers) and do not include administrative and other costs;

- increased annual leave is likely to produce benefits (which we are unable to quantify) as well as increased costs;

- it is not possible, in our estimates, to allow for the manner in which firms implement the changes; and

- the estimates presented here assume 100 per cent compliance.

The Views of Interested Parties

5.22 Our consultations inform our interpretation of the data. A formal written exercise was carried out over the Summer of 2007. In addition, we visited many different parts of the United Kingdom over the course of the year to listen to individuals and businesses directly affected by the minimum wage. In November we spent two days taking oral evidence from key interested groups. The Low Pay Commission Secretariat took part in many more informal meetings and visits with firms and other groups. A list of the organisations and individuals that were involved in our consultation and gave consent for us to publish their names can be found at Appendix 1.

5.23 When it came to a discussion of the appropriate level of the minimum wage for October 2008, the responses to our formal consultation exercise largely followed the pattern of previous years. The majority of unions supported a substantial increase in the rates while most employers called for restraint. The unions tended to name a specific figure (often £6 or thereabouts), whereas employer organisations preferred to use a form of words ('only a modest rise').

5.24 The CBI described the overall economic outlook for the UK as uncertain and warned that a rise in the rate of the minimum wage above average earnings could do serious damage if the economy were to slow. The

Our view is that the labour market and the economy is strong enough to bear an increase that is both somewhat ahead of the predicted growth in average earnings in 2008/2009 and picks up the modest amount of slack generated by the 2007/2008 increases in the rates.

TUC evidence

CBI's caution about the future economic prospects was mirrored in the submissions of the British Chambers of Commerce (BCC) and the Institute of Directors, both of which argued that the impact of any large increases would be magnified in an economic downturn.

5.25   The TUC, on the other hand, maintained that, although growth was expected to be slightly slower in 2008, the fundamentals of the UK economy were sound. Most low-paying sectors had either experienced job growth or been stable during the past year and the UK economy was sustaining record levels of employment – all of which supported their view that the UK economy as a whole remained robust and healthy. Individual union submissions made broadly similar points: the UK economy was doing well and conditions were set fair for a substantial increase in minimum wage rates.

5.26   The CBI argued that the UK's minimum wage was high by international standards. Although it did not want the minimum wage to 'wither on the vine', it believed that the minimum wage had now reached an appropriate level when compared to the average wage and it advised that the Commission should, as last year, remain cautious in its approach. The BCC believed future increases should be held below the forecast increase in average earnings. The British Hospitality Association (BHA), British Beer and Pub Association (BBPA) and Business in Sport and Leisure (BISL) called for a modest rise no higher than the increase for 2007. The EEF argued that it was inappropriate to link the minimum wage to average earnings growth and argued for a formulaic approach based on average pay settlements. The National Hairdressers' Federation sought an increase no higher than average earnings growth over the past 12 months. The British Apparel & Textile Confederation saw no justification for an increase in excess of 3 per cent and thought that the figure should be closer to 2 per cent, in line with the Chancellor's targets for public sector pay. The Federation of Small Businesses (FSB) called for no increases at all and, at the very least, none above inflation. The National Farmers' Union argued for the increase to be limited to the level of the CPI to minimise disruption to pay differentials. The British Retail Consortium (BRC) repeated its claim that the minimum wage had arrived at 'the tipping point' and argued for reform of the process. It did not, however, make any clear proposal for the rate of the minimum wage in October 2008.

5.27 The unions, on the other hand, were of the view that the next upratings should be sizeable. The TUC called for a minimum wage of more than £6 an hour by October 2008. It did not accept the view put forward by the CBI and others that the minimum wage had reached its highest sustainable level and therefore looked for an increase that was above the projected increase in average earnings. It was supported in this call by Usdaw and the Communication Workers' Union. GMB and Unite also supported the TUC line but then went further, arguing that such an increase should be seen merely as a first step on the road to their ultimate goal of a living wage, currently pitched somewhere between £7 and £8 an hour. Other unions went higher than £6 an hour. UNISON argued for a minimum wage of £6.75 and the Public and Commercial Services Union wanted £8 an hour in October 2008 to reflect the rising costs of housing and utilities.

5.28 The CBI continued to support strongly the retention of lower rates for young people as did other employer organisations. The unions' position was also unchanged in that most unions argued for the adoption of the adult rate for all, while recognising that this might have to be achieved over a period of years. The responses on the youth rates from organisations representing young people were more forceful than in previous years. The British Youth Council (BYC) accompanied its submission with a petition of letters signed by around 600 young people calling for equal treatment under the minimum wage. The BYC claimed that the youth rates were deeply discriminatory and contravened the spirit, if not the letter, of the age discrimination legislation. The National Union of Students took a similar line, arguing that the youth rates militated against young people staying in education. The Children's Rights Alliance for England went further, arguing for a single minimum wage from the age of 13 (the age at which a person may legally work) and citing the UN Convention on the Rights of the Child as support for their position.

5.29 As last year, the unions argued that minimum wage upratings should not be reduced because of the parallel introduction of better minimum leave entitlements. The CBI and employers disagreed. The BHA and other hospitality bodies expected the impact to be significant in their sector. The Association of Licensed Multiple Retailers (ALMR) believed that there would be a significant increase in wage bills arising from the

> *Increasing numbers of firms and sectors are now being affected by the National Minimum Wage ... Over the same period, firms have faced a multitude of additional regulatory costs (estimated at over £43 billion since 1998), reducing their ability to absorb further large increases.*
>
> **CBI evidence**

new entitlement. Similarly, representatives of the care sector predicted a substantial impact on their business. The FSB thought the costs would be considerable for small firms.

5.30 The Commission's decision to move from bi-annual to annual recommendations (made in order to ensure decisions are made on the latest available data) was mentioned by five respondents – Tesco, BHA, the Cleaning and Support Services Association, BRC and the GMB. The first four of these argued that the move to an annual cycle gave insufficient time for employers to manage the upratings. The fifth, the GMB, argued against the move to annual cycles on the grounds that a longer lead-in time would allow the Commission to recommend larger increases and afford employers more time to absorb them.

5.31 A number of stakeholders asked us to consider the impact of the minimum wage in the context of other regulatory changes faced by business. Many referred to increases in statutory leave entitlement, which we cover elsewhere in this chapter. BCC estimated that the cost of new regulatory burdens on business since 1998 now totalled £55 billion. The Forum of Private Business quoted from its research report '*Cost of Compliance*', which had found that smaller firms feel overburdened by employment law.

5.32 Social care providers alerted us to the decision of the Border and Immigration Agency not to issue new work permits for care staff workers from non-EU and non-EEA countries, and to limit extensions to work permits for existing senior care staff to those paid at least £7.02 an hour. This would have an impact on both wage costs and their ability to fill vacancies. The Scottish Licensed Trade Association was concerned at the effects of the smoking ban introduced in Scotland in 2006. The Association of Labour Providers (ALP) suggested that the Commission should study the interaction between the National Minimum Wage and the Agricultural Minimum Wage and the problems which arose for those who had to operate with both of them.

5.33 A few employer representatives proposed that the level of the minimum wage should vary by region. In support of their case they pointed to a higher 'bite' of the minimum wage in low-income regions. Others thought there was a case for a limited, two-tier, arrangement, with one level of minimum wage for London / the South East and another for the rest of the UK. However, groups arguing for a regional minimum wage were a very small minority, perhaps reflecting the CBI's view, expressed in oral evidence, that a regional minimum wage would bring great complexity and much confusion for little benefit. The TUC also rejected the idea of regional minima, saying it believed that the minimum wage should remain a National Minimum Wage providing a nationwide floor on wages. In fact the concept of a minimum wage that varied by region would be in conflict with the primary legislation which established a National Minimum Wage.

The Recommended Rates

5.34   A year ago, in January 2007, we agreed to recommend an increase of 3.2 per cent in the adult rate of the minimum wage for October 2007. When, a year later in January 2008, we came to review the relevant evidence and consider what recommendations we should make regarding the rates for October 2008, we took as our starting point the agreed aim of the Commission – 'to produce a minimum wage that helps as many low-paid workers as possible without significant adverse impact on employment or the economy' – and the following two passages from Chapter 7 of our last report.

> "This [recommended increase of 3.2 per cent] is less than the predicted annual increase in average earnings, but more than the predicted increase in prices and is in line with current pay settlements." (Paragraph 7.44)

> "Our present view, drawing on the analysis we have made for this report, is that the increases we are likely to recommend for 2008 will be around the predicted rise in average earnings, but much will depend on what happens between then and now in the economy and the labour market. Two of the most important factors will be the movement in average earnings and the level of employment – especially employment in the most affected sectors. We will also want to take account of price inflation and whether it falls back in 2007 as predicted." (Paragraph 7.45)

5.35   Looking back, the 3.2 per cent increase we recommended last year turned out, as we expected, to be lower than the growth in average earnings. But the actual increase in average earnings over the past year was 4 per cent, a little lower than the predicted growth of 4.3 per cent that we had factored into our calculations when we made our recommendation. In a sense, therefore, the 3.2 per cent uprating ended up being slightly higher, relative to the average increase, than we had envisaged.

5.36   Conversely, in January 2007 the HM Treasury Panel of Independent Forecasts was predicting that the RPI inflation rate (which then stood at 4 per cent) would moderate to 2.9 per cent over the coming year. However, RPI inflation did not come down as forecast but remained relatively high, standing at 4 per cent in December 2007. This meant that our expectation that an increase of 3.2 per cent would lead to a modest real terms rise in the hourly wage of the lowest paid was not realised. In that sense the effect of the increase we recommended was less beneficial to low-paid workers than we had envisaged.

5.37   Reviewing the most recent data on employment, we found the figures predominantly positive, with unemployment down and record numbers in work. We continued to find little evidence to suggest that the minimum wage had harmed job prospects, even in the most vulnerable sectors. Overall, employment in the low-paying sectors proved more robust than last year's figures had suggested. Indeed, the latest figures, from September 2006 to September 2007, showed that the number of jobs in low-paying sectors had increased by 71,000, showing slightly stronger growth than in the economy as a whole, and job figures for the two largest low-paying sectors, retail and hospitality, were buoyant.

5.38   However, against the positive picture generated by an analysis of the data for the past year, a less positive scenario was presented by a preview of the economic prospects for the coming year. Most indicators were predicting a period of greater uncertainty in the UK economy than a year ago. Nevertheless, the Treasury, the CBI and the majority of reputable forecasters were predicting a downturn, not a recession, with predicted growth of around 1.8 per cent in the UK economy for 2008, to be followed by a recovery towards trend in 2009.

5.39   Against this background, we rehearsed the arguments for and against maintaining the caution of last year. There were several arguments put forward in favour of the Commission taking a bolder line this time and proposing an increase in the minimum wage above the projected 4 per cent increase in average earnings predicted for 2008. One argument was that last year's rise of 3.2 per cent had been over-cautious in the light of the stronger than expected performance of the UK economy, which had grown at a rate of 3.1 per cent against the predicted 2.5 per cent. Another was that there was growing recognition and acceptance amongst employers and society generally of the need for the wages of the least well-paid to increase in line with wage growth in the wider economy. It was also pointed out that it had not been the Commission's intention, last time round, to propose an increase that would be lower than the increase in RPI and it was suggested that we had the opportunity to remedy the situation by being more, rather than less, generous in our approach to October 2008. Another line of reasoning advanced was that the forthcoming increase in annual leave entitlement would have no more than a modest impact, probably lower than most official estimates. Also, it was pointed out that, whereas last year there were signs of some job losses in low-paying sectors, the most recent ONS data indicated that the employment situation was healthy and jobs were continuing to grow in most low-paying sectors. Finally, it was suggested that we should have an eye to the growing gap between the best and worst rewarded workers and we were reminded that pay of the very highest earners had continued to rise steeply relative to the pay of just about everyone else.

5.40 Against these arguments for boldness were set others that pointed to the need for further caution and a recommended figure below the predicted increase in average earnings. These counter-arguments started by pointing to the uncertain outlook for the UK economy in 2008. There were growing concerns about a serious slow-down. Recent consumer confidence indicators had declined sharply, which did not augur well for some low-paying sectors such as much of hospitality and some parts of the retail sector. In addition, we were reminded that, although we had monitored developments closely, the impact of the large minimum wage upratings of 2003 and onwards had yet to be fully assessed and that we would not have the results of the relevant research projects until the end of 2008. The continuing employer concern about the impact on differentials was another argument for caution. Moreover, it was pointed out that the increase in annual leave entitlement would undoubtedly add to costs of many firms in the low-paying sectors. And, although we had already taken account last year of the first tranche of increased holiday entitlement, we had yet to factor in the effect of the second stage. Finally, it was pointed out that, in seven of the last ten years the independent forecasts of future average earnings growth had proved to be an over-estimate. It was suggested that we should factor this into our calculations when considering what rate we ought to recommend for future years.

5.41   After weighing the arguments, consulting the evidence and reflecting on the insights we had gained from our many meetings with interested parties over the past year, we agreed that, on balance, the uncertain economic outlook made a degree of caution advisable, despite the generally encouraging labour market data. **We therefore recommend that the adult rate of the minimum wage should be increased from £5.52 to £5.73 an hour in October 2008**. This is close to, but less than, the predicted annual increase in average earnings. It is higher than the predicted increase in prices and marginally higher than the average increase in current pay settlements. We see this recommendation as balancing the generally positive messages in the data with the need for caution implied by the uncertain economic outlook.

5.42   In reaching this decision, we have, as our remit required, taken account of the forthcoming increase in annual leave entitlement. However, given that the evidence available to inform our view of the impact of the increased entitlement to annual leave is less than perfect, and that it should be possible in the near future to get an indication of the actual rather than the hypothetical impact, we intend to keep the matter under review during the coming year in the light of our analysis of relevant data from the LFS and the results of our ongoing consultations with stakeholders.

5.43   Looking forward to 2009, we will agree our recommendations for October 2009 based on careful consideration of the evidence gathered in the course of the year from visits, official data and the formal consultation exercise. The increases we recommend for October 2009 will be particularly influenced by three factors. We will take account of the nature of the broad economic environment. We will also look closely at the findings of the wide-ranging research programme we have instigated for the next report which is designed to assess the impact of the series of above average earnings increases in the minimum wage implemented from 2003 onwards. Finally, we will take account of developments in the low-paying sectors. We expect the recommendation to be broadly around the predicted increase in average earnings, but our decision, as always, will depend on the evidence.

5.44 In considering the Youth Development Rate and the 16–17 year old rate, we noted the calls from some unions and youth organisations for a single minimum wage rate for all, regardless of age. However, in view of the evidence from other countries of the potentially negative impact of a single rate on younger workers and the relatively poor showing of young people in the UK labour market, we believe that lower minimum wage rates for workers under the age of 21 are justified to protect their employment prospects. We therefore decided, after some discussion, to recommend that the value of the youth rates relative to the adult rate should be maintained. **In line with our approach to the adult rate, we recommend that in October 2008 the Youth Development Rate should increase from £4.60 to £4.77 an hour and that the 16–17 rate should increase from £3.40 to £3.53 an hour.**

The Accommodation Offset

5.45 The accommodation offset is a mechanism that enables employers to set the cost of accommodation provided to workers against the minimum wage up to a maximum daily limit. It is the only benefit-in-kind that may be counted towards the minimum wage. The provision of accommodation is significant in some low-paying sectors, particularly hospitality and agriculture, and the offset was designed to recognise its importance to both employers and workers. When introduced, the arrangement was supported by both employer and worker representatives and it was pitched at a level that reflected former Wages Council and industry agreements. It provides protection to the worker and gives limited recognition of the value of the benefit, but it is not intended to reflect the actual costs of provision to the employer or the commercial market value.

5.46 IDS (2007a) found that the provision of accommodation by employers was common in the hospitality sector. The research found a wide range of charges in hotels, from £15 to £85 per week, but with lower-paid staff sometimes charged less. In the pubs sector the deductions were found to be slightly lower or well below the maximum offset allowed, with no evidence that the guidelines were being breached.

5.47 Employer stakeholders in the hospitality and leisure sectors submitted written evidence calling for a more substantial rise in the offset level. The ALMR argued that the low level of the offset acts as a disincentive leading to the potential loss of this facility to the low paid, who would then face higher alternative rental costs, extended commuting and possibly reduced employment opportunities. The ALMR called for the offset to be increased to £40 per week to act as more of an incentive to provide accommodation. The CBI supported the retention of the offset, but was concerned that, for many hotels, the benefit provided was not reflected in the offset value. The BHA, BISL and BBPA maintained their support for an offset, but raised similar concerns, asking the Commission to consider increasing it towards what they regarded to be a more realistic level. They maintained that the realistic market rate would be around double the existing level. During the Commission visit to Aviemore, Macdonald Hotels also argued that the offset did not reflect the true cost of accommodation and that it penalised those who tried to offer a higher standard. They suggested different levels of offset to reflect different standards of accommodation.

5.48 The ALP repeated its contention that accommodation should be regarded as a matter of free choice where it was provided by employers outside of the employment contract. It said that, as a result of our 2006 Report (in which we decided against the adoption of such an approach), most labour providers had ceased to provide housing and such provision was now restricted to areas of low cost accommodation, such as farms. Consequently, workers were forced to look for accommodation on the open market where landlords were free to charge whatever they wished. The ALP called on the Commission to conduct a study of accommodation costs paid by low-paid workers, including 'key-worker' assisted schemes and those operated by employers, to enable a more informed debate to take place on the merits of applying restrictions on the rents which could be charged to low-paid workers by employers.

5.49 The TUC and trade unions supported the retention of the offset, but submitted little evidence relating to the level. Their concerns about the application of the offset were largely related to enforcement and a number of issues which particularly affect vulnerable workers, such as illegal or excessive deductions from their wages. Housing quality was also a particular concern. The Scottish Low Pay Unit observed that deductions from wages often exceeded the maximum permitted by the offset rules.

5.50 To date, the accommodation offset has risen broadly in line with the adult rate, remaining at around 77–79 per cent of the adult National Minimum Wage. It currently stands at £4.30 per day. We received no compelling evidence that has persuaded us to deviate from our normal practice, and concluded that the accommodation offset should be increased in line with the minimum wage upratings. **We therefore recommend that the value of the accommodation offset should rise from £4.30 per day to £4.46 per day from October 2008.**

The Impact of Our Recommendations

Coverage

5.51 As last year, the recommended minimum wage rates for October 2008 are slightly below the forecast increase in average earnings. If implemented, these upratings are therefore likely to cover a similar proportion of jobs to the proportion covered by the 2007 upratings and slightly fewer jobs than in years when the upratings were in line with, or exceeded, the growth in average earnings.

5.52 In April 2007, according to ASHE, there were just under 2 million jobs that paid less than the minimum wage rates we are recommending for October 2008. These were made up of around 1.82 million jobs held by those aged 21 and over (7.7 per cent), about 141,000 jobs held by 18–20 year olds (14.5 per cent) and 36,000 jobs held by 16–17 year olds (9.3 per cent).

5.53 However, in order to estimate coverage, we need to make assumptions about how the wages of the low paid would have increased in the absence of any minimum wage upratings. In other words, we need to estimate the real value of the October 2008 minimum wage at April 2007 (the date of the latest earnings data) by downrating using estimated prices or earnings growth.

5.54   Assuming that, in line with our recommendation, 21 year olds would be entitled to the adult minimum wage from October 2008 and that the wages of the lowest paid would increase in line with forecast average earnings, we estimate that about 0.89 million jobs or 3.7 per cent of all jobs held by those aged 21 and over would be covered by the new rate of £5.73 in October 2008. If we assumed instead that the wage growth of the lowest paid would just match forecast price inflation, a greater number of jobs would be covered – between 1.07 and 1.37 million jobs (4.5 to 5.8 per cent) held by the adult workforce depending on the price index used. On this basis we estimate that the new adult rate for the minimum wage will achieve a slightly lower level of coverage than the £5.52 uprating in October 2007 (when 1.02 million or 4.3 per cent of jobs held by those aged 21 and over were covered based on the earnings assumption)[1].

Table 5.2

Estimated Number and Percentage of Jobs Covered by the Recommended October 2008 National Minimum Wage Upratings, UK, 2008

Estimated number and percentage of jobs covered		Earnings basis	Price basis	
	October 2008 hourly minimum wage rates	AEI including bonuses	RPI	CPI
Adult rate (21 and over)	£5.73	0.89 million 3.7%	1.07 million 4.5%	1.37 million 5.8%
Development Rate (18–20 year olds)	£4.77	90,000 9.2%	108,000 11.1%	118,000 12.1%
16–17 year old rate	£3.53	26,000 6.7%	27,000 7.0%	29,000 7.6%
Total		1.00 million 4.0%	1.21 million 4.8%	1.52 million 6.1%

Source: LPC estimates based on ONS ASHE 2007 methodology, low-pay weights, UK, April 2007.
AEI including bonuses (ONS code LNNC), RPIX (ONS code CDKQ), RPI (ONS code CZBH) and CPI (code D7G7), seasonally adjusted, UK (GB for AEI), October 2007. HM Treasury Panel of Independent Forecasts for 2008, UK, January 2008.

5.55   We have recommended increases in the Youth Development Rate and the 16–17 year old rate in line with our recommendation for the adult minimum wage – an uprating of 3.8 per cent in October 2008. Assuming that young workers' wages would increase in line with average earnings, we estimate that 90,000 jobs held by those aged

[1]   These numbers differ from those stated in Chapter 2 as the estimates in Chapter 2 use adults aged 22 and over.

18–20 will be covered by the October 2008 Youth Development Rate – representing around 9.2 per cent of jobs held by these young workers. Based on the price assumption, the coverage estimates range between 109,000 and 118,000 jobs (about 11.1 to 12.1 per cent of all jobs held by that age group)[2].

5.56   As for 16–17 year olds, we estimate, based on the earnings assumption, that 26,000 jobs (or 6.7 per cent of all jobs held by 16–17 year olds) will be covered by the October 2008 uprating. Using the price assumption, the coverage increases to 27,000–29,000 jobs for that age group (between 7.0 and 7.6 per cent of all jobs).

5.57   Overall, we therefore estimate that the total coverage of the recommended October 2008 upratings will be approximately one million jobs (4.0 per cent of all jobs) if the wages of the low paid were to increase by the forecast growth in average earnings between April 2007 and October 2008, or between 1.21 million jobs (4.8 per cent of all jobs) and 1.52 million jobs (6.1 per cent of all jobs) based on the price assumption.

Coverage by Gender

5.58   As we discussed in Chapter 2, women are more likely than men to be working in low-paid jobs. Based on the earnings assumption, we estimate that the October 2008 adult minimum wage will cover around 300,000 jobs held by men and 586,000 jobs held by women. Using our alternative price assumption, we expect that up to 441,000 jobs held by men and 927,000 jobs held by women would be covered by the uprating to £5.73. On all measures, jobs held by women aged 21 and over are expected to make up around two-thirds of all jobs covered by the 2008 October uprating in the adult rate.

Position Relative to Average Earnings

5.59   The 'bite' of the minimum wage, that is its relationship to average earnings (measured at the median or the mean), is another way of assessing the impact of the minimum wage on the earnings distribution. In April 2007, according to ASHE, the median gross hourly

---

[2]   These estimates are higher than from those stated in Chapters 2 and 3 as those estimates use youths aged 18–21.

earnings (excluding overtime) of all employees aged 21 and over (full and part-time) were £10.33 an hour. In order to be able to compare median earnings with the October 2008 adult rate, we need to uprate it by the growth in average earnings (including bonuses), both actual and predicted. On that basis, the adult rate of £5.73 in October 2008 is expected to be about 52.3 per cent of forecast average earnings of £10.96. This compares with a bite of 46.2 per cent when the minimum wage was introduced in 1999, a bite of 54 per cent for the October 2006 rate of £5.35 and a bite of about 52.4 per cent for the October 2007 rate of £5.52. Using the mean, we estimate that the bite in October 2008 will be about 40.4 per cent for employees aged 21 and over based on the earnings assumption[3].

Wage Bills

5.60   We anticipate that the direct impact of our recommendations on the average wage bill is likely to be modest as the recommended increase in the minimum wage is below the predicted rise in average earnings. However, our recommendation that 21 year olds should be entitled to the adult minimum wage could lead to an increase of more than 3.8 per cent for the small number who would be directly affected. As we saw in Chapter 3, around 90 per cent of jobs held by 21 year olds are already paying at least the adult rate and so the impact of this recommendation on the wage bill should be small.

Public Sector

5.61   The lowest rates of pay in the public sector generally tend to be above minimum wage levels and, as we saw in Chapter 2, very few jobs in the public sector are low-paid. We therefore expect that the impact of the recommended October 2008 rates on the public sector wage bill will be very small. However, given that many public bodies employ private sector firms under contract to provide services such as cleaning, there may be some indirect impact.

---

[3]   These bite figures differ from those in Chapter 2 as the estimates here also cover workers aged 21.

5.62 The minimum wage can also affect the public sector through the impact on the Exchequer of any savings resulting from reduced benefits and increased tax receipts as the minimum wage increases. Table 5.3, based on information supplied by the Government[4], illustrates the impact of the 21 pence increase in the minimum wage. We estimate that total Government savings from the 2008 minimum wage upratings will be around £245 million, composed mainly of an increase of over £100 million in income tax and over £50 million in National Insurance receipts as the earnings of minimum wage earners rise. The Government also stands to make significant savings from reductions in Working Tax Credits (just under £50 million) and other benefits (over £40 million in total).

Table 5.3:
Government Savings from the 2008 National Minimum Wage Upratings, £ Million, UK, 2008–2009

£ million	Government savings from the increase in the minimum wage to £5.73 in October 2008
Income tax	105
National Insurance Contributions	51
Working Tax Credit	48
Child Tax Credit	17
Income Support	6
Housing Benefit	14
Council Tax Benefit	5
Total	**245**

Source: LPC estimates based on HM Treasury calculations using ten pence increases in the minimum wage based on Family Resources Survey 2005/2006, uprated to 2008/09, UK, 2008–2009.
Note: These figures take account of changes in tax credits, benefits, taxes and National Insurance Contributions but do not take any account of likely behavioural change caused by a rise in hourly pay, such as changed levels of employment or hours worked. They also do not include the effect of the £25,000 disregard in tax credits, which allows income to rise between one year and the next by up to £25,000 before tax credits begin to be withdrawn. This means that the reductions in tax credits would in practice be significantly smaller, at least in the initial tax year.

---

[4] After the Pre-Budget Report in November 2007, the Government provided us with estimates of savings for hypothetical increases in the minimum wage of 10 pence, 20 pence and 30 pence.

Conclusion

5.63 This year, influenced by the uncertain economic prospects for the coming year, we have again exercised caution and recommended an increase that is slightly below the projected increase in average earnings. As we have said earlier, our long-term aim is to create and maintain a minimum wage that helps as many low-paid workers as possible without significant adverse impact on employment or the economy. We recognise that there are conflicting views as to the appropriate long-term level of the National Minimum Wage. As a Commission, we continue to look to the evidence to guide us. Next year, in addition to our usual sources of evidence, we will have the advantage of a series of research projects reporting on the impact of the above average earnings upratings of the minimum wage between 2003 and 2006 on the economy, the labour market and the low-paying sectors. In line with our recommendation, we also hope to have the benefit of improved data from the Office for National Statistics.

Consultation

We are grateful to all the people and organisations that helped us by providing oral and written evidence, and by organising or participating in visits and meetings. All organisations which participated, and gave consent for us to publish their names, are listed below according to the nature of their contribution.

Oral Evidence to the Commission

Association of Convenience Stores
British Beer & Pub Association
British Hospitality Association
British Retail Consortium
British Youth Council
Business in Sport and Leisure
Confederation of British Industry (CBI)
Cleaning and Support Services Association
English Community Care Association
National Care Association
National Group on Homeworking
Trades Union Congress (TUC)
Union of Shop, Distributive and Allied Workers
UNITE

Written Evidence to the Commission

Association of Convenience Stores
Association of Labour Providers
Association of Licensed Multiple Retailers
British Apparel & Textile Confederation
British Beer & Pub Association (Joint submission with British Hospitality Association, Business in Sport and Leisure)
British Chambers of Commerce
British Furniture Manufacturers
British Hospitality Association (Joint submission with British Beer & Pub Association, Business in Sport and Leisure)

British Retail Consortium

British Shops and Stores Association

British Youth Council and 600 letters from Young People

BUPA Care Services

Business in Sport and Leisure (Joint submission with British Beer & Pub
Association, British Hospitality Association)

CBI

Central Council of Physical Recreation

Children's Rights Alliance for England

Citizens Advice Northern Ireland

Cleaning and Support Services Association

Communication Workers Union

Daycare Trust

Dyfed Cleaning Services Limited

EEF The Manufacturers' Organisation

Employment Information Services

English Community Care Association

Equality Commission for Northern Ireland

Equal Opportunities Commission

Federation of Licensed Victuallers Associations

Federation of Small Businesses

Food and Drink Federation

Forum of Private Business

Glasgow Chamber of Commerce

GMB

Her Majesty's Government

Independent Retailers Confederation

Institute of Directors

Leicester City Council

Local Government Employers

Mark Watson

National Care Association

National Centre for Social Research

National Day Nurseries Association

National Farmers' Union

National Group on Homeworking

National Hairdressers' Federation

National Union of Students

Northern Ireland Public Service Alliance

Public and Commercial Services Union

Rural Shops Alliance

Scottish Association of Master Bakers

Scottish Licensed Trade Association

Scottish Low Pay Unit

Scotland Office

Scottish Textiles Industry Association

Tesco Stores Limited

The Newspaper Society

The Northern Ireland Committee, Irish Congress of Trade Unions

Trades Union Congress

Triangle Supported Employment Service

Union of Shop, Distributive and Allied Workers

Union of Shop, Distributive and Allied Workers Northern Ireland

UNISON

Unite

United Kingdom Home Care Association

Unquoted Companies Group

Welsh Assembly Government

White Horse Child Care Ltd

YWCA England & Wales

Visits and Meetings

Abbey Quilting Ltd

Agricultural Wages Board for England & Wales

Agricultural Wages Board for Northern Ireland

All Aspects Labour Ltd

Association of Licensed Multiple Retailers

Bank of England

Barking & Dagenham Citizens Advice Bureau

British Apparel & Textile Confederation

British Beer & Pub Association

British Beer & Pub Association Midland Counties

British Chambers of Commerce

British Hospitality Association

British Youth Council

Business in Sport and Leisure

CBI

CBI Wales

Central Council of Physical Recreation

Cleaning and Support Services Association

Colwall Park Hotel, Bar & Restaurant

Desk-Link Office Furniture Ltd

English Community Care Association

Federation of Small Businesses

Freshtime UK Ltd

Fuller, Smith and Turner Plc

Gangmasters Licensing Authority

GMB, Birmingham & West Midlands Region

GMB, Midland & East Coast Region

Hartley Dyke Farm Shop

Hayloft Plants Ltd

Home Retail Group

John Cruddas MP

Johnson's of Sandhurst

Learning and Skills Council

Leonard Cheshire Disability

Lincolnshire Chamber of Commerce and Industry

McDonald's Restaurants Limited

Macdonald Hotels and Resorts

MS Agricultural Services Ltd

MSS Group

National Care Association

National Day Nurseries Association

National Farmers' Union

Northern Ireland Executive

Northern Ireland Public Services Alliance

Poverty Alliance

Registered Nursing Home Association

Rural Kent

S.A. Brain & Co. Ltd

Scottish Government

Scottish Low Pay Unit

Scottish Youth Parliament

Spar, Sissinghurst, Kent

The Peacock Group

Trades Union Congress

Ulster Farmers Union

Union of Shop, Distributive and Allied Workers

UNISON

UNISON Northern Ireland

Welsh Assembly Government

Appendix 2

Low Pay Commission Research Reports

Overview

1   We commissioned two research projects for our 2008 Report. Incomes Data Services (IDS) were commissioned to monitor the impact of the October 2006 minimum wage upratings. Jonathan Wadsworth (Centre for Economic Performance, London School of Economics (LSE)) was invited to supplement his previous research investigating the impact of the National Minimum Wage on prices.

2   In addition, we undertook three research projects in-house. The first was carried out by Heather Holt, Mouna Kehil (both members of the LPC Secretariat) and Geoff White (University of Greenwich) and looked at the change in pay composition since 1997. The second, by Heather Holt, Jamie Jenkins and Jenny Johnson (both ONS) attempted to investigate the level of minimum wage non-compliance. Third, Heather Holt also investigated the characteristics of low-paid jobs.

3   Further information on these projects is provided in the Table below.

Table A2.1

Low Pay Commission Research Projects for the 2008 Report

Project Title and Researchers	Aims and Methodology	Key Findings and Results

Monitoring the Impact of the National Minimum Wage.
 	
Nicola Allison, Fernando Arrieta, Angela Bowring, Alastair Hatchett, Catherine Kirk, Simone Melis, Ken Mulkearn, Louisa Potter and Lois Wiggins (Incomes Data Services)
	Incomes Data Services monitored the impact of the 2006 increase in the minimum wage, and employers' continuing responses to earlier increases in the minimum wage. This represented a continuation of previous work for the Commission. IDS also examined the impact of the changes made by employers in response to the forthcoming 2007 upratings.
	
	The same methodology as in previous years was employed. This involved a mixture of telephone and postal survey work (of around 1000 organisations), and further telephone-based follow-up work.
	
	IDS concentrated on the low-paying sectors such as hospitality (including fast food, pubs, hotels and restaurants); care homes; childcare; leisure and retail.
	
	IDS also looked at rates of pay for apprentices and the impact of the October 2007 increase in annual leave entitlement.
		IDS found that:
		
		• the minimum wage continues to have a substantial impact on the lowest rates of pay across low-paying sectors, particularly pubs and fast food;
		
		• the 2006 upratings narrowed differentials or caused changes to pay structures in retail and fast food;
		
		• the divergence in youth pay has continued;
		
		  – some firms now pay adult rates at 16,
		
		  – most retailers pay adult rates at 18,
		
		  – but fast food outlets use lower rates for under 22s.
		
		• October has become the most popular month for pay reviews in retail;
		
		• median pay for some jobs in hotels were less in London and the South East than in rest of UK;
		
		• there was little evidence of substitution between groups of workers;
		
		• recruitment and retention problems do not seem to have been affected by recent minimum wage rises;
		
		• few employers reported that the increase had adversely affected employment or hours;
		
		• an entitlement of just 20 days annual leave including Bank Holidays was common in some low-paying sectors such as fast food, pubs, restaurants and leisure; and
		
		• the 2007 increase in annual leave entitlement cost many firms 1.3 to 1.6 per cent of the wage bill.

Did the UK Minimum Wage Affect Prices? Jonathan Wadsworth, Centre for Economic Performance, LSE	In previously commissioned research, Wadsworth (2007) suggested that the introduction and subsequent uprating of the minimum wage may have induced certain industries and services that employed a high share of minimum wage workers among the workforce to raise prices more than in sectors which employed fewer minimum wage workers. However, these findings were tentative, due to data limitations, data availability and time constraints which precluded a more in-depth analysis of these issues. This new study looked further at the effects of the minimum wage on the prices of UK goods and services. Wadsworth used the Labour Force Survey (LFS) and the Annual Survey of Hours and Earnings (ASHE) to estimate the employee and the wage bill shares relating to minimum wage workers in each three or four digit industry sector and so define minimum wage goods and services. He then matched these data to sectoral-level data on retail prices and looked to see if there was any evidence that prices in minimum wage sectors were changed more by the introduction of, and subsequent changes in, the minimum wage.	The research found that, while it is hard to detect much evidence of a significant change in prices in the month in which the minimum wage changed, prices in several minimum wage sectors appear to have risen relatively faster than prices in non-minimum wage sectors in the period after the minimum wage was introduced.

Project Title and Researchers	Aims and Methodology	Key Findings and Results
The Pay Composition of the Low Paid: An Analysis from 1997 to 2006 Heather Holt, Mouna Kehil (both LPC Secretariat) and Geoff White (University of Greenwich)	This research updated previous Commission research on the change in pay composition since the introduction of the National Minimum Wage. ASHE data from 1997 to 2006 were used to investigate the incidence of additional pay components among the low paid and their contribution to gross pay, as well as industry variations and changes over time. LFS and ASHE were used to assess the prevalence of a range of benefits such as pension provision, tied accommodation, annual leave entitlement and other non-wage benefits among low-paid employees.	Researchers found that, in the last ten years, the incidence of additional payments among low-paid employees increased while it declined for better paid employees. However, low-paid employees were still less likely to be receiving shift premia, incentive payments or additional pay components such as car allowances or on call/stand-by allowances. By contrast, low-paid employees were now as likely to be paid overtime as better paid employees. The sectors with the highest increases in the incidence of overtime among the low-paid since 1997 were food processing, leisure, social care and agriculture. Further, they found that the low paid continued to receive much less generous benefits packages. Over 80 per cent of low paid employees were without an occupational pension. The low paid also got fewer days annual leave and were more likely to work on Bank Holidays or not get paid for the Bank Holidays not worked.
Characteristics of Those Paid Below the National Minimum Wage Heather Holt (LPC Secretariat), Jamie Jenkins and Jennie Johnson (both ONS)	Each year, around one per cent of the workforce is found by ONS to be paid less than the minimum wage. This is not necessarily due to non-compliance. Using ASHE and the LFS, these two research projects attempted to get behind the reasons why around 300,000 employees each year are recorded in official surveys as being paid less than the minimum wage. The research explored likely legitimate reasons for being paid less than the minimum wage and attempted to gauge the extent of training and apprenticeship exemptions; the use of the accommodation offset; and the possibility that piece rates might also be a factor. The research also looked in detail at possible measurement issues with regards to rounding, stated versus derived hourly rates and proxy responses.	The research found that it was not possible to identify the extent of non-compliance using the data available. However, making various assumptions concerning measurement error and legitimate exemptions and offsets, the research found that it was possible to explain between a quarter and a half of the number of jobs estimated to be paid below the minimum wage. The researchers were unable to determine whether the remainder was due to non-compliance or whether it was the result of factors they had been unable to take into account.
An Analysis of Low-paid Jobs Heather Holt (LPC Secretariat)	Each year, around one per cent of the workforce is found by ONS to be paid less than the minimum wage. Using ASHE this research explored the characteristics of the jobs paid below the minimum wage. The research then uses the ASHE/New Earnings Survey panel data to explore the persistence of jobs paid below the minimum wage and the impact of working in a job of this kind in the past on working in a similar job currently.	The research found that jobs paid below the minimum wage were more likely to be undertaken by employees who: were female; were younger (22–34) or older (aged 59/64+); were part-time; were on a temporary contract; had worked for the firm for less than one year; or who held more than one job. It also found that these jobs were more likely to be: in the private sector; not covered by collective agreements; in a sales and customer service, skilled trade, personal service, process, plant and machine operative or elementary occupation; in the wholesale and retail trade or hotel and restaurant sector; in small firms (fewer than 10 employees); and in a region other than the South East. The research concluded that the persistence of below minimum wage jobs was low with a high probability that employees would leave these jobs after a short time. The average tenure in these jobs was estimated to be 1.25 years. However, it also found evidence of a scarring effect. That is, earning below the minimum wage in the past significantly increased the chance of currently earning below the minimum wage (or being low-paid).

Future Research

4   We have commissioned the following projects to inform the recommendations in our next report:

- **An Assessment of the Impact of Recent Upratings of the National Minimum Wage: Considering its Effect on Competitiveness, Performance and Sector Dynamics in Britain:** Robinson, Forth, Rincon-Aznar from the National Institute of Economic and Social Research (NIESR) and Harris (University of Glasgow);

- **Research on the Impact of the Minimum Wage on Staff Turnover, Retention and Recruitment:** McVittie, Blake, Inskip, Lyne and Wong (all Experian);

- **Econometric Study of the Employment and Hours of Work Effects of the National Minimum Wage:** Riley, Wilkinson (NIESR) and Dickens (University of Sussex);

- **The Geography of the National Minimum Wage:** Dolton and Wadsworth (both Royal Holloway University of London); and

- **Monitoring the Impact of the National Minimum Wage:** Allison, Bowring, Chubb, Hatchett, Mulkearn, Potter, Warberg and Wiggins (IDS).

In addition, we will also conduct two in-house research projects:

- **The Impact of the Minimum Wage on Differentials:** Manning (LSE), Dickens (University of Sussex) and Butcher (LPC Secretariat); and

- **The Impact of the 2007 Increase in Annual Leave Entitlement:** Analytical Team (LPC Secretariat).

Further, we will also be looking to commission research on the working of the apprenticeship exemptions and the interaction with the youth labour market.

Summary of Changes to Main Data Sources

Introduction

1   In this appendix, we outline the main data sources used in our analyses of employment and earnings and review the principal changes made since our 2007 Report.

2   There are two main sources of data that we use in this report to measure earnings, the Annual Survey of Hours and Earnings (ASHE) and the Labour Force Survey (LFS), both of which are produced by the Office for National Statistics (ONS). In addition, but to a lesser extent, we use two other ONS sources of earnings information, the Average Earnings Index (AEI) and Average Weekly Earnings (AWE).

3   There are also two main sources of employment information, the LFS and the ONS employee jobs series. The LFS captures the number of people in employment, while the employee job series measures the number of jobs in the economy.

Annual Survey of Hours and Earnings

4   ASHE is the main source of structural earnings data in the UK and is regarded by the ONS as the best source of earnings information. It provides information on the levels, distribution and make-up of earnings, as well as on hours, gender, age, geography, occupation and industry. It is a survey of employees completed by employers and conducted in April each year. Results are based on a sample of employees in Pay-As-You-Earn income tax schemes. The self-employed are excluded.

5   In 2007 the ASHE sample was cut by 20 per cent.[1] The ONS states that this has not introduced a discontinuity in the series and that these cuts have had a limited impact on the precision of estimates at an

---

[1]   http://www.statistics.gov.uk/downloads/theme_labour/ASHE/ChangeInASHE07.pdf

aggregate level. However, ONS conducted a very limited impact analysis for lower levels of disaggregation before the sample was cut. Subsequent ONS investigations and our own analysis of the 2007 data confirm the ONS view at the aggregate level, but shows that the sample reduction has affected the precision of some estimates at more disaggregated levels such as 4-digit industry.

6   As well as reducing the sample, ONS made two further key methodological changes to the 2007 ASHE, designed to improve the quality of ASHE estimates. These changes were:

- the introduction of automatic occupation coding, which led to a small reduction in the estimates of median gross weekly pay for most two-digit occupation groups; and

- those businesses responding to the ASHE survey that have special reporting arrangements are now treated as a separate stratum with a separate weight.

7   While we understand that these changes are aimed at improving the quality of the data in the long-term, they have resulted in a break in the series. ONS were able to implement automatic coding and the treatment of those with special arrangements as a separate stratum to the 2006 data to make it consistent with 2007. However, due to a change to the occupation question between 2005 and 2006, automatic coding of occupation cannot be carried out for 2005 on a consistent basis. As a result, data prior to 2006 could not be adjusted to make it directly comparable with 2006 and 2007. We are, therefore, not able to make consistent comparisons between the current data for 2007 and years prior to 2006.

8   Taken along with other changes in recent years, there are now four earnings datasets:

- 1970–2003 New Earnings Survey;

- 1997–2004 ASHE excluding supplementary information;

- 2004–2006 ASHE including supplementary information; and

- 2006–2007 ASHE 2007 methodology.

Low Pay Weights

9   In our report, estimates of the number of jobs paid below certain
           thresholds using ASHE are based on low-pay weights which have been
           developed by ONS. These weights remove those employees whose
           pay in the reference period of the survey has been affected by absence
           and weight the remaining employees up to UK population estimates.
           Estimates of the level of earnings use the standard ASHE weights;
           these weight all employee responses up to the UK population and then
           remove (after weighting) those whose pay has been affected by
           absence. Our analyses of earnings differ from those available on the
           ONS website as ONS remove (after weighting) those employees not
           on what the employer considers to be an adult rate as well as those
           whose pay is affected by absence in the reference period.

Low Pay Statistics

10   According to the 2006 ASHE, published in October 2006, 336,000
           employee jobs paid below the minimum wage. On 7 November 2007,
           the figure for 2006 was revised downwards to 296,000 as a result of
           new information regarding age (ONS used a default age of 25 for
           missing data but new information on actual age from Her Majesty's
           Revenue and Customs revealed that many of those employees paid
           below the minimum wage were actually aged 16–21). The provisional
           2007 data are broadly in line with the revised 2006 data. The number of
           jobs paid below the minimum wage was 292,000 in April 2007; this is
           equivalent to 1.2 per cent of all jobs.

Average Earnings Index and Average Weekly Earnings

11   The AEI and AWE are both based on data from the Monthly Wages
           and Salary Survey, but they differ in terms of weighting, estimation,
           imputation, the handling of outliers and the treatment of smaller firms.
           AWE was introduced in August 2005 following the Turnbull-King review
           but is still an experimental series. ONS regard the AEI as the best
           short-term measure of growth in average earnings, while the AWE is
           best used to measure the level of average earnings. Changes in AWE
           reflect monthly changes in the composition of employment (both within

and between industries) whereas the AEI only captures changes in the annual composition of employment between industries (due to fixed industry weights).

12   From the time when AWE data was first made available in 2001, there has been some variation in the growth of the two measures but, since 2005, growth in AWE has on most occasions exceeded that in AEI. ONS has been working to reconcile these two series however, as AWE is still experimental, the main measure of short-term earnings growth for our analyses continues to be the AEI.

Labour Force Survey

13   The LFS is the official data source used to measure the number of employed and unemployed people. It is a quarterly survey of around 52,000 UK households and provides information on employment, earnings and personal and socio-economic characteristics including gender, ethnicity and disability.

14   In this report, analyses of aggregate employment, unemployment and hours worked use monthly and quarterly LFS data published on the ONS website, which are seasonally adjusted estimates, interim re-weighted to the latest population estimates. For detailed analyses of the labour market by age, ethnic status and disability, we have used the LFS Microdata, which are not seasonally adjusted and are weighted to population estimates published in Spring 2003. As the population estimates published in Spring 2003 are lower than the most current estimates, the analyses based on the LFS Microdata produce estimates of levels which are lower than those using the interim re-weighted data. Estimates showing proportions are not affected as much as both the numerator and denominator are lower.

15   ASHE does not provide information on disability, ethnic background or education level. The LFS is therefore the main source of data on earnings for these groups of employees. Data on pay and hours in the LFS may be less reliable than in ASHE because people often answer the earnings questions without reference to pay documentation and some information is provided by proxy respondents. ASHE collects information from employers about employees' paid hours, whereas the LFS collects information from individuals about their actual and usual

hours of work, which might include unpaid hours. This generally leads the derived hourly earnings variable in LFS to be below the derived hourly pay rate recorded in ASHE. ONS applies a methodology that uses a stated hourly rate for each individual where available or an imputed hourly rate using a nearest neighbour regression model otherwise. This reduces the differences between estimates from the LFS and ASHE. This method also takes account of information on second jobs in the LFS.

16   In January 2006, in order to comply with EU requirements, the ONS moved to produce LFS Microdata on calendar, rather than seasonal, quarters. Despite an initial statement that suggested a back series would become available, the ONS has still only released a limited back-series on a calendar quarter basis. The calendar quarter series currently covers Q2 and Q4 of 1997, 1999, 2001–2004 and each quarter from Q1 2005 onwards. As a result, in the 2007 Report and in this report, there is a break in the LFS series between Summer 2004 and Q4 2004. Any comparisons across these quarters should therefore be avoided. However, we welcome the assurances we have received that the back series will be available later this year.

Employee Jobs

17   The employee job series provide a timely industrial breakdown of jobs in the UK. A number of Short Term Employer Surveys are used to collect data to compile the employee jobs series. The surveys collect information from businesses across the economy. However, figures at a more detailed level are only available for Great Britain and are not seasonally adjusted making quarter to quarter comparisons problematic, particularly as much employment in the low-paying sectors is of a seasonal nature. However, comparisons between one quarter and the same quarter a year ago overcome this particular problem.

18   The employee jobs series is published quarterly and is benchmarked annually to the latest results from the Annual Business Inquiry (ABI/1). The annual benchmark moved from December to September in 2006. ONS also introduced some methodological changes designed to produce an improvement in the estimates of both the levels and

changes moving forward. However, this has resulted in a break in the employee job series between December 2005 and September 2006.[2]

19   The changes have produced a considerable discontinuity in our time series analysis of annual changes in employee jobs between December 2005 (which can be compared with December 2004 on the old basis) and September 2007 (which can be compared with September 2006) and has seriously affected our ability to track the impact of the National Minimum Wage on jobs in the low-paying sectors across time.

20   Further, in January 2007, the sample size for two of the constituent surveys was cut by 12–15 per cent, however, ONS re-optimised the samples to offset the impact of reducing their size. It considers the discontinuities introduced by these survey cuts to be minimal.

---

[2] More information on the revisions can be found here
http://www.statistics.gov.uk/cci/article.asp?id=1802

Comparison of Minimum Wages Across Countries

Table A4.1

Comparison of Level of Minimum Wages[a] Across Countries, End 2007

	In national currency expressed as hourly rate[b]	In UK £, using: Exchange rates[c]	PPPs[d]	Date of last uprating	Age full minimum wage usually applies[e]
Australia[f]	Aus $13.74	5.76	5.76	October 2007	21
Belgium	€7.41 (€1283.91/month)	5.11	5.00	April 2007	21
Canada[g]	Can $7.92	3.82	3.78	[h]	16
France	€8.44	5.81	5.54	July 2007	18
Greece[i]	€3.67 (€29.37/day)	2.53	2.91	May 2007	15
Ireland	€8.65	5.96	4.51	July 2007	20
Japan[j]	Yen 687	2.96	2.90	October 2007	16
Netherlands	€7.60[k] (€303.90/week)	5.24	5.08	July 2007	23
New Zealand	NZ $11.25	4.00	4.35	April 2007	18
Portugal[l]	€2.33 (€403/month)	1.61	2.03	January 2007	16
Spain[l]	€3.29 (€570.60/month)	2.27	2.55	January 2007	16
United Kingdom	£5.52	5.52	5.52	October 2007	22
United States	US $5.85[m]	2.90	3.45	July 2007	20

Sources: British Embassies and High Commissions. OECD Minimum Wage Database. LPC calculation of exchange rates and PPPs. PPPs derived from CPLs, OECD Main Economic Indicators, September 2007. For exchange rates, Bank of England monthly average spot exchange rate, September 2007.

Notes:
(a) In all cases, the minimum wage refers to the basic rate for adults.
(b) For countries where the minimum wage is not expressed as an hourly rate, the rate has been converted to an hourly basis assuming a working time of 8 hours per day, 40 hours per week and 173.3 hours per month.
(c) September 2007.
(d) Purchasing Power Parities (PPPs) derived by applying OECD Comparative Price Levels (CPLs) – ratio of PPPs for private consumption to exchange rates – for September 2007.
(e) Exemptions and special rules apply in many cases. For example, in France and the United States the full adult rate applies to young workers with a tenure of more than 6 and more than 3 months respectively.
(f) Federal minimum wage – hourly rate under Fair Pay Commission arrangements.
(g) Weighted average of provincial/territorial rates.
(h) Date of last uprating varies between provinces.
(i) For blue collar workers. Wage used in Figure A4.1 overleaf is for white collar workers (€767.54 per month, representing minimum wage of €657.89 per month plus entitlement to two additional months of wages).
(j) Weighted average of prefectural rates.
(k) Excludes 8 per cent supplement for holiday pay.
(l) Not including annual supplementary pay of two additional months of salary for full-time workers.
(m) Federal minimum wage. Tipped employees receive a lower minimum wage of $2.13 per hour in direct wages.

Table A4.2

Adult Minimum Wages Relative to Full-time Median Earnings, Mid-2006[a]

Country	Percentage
France	61.4
New Zealand	56.9
Australia[b]	
– LFS	53.8
– ES	51.9
Greece[c]	52.7
Belgium	51.6
Ireland	48.0
UK[d]	45.0
Netherlands[e]	44.6 (52.1)
Canada	40.5
Portugal[f]	38.7 (45.1)
Spain[f]	33.6 (39.2)
Japan	33.3
US	30.7

Sources: Minimum wages and median earnings for full-time workers: OECD estimates and OECD Earnings Structure Database.

Notes:

(a) In all cases the minimum wage refers to the basic rate for adults. In some cases, the median earnings data for full-time workers for mid-2006 are estimates based on extrapolating data for earlier years in line with other indicators of average earnings growth. All earnings data are gross of employee social security contributions.

(b) Two estimates of median earnings are available based on the Labour Force Survey (LFS) and an Enterprise Survey (ES). In each case, the data refer to weekly earnings. The minimum wage refers to the Federal Minimum Wage.

(c) Minimum wage for blue collar workers.

(d) Differs from the LPC estimate in Chapter 2 (Table 2.4), as the OECD estimate is for the minimum wage relative to the median earnings of full-time, rather than all, employees.

(e) The ratio including 8 per cent supplement for holiday pay is given in parentheses.

(f) The ratio including annual supplementary pay of two additional months of salary is given in parentheses.

Figure A4.1

Adult Minimum Wages Relative to Mean Earnings[a][b]

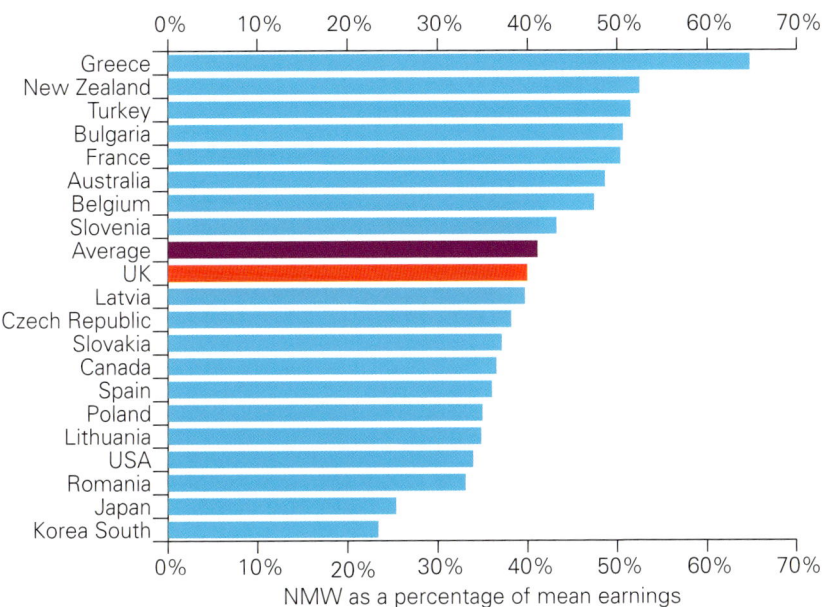

NMW as a percentage of mean earnings

Source: Government evidence to the Low Pay Commission on the economic effects of the National Minimum Wage, November 2007. (www.berr.gov.uk)

Notes:

(a)   National minimum wage rates used may vary from those used in both Table A4.1 and Table A4.2

(b)   Earnings periods used vary between countries, and in most cases differ from that used in Table A4.2. In addition Table A4.2 uses median earnings of full-time, rather than all, employees.

Abbreviations

A2	Romania and Bulgaria, both of which joined the EU in January 2007
A8	The eight central and eastern European Accession countries that joined the EU in May 2004: the Czech Republic, Estonia, Hungary, Latvia, Lithuania, Poland, Slovakia and Slovenia.
ABI	Annual Business Inquiry
ACS	Association of Convenience Stores
AEI	Average Earnings Index
ALMR	Association of Licensed Multiple Retailers
ALP	Association of Labour Providers
ASHE	Annual Survey of Hours and Earnings
AWB	Agricultural Wages Board
AWE	Average Weekly Earnings
BATC	British Apparel & Textile Confederation
BBPA	British Beer and Pub Association
BCC	British Chambers of Commerce
BERR	Department for Business, Enterprise and Regulatory Reform
BHA	British Hospitality Association
BIA	Border and Immigration Agency
BISL	Business in Sport and Leisure
BRC	British Retail Consortium
BSSA	British Shops and Stores Association
BYC	British Youth Council
CBI	Confederation of British Industry
CPI	Consumer Price Index

CPL	Comparative Price Level
CSSA	Cleaning and Support Services Association
DCSF	Department for Children, Schools and Families
DDA	Disability Discrimination Act
DfES	Department for Education and Skills
DTI	Department of Trade and Industry
DWP	Department for Work and Pensions
EAS	Employment Agency Standards
ECCA	English Community Care Association
EIS	Employment Information Services
EOC	Equal Opportunities Commission
ES	Enterprise Survey
ET	Employment Tribunal
EU	European Union
FSB	Federation of Small Businesses
FTE	Full-time education
GB	Great Britain
GDP	Gross Domestic Product
GLA	Gangmasters Licensing Authority
HMRC	Her Majesty's Revenue and Customs
IDS	Incomes Data Services Ltd
ILO	International Labour Organisation
IMF	International Monetary Fund
JWEP	Joint Workplace Enforcement Pilot
LFS	Labour Force Survey
LPC	Low Pay Commission
LSC	Learning and Skills Council
LSE	London School of Economics and Political Science
MOD	Ministry of Defence

MWSS	Monthly Wages and Salary Survey
NCA	National Care Association
NEET	Not in Education, Employment or Training
NFU	National Farmers' Union (England and Wales)
NGH	National Group on Homeworking
NHF	National Hairdressers' Federation
NICs	National Insurance Contributions
NIESR	National Institute of Economic and Social Research
NMW	National Minimum Wage
OECD	Organisation for Economic Co-operation and Development
ONS	Office for National Statistics
PPP	Purchasing Power Parity
Q	Quarter
RPI	Retail Price Index
RPIX	Retail Price Index excluding mortgage interest payments
TUC	Trades Union Congress
UK	United Kingdom
UKHCA	United Kingdom Home Care Association
Usdaw	Union of Shop, Distributive and Allied Workers
VAT	Value Added Tax
WRS	Worker Registration Scheme
YDR	Youth Development Rate

Bibliography

Bank of England, 2007a. *Quarterly Bulletin.* Volume 47 No.1.

Bank of England, 2007b. *Inflation Report.* November.

Bank of England, 2008. *Agents' summary of business conditions.* January.

Bank of England, ongoing. *Minutes of Monetary Policy Committee Meeting.*

Barford, N., 2007. Revisions to workforce jobs. *Economic & Labour Market Review.* 1(5), pp. 56–59.

Battistin, E., C. Emmerson, E. Fitzsimons, S. Maguire, S. Middleton, K. Perren and J. Rennison, 2005. *Evaluation of Education Maintenance Allowance Pilots: Young People Aged 16–19 Years Final Report of the Quantitative Evaluation.* Research Report RR678, October. (Department for Education and Skills.)

Blanchflower, D. G., 2006. *Reflections on my first four votes on the MPC.* Speech. September.

Blanchflower, D. G., 2007a. *Recent Developments in the UK Economy: the Economics of Walking About.* Bernard Corry Memorial Lecture. May.

Blanchflower, D. G., 2007b. *Entrepreneurship in the UK.* Speech at the Max Planck Summer Institute on Entrepreneurship Research. July.

Blanchflower, D. G., 2007c. *Is unemployment more costly than inflation?* September.

Blanchflower, D. G., 2007d. *Trends in European labour markets and preferences over unemployment and inflation.* Keynote address. September.

Blanchflower, D. G. and A. Bryson, 2007. *The Wage Impact of Trade Unions in the UK Public and Private Sectors.* September.

Blanchflower, D. G., J. Saleheen and C. Shadforth, 2007. *The Impact of Recent Migration from Eastern Europe on the UK Economy.* January.

Blanchflower, D. G. and C. Shadforth, 2007. *Fear, Unemployment and Migration.* NBER Working Paper 13506. October.

Border and Immigration Agency and Department for Work and Pensions, 2007a. *Bulgarian and Romanian Accession Statistics January–March 2007.* Online report. (www.bia.homeoffice.gov.uk)

Border and Immigration Agency and Department for Work and Pensions, 2007b. *Bulgarian and Romanian Accession Statistics April–June 2007.* Online report. (www.bia.homeoffice.gov.uk)

Border and Immigration Agency and Department for Work and Pensions, 2007c. *Bulgarian and Romanian Accession Statistics July–September 2007.* Online report. (www.bia.homeoffice.gov.uk)

Border and Immigration Agency, Department for Work and Pensions, HM Revenue and Customs and Department for Communities and Local Government, 2007d. *Accession Monitoring Report May 2004–September 2007.* Online report. (www.bia.homeoffice.gov.uk)

Brewer, M., L. Sibieta and L. Wren-Lewis, 2008. *Racing away? Income inequality and the evolution of high incomes.* IFS Briefing Note No. 76, January.

Brindley, P., A. Geddes, K. B. Nielsen and S. Scott, 2007. *Gangmasters Licensing Authority: Annual Review.* November.

British Retail Consortium, KPMG, 2008. BRC-KPMG Retail Sales Monitor December 2007. *News Release.* January.

Brown, W., 2007. The Process of Fixing the British National Minimum Wage, 1997–2007. Paper given at the BJIR Conference *100 Years of Minimum Wage Regulation.* December.

Camus, D., 2007. Publishing productivity measures in ONS. *Economic & Labour Market Review.* 1(7), pp. 19–21.

Clark, K. and S. Drinkwater, 2006. *Changing Patterns of Ethnic Minority Self-Employment in Britain: Evidence from Census Microdata.* Discussion Paper No. 2495, December. (Institute for the Study of Labor.)

Cooke, G. and K. Lawton, 2008. *Working Out of Poverty. A study of the low-paid and the 'working poor'.* January. (Institute for Public Policy Research).

Croucher, R. and G. White, 2007. *Awareness of the Minimum Wage in the Hairdressing Industry: An Evaluation of the DTI/HMRC Targeted Campaign.* Research Report for the Low Pay Commission. University of Middlesex Business School and University of Greenwich Work and Employment Research Unit.

Dearden, L., C. Emmerson, C. Frayne and C. Meghir, 2006. *Education Subsidies and School Drop-Out Rates.* January. (Centre for the Economics of Education, London School of Economics.)

Department for Business, Enterprise and Regulatory Reform, 2007a. *Government evidence to the Low Pay Commission on the economic effects of the National Minimum Wage.* URN 07/1650, November. (www.berr.gov.uk)

Department for Business, Enterprise and Regulatory Reform, 2007b. *National Minimum Wage and Voluntary Workers: Government Response to the Consultation.* URN 07/1663, November. (www.berr.gov.uk)

Department for Business, Enterprise and Regulatory Reform, 2007c. *National Minimum Wage and Employment Agency Standards Enforcement: Government Response to Public Consultation.* URN 07/1676, December. (www.berr.gov.uk)

Department for Children, Schools and Families, 2007. *2006 Childcare and Early Years Providers Surveys. Overview Report.* Robert Kinnaird, Susan Nicholson and Emma Jordan. BMRB Social Research. Research Report DCSF-RR009.

Department of Communities and Local Government, 2008. *House Price Index, November 2007.* Statistical Release HPI–01–08, January.

Department for Constitutional Affairs, 2006. *The Draft Tribunals, Courts and Enforcement Bill.* Cm 6885, July. (The Stationery Office.)

Department for Education and Skills, 2005. *Apprenticeship Pay: A Survey of Earnings by Sector.* Anna Ullman and Gemma Deakin. BMRB Social Research. Research Report RR674, October.

Department for Education and Skills, 2007. *Participation in Education, Training and Employment by 16–18 Year Olds in England: 2005 and 2006.* SFR 22/2007, June.

Department of Trade and Industry, 2004a. *Regulations to Introduce Fair Piece Rates for Output Workers, including Homeworkers, Full Regulatory Impact Assessment.* February. (www.berr.gov.uk)

Department of Trade and Industry, 2004b. *A Detailed Guide to the National Minimum Wage.* URN 04/1253, October. (www.berr.gov.uk)

Department of Trade and Industry, 2006. *Success at Work. Protecting Vulnerable Workers, Supporting Good Employers.* URN 06/1024, March (www.berr.gov.uk)

Department of Trade and Industry, 2007a. *The Minimum Wage and Therapeutic Work.* Information Note. URN 07/593, January. (www.berr.gov.uk)

Department of Trade and Industry, 2007b. *Guidelines for Television Employers Offering Work Experience Placements to Individuals.* URN 06/2214, February. (www.berr.gov.uk)

Department of Trade and Industry, 2007c. *National Minimum Wage and Accommodation Offset.* URN 07/841, April. (www.berr.gov.uk)

Department of Trade and Industry, 2007d. *National Minimum Wage and Employment Agency Standards Enforcement: Consultation Document.* URN 07/961, May. (www.berr.gov.uk)

Department of Trade and Industry, 2007e. *National Minimum Wage and Voluntary Workers: Consultation Document.* URN 07/962, June. (www.berr.gov.uk)

Department of Trade and Industry, 2007f. *Increasing the holiday entitlement – A further consultation. Final Regulatory Impact Assessment.* URN 07/1095, June. (www.berr.gov.uk)

Department for Work and Pensions, 2007. *Explanatory Memorandum to the Social Security (Miscellaneous Amendments) (No.5) Regulations 2007.* (No. 2618) (www.opsi.gov.uk/si/si200726)

Dobbs, C., 2007. Patterns of pay: results of the Annual Survey of Hours and Earnings, 1997 to 2006. *Economic & Labour Market Review.* 1(2), pp. 44–51.

Duff, H., 2007a. A preliminary analysis of the differences between AWE and the AEI. *Economic & Labour Market Review.* 1(9), pp. 48–56.

Duff, H., 2007b. The effect of bonuses on earnings growth in 2007. *Economic & Labour Market Review.* 1(10), pp. 43–45.

Dustmann, C., T. Frattini and I. Preston, 2007. *A Study of the Migrant Workers and the National Minimum Wage and Enforcement Issues.* Research Report for the Low Pay Commission. University College London.

EEF, 2007. Pay Bulletin. December 2007.

Elekdag, S. and S. Lall, 2008. *Global Growth Estimates Trimmed After PPP Revisions.* January. International Monetary Fund.

Elmeskov, J., 2007. *OECD Economic Outlook No. 82.* December. Organisation for Economic Co-operation and Development.

Employment Tribunals Service, 2007. Annual Statistics 2006–2007. (www.employmenttribunals.gov.uk/publications)

Ernst & Young, 2007. *Economic Outlook for Business.* Issue No. 41, Autumn.

Eurostat, 2007. Young Europeans through statistics. *News Release* 44/2007, March.

French, S. and J. Möhrke, 2006. *The Impact of 'New Arrivals' Upon the North Staffordshire Labour Market* Research Report for the Low Pay Commission. Centre for Industrial Relations, Institute of Public Policy and Management, Keele University.

Gangmasters Licensing Authority, 2006. *Licensing Standards. Agriculture, Horticulture, Shellfish Gathering and Processing and Packaging for Food, Fish and Shellfish.* October. (Nottingham: GLA.)

GfK NOP, 2008. Consumers are suffering from a dose of realism! *News Release.* January.

Gilpin, N., M. Henty, S. Lemos, J. Portes and C. Bullen, 2006. *The Impact of Free Movement of Workers from Central and Eastern Europe on the UK Labour Market.* Working Paper No 29. (Department for Work and Pensions).

Goodridge, P., 2007. *New labour productivity measures from the ABI – 1998 to 2005. Economic & Labour Market Review.* 1(9), pp. 25–39.

Grimshaw, D. and J. Rubery, 2007. *Undervaluing women's work.* Working Paper Series No. 53. Equal Opportunities Commission.

Heath, A. and S. Y. Cheung, 2006. *Ethnic penalties in the labour market: Employers and discrimination.* Research Report No 341. (Department for Work and Pensions.)

HM Revenue and Customs, 2008. *Tips, Gratuities, Service Charges and Troncs.* Booklet E24 (2008). (www.hmrc.gov.uk/helpsheets/e24)

HM Treasury, 2006. *Pre-Budget Report 2006. Investing in Britain's Potential: Building our Long-term Future.* Cm 6984, December. (The Stationery Office.)

HM Treasury, 2007a. *Pre-Budget Report 2007. Meeting the aspirations of the British people.* Cm 7227, October. (The Stationery Office.)

HM Treasury, 2007b. *Budget 2007. Building Britain's long-term future: Prosperity and fairness for families.* HC 342, March. (The Stationery Office.)

HM Treasury, 2008. Pocket Databank. January.

HM Treasury, ongoing. *Forecasts for the UK Economy: A Comparison of Independent Forecasts.*

Holt, H., 2008a. *Characteristics of Those Paid Below the National Minimum Wage Using the Annual Survey of Hours and Earnings.* Research Report for the Low Pay Commission. (www.lowpay.gov.uk)

Holt, H., 2008b. *An Analysis of Low-paid Jobs.* Research Report for the Low Pay Commission. (www.lowpay.gov.uk)

Holt, H., M. Kehil and G. White, 2008. *The Pay Composition of the Low Paid: An Analysis from 1997 to 2006.* Research Report for the Low Pay Commission. (www.lowpay.gov.uk)

Home Office and Department for Work and Pensions, 2007. *The Economic and Fiscal Impact of Immigration. A Cross-Departmental Submission to the House of Lords Select Committee on Economic Affairs.* Cm 6768, October. (The Stationery Office.)

House of Commons Trade and Industry Committee, 2007. *Europe moves East: The impact of the new EU Member States on UK business. Eleventh Report of Session 2006–07.* HC 592 October. (The Stationery Office.)

Income Data Services Ltd, 2007a. *Monitoring the Impact of the National Minimum Wage.* Research Report for the Low Pay Commission.

Income Data Services Ltd, 2007b. *IDS Pay Report No. 992.* January.

Jenkins, J. and J. Johnson, 2008. *Characteristics of Those Paid Below the National Minimum Wage Using the Labour Force Survey.* Online report. (www.statistics.gov.uk)

Kent, K., 2007. New LFS questions on economic inactivity. *Economic & Labour Market Review. 1(12), pp. 30–36.*

KPMG/CIPD, 2007. *Labour Market Outlook.* Autumn.

Laing & Buisson, 2007. *Care of Elderly People. UK Market Survey 2007.* Twentieth Edition.

Learning and Skills Council, 2006. *Young people aged 16–18 who are not in Education, Employment or Training.* LSC 45/2006, October.

Low Pay Commission, 1998. *The National Minimum Wage. First Report of the Low Pay Commission.* Cm 3976, June. (The Stationery Office.)

Low Pay Commission, 2006. *National Minimum Wage. Low Pay Commission Report 2006.* Cm 6759, March. (The Stationery Office.)

Low Pay Commission, 2007. *National Minimum Wage. Low Pay Commission Report 2007.* Cm 7056, March. (The Stationery Office.)

Meader, R., 2007. Revisions to quarterly GDP growth and its components. *Economic & Labour Market Review.* 1(11), pp. 28–35.

Metcalf, D., 2007. Nothing new under the sun: The prescience of George Sanders' 1906 Fabian Tract. Paper given at the BJIR Conference *100 Years of Minimum Wage Regulation.* December.

National Institute of Economic and Social Research, 2007. *National Institute Economic Review.* No. 202, January.

Nationwide, 2008a. *Nationwide Consumer Confidence Index in partnership with TNS. December 2007.* January.

Nationwide, 2008b. Rate of annual house price growth slows in all UK regions. *News Release.* January.

NatWest and RBS, 2007. *NatWest and RBS Small Business Monitor.* H1.

Office for National Statistics, 2007a. *Low Pay Estimates, Spring 2007.* December. (www.statistics.gov.uk)

Office for National Statistics, 2007b. *Plans for the ONS Statistical Work Programme Technical Annex.* (www.statistics.gov.uk)

Office for National Statistics, 2007c. *Changes to ASHE 2007.* (www.statistics.gov.uk)

Office for National Statistics, ongoing. Consumer Price Indices.

Office for National Statistics, ongoing. Gross Domestic Product.

Office for National Statistics, ongoing. Index of Distribution.

Office for National Statistics, ongoing. Index of Production.

Office for National Statistics, ongoing. Labour Market Statistics.

Office for National Statistics, ongoing. Monthly Digest of Statistics.

Office for National Statistics, ongoing. Producer Prices.

Office for National Statistics, ongoing. Productivity.

Office for National Statistics, ongoing. Profitability of UK Companies.

Office for National Statistics, ongoing. Public Sector Employment.

Office for National Statistics, ongoing. Retail Sales.

Office for National Statistics, ongoing. UK Economic Accounts.

Office for National Statistics, ongoing. UK Output, Income and Expenditure.

Ormerod, C., 2007. What is known about the numbers and 'earnings' of the self-employed? *Economic & Labour Market Review.* 1(7), pp. 48–56.

Ormerod, C. and F. Ritchie, 2007a. Linking ASHE and LFS: can the main earnings sources be reconciled? *Economic & Labour Market Review.* 1(3), pp. 24–31.

Ormerod, C. and F. Ritchie, 2007b. Measuring low pay: The importance of timing? *Economic & Labour Market Review.* 1(4), pp. 18–22.

Ormerod, C. and F. Ritchie, 2007c. Issues in the measurement of low pay. *Economic & Labour Market Review.* 1(6), pp. 37–45.

Palmer, N. and M. Hughes, 2008. Labour Force Survey: interim reweighting 2007. *Economic & Labour Market Review.* 2(1), pp. 49–53.

Palmer, N. and J. Hynard, 2007. Comparing ONS's retail sales index with the BRC's retail sales monitor. *Economic & Labour Market Review.* 1(4), pp. 47–49.

Platt, L., 2006. *Pay Gaps: The position of ethnic minority women and men.* Equal Opportunities Commission.

Platt, L., 2007. *Poverty and Ethnicity in the UK.* Joseph Rowntree Foundation.

Ram, M., P. Edwards and T. Jones, 2004. *Informal Employment, Small Firms and the National Minimum Wage.* Research Report for the Low Pay Commission. Small Business and Enterprise Research Group, Leicester Business School, de Montford University and Industrial Relations Research Unit, Warwick Business School, University of Warwick.

RBS, 2007. *UK Economic Outlook.* November.

RBS, 2008. *Chief Economist's Weekly Brief.* January.

Richardson, I., 2007. Services Producer Price Index (experimental) – fourth quarter 2006. *Economic & Labour Market Review.* 1(11), pp. 28–35.

Rigg, J., 2005. *Labour Market Disadvantage amongst Disabled People: A Longitudinal Perspective.* CASE/103, November. London School of Economics.

Scruton, J., 2007. Introduction of automatic occupation coding in ASHE. *Economic & Labour Market Review.* 1(8), pp. 29–32.

The Prince's Trust, 2007. *The Cost of Exclusion. Counting the cost of youth disadvantage in the UK.* April.

Wadsworth, J., 2007. *Did Increases in the Minimum Wage Change Consumption Patterns?* Research Report for the Low Pay Commission. Royal Holloway College, University of London.

Wadsworth, J., 2008. *Did the UK Minimum Wage Affect Prices?* Research Report for the Low Pay Commission. Centre for Economic Performance, LSE.

Waldron, M. and G. Young, 2007. Household debt and spending: results from the 2007 NMG Research survey. *Bank of England Quarterly Bulletin.* 47(4), pp. 512–521.

Walling, A., 2007. Understanding statistics on full-time/part-time employment. *Economic & Labour Market Review.* 1(9), pp. 48–56.

Walton, A., R. Youll and C. Hunt, 2008. Planned methodological changes to the Index of Production. *Economic and Labour Market Review.* 2(1), pp. 30–37.

Wingfield, D., 2007. CPI and RPI: the 2007 basket of goods and services. *Economic & Labour Market Review.* 1(4), pp. 39–46.

Printed in the UK for The Stationery Office Limited
on behalf of the Controller of Her Majesty's Stationery Office
ID5734628   03/08

Printed on Paper containing 75% recycled fibre content minimum.